Yale Studies in Political Science, 9
David Horne, Editor

Published under the direction
of the Department of Political Science

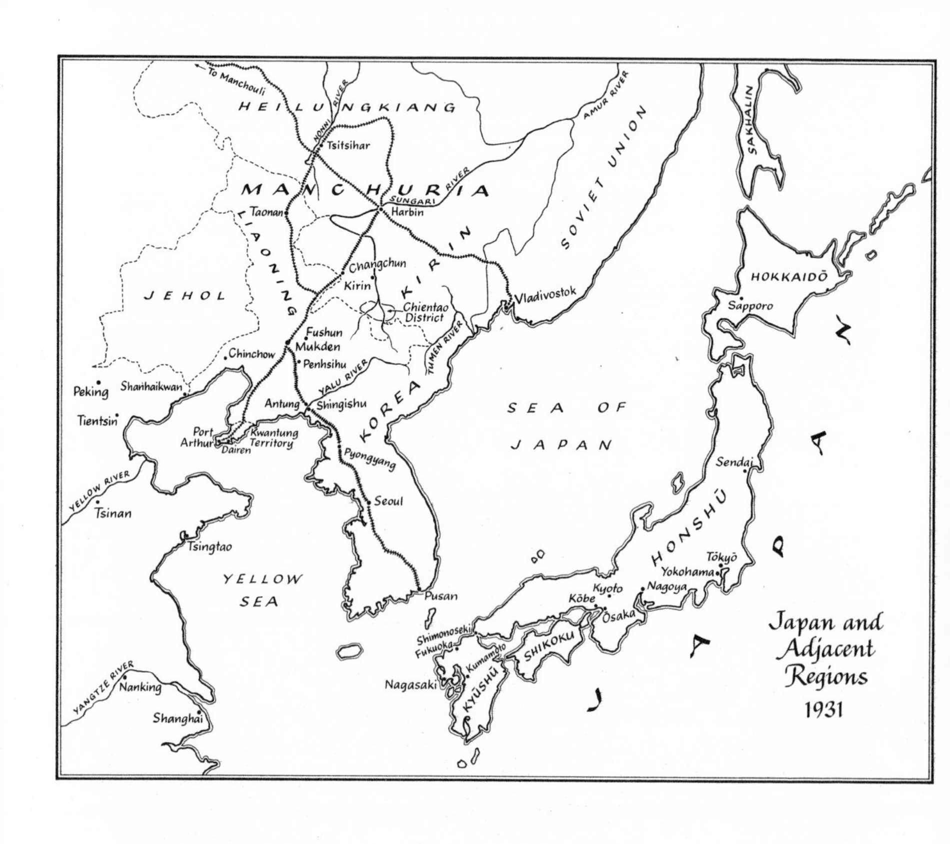
To Manchouli
HEILUNGKIANG
NONNI RIVER
AMUR RIVER
SAKHALIN
Tsitsihar
MANCHURIA
SUNGARI RIVER
Harbin
SOVIET UNION
Taonan
LIAONING
KIRIN
Changchun
Kirin
JEHOL
Chientao District
Vladivostok
HOKKAIDŌ
Sapporo
Fushun
Mukden
Chinchow
Penhsihu
TUMEN RIVER
YALU RIVER
Peking
Shanhaikwan
KOREA
Antung
Shingishu
SEA OF JAPAN
Tientsin
Port Arthur
Dairen
Kwantung Territory
Pyongyang
Sendai
YELLOW RIVER
Seoul
Tsinan
HONSHŪ
Tsingtao
Tōkyō
Yokohama
YELLOW SEA
Pusan
Kyoto
Kōbe
Nagoya
Ōsaka
JAPAN
Shimonoseki
Fukuoka
Kumamoto
SHIKOKU
YANGTZE RIVER
Nanking
Nagasaki
KYŪSHŪ
Shanghai
Japan and Adjacent Regions 1931

CONSPIRACY AT MUKDEN

The Rise of the Japanese Military

By TAKEHIKO YOSHIHASHI

New Haven and London, Yale University Press, 1963

Designed by Crimilda Pontes,
set in Times Roman type,
and printed in the United States of America by
The Carl Purington Rollins Printing-Office
of the Yale University Press.

Library of Congress catalog card number: 63–17025

TO MY FATHER AND MOTHER

PREFACE

Japan was confronted in the early nineteen thirties with two crucial problems. Her economy had been in a state of chronic malaise for three years when the world-wide depression engulfed the nation and threatened disaster. In China and Manchuria, because of the intense antiforeign sentiment which the "rights recovery" movement aroused, Japan was being prevailed upon to relinquish rights and privileges which in the course of decades she had come to assume were rightfully hers. The growing feeling that the government was impotent to cope with the crises at home and abroad, reinforced by rumors of corruption in high places, discredited the Diet and political parties—that is to say, the civilian government—rather convincingly in the eyes of the people.

Hardly a more opportune time could have presented itself for self-styled patriots—ultranationalists, expansionists, activists, and young officers—to step forward with a dynamic plan of expansion. Politically, economically, and socially Japan was in ferment and ripe for momentous change.[1] On the night of September 18, 1931, a handful of officers of the Kwantung Army, seizing the moment, engineered the Mukden Incident by setting off a bomb

1. John W. Burton in *Peace Theory: Preconditions of Disarmament* (New York, 1962), pp. 8–11, 22–23, attributes Japan's aggressive behavior in the thirties to her economic hardship, which in turn was caused by trade restrictions imposed on her by Western nations; also see Robert A. Scalapino, *Democracy and the Party Movement in Prewar Japan* (Berkeley, 1953), pp. 233–34.

on a rail just outside the city of Mukden. The Kwantung Army immediately went into action and by the following morning was in full control of the city. Its subsequent unbridled military campaign into the plains of northern Manchuria, which precipitated the Manchurian crisis, seriously threatened world peace.

Equally momentous but less appreciated were the domestic repercussions of the Incident. In its wake the Army extremists made an unsuccessful attempt at another coup d'état, the October Plot—a successor to the abortive March Plot of seven months earlier. The succession of crises at home and abroad strengthened the influence of the military in national affairs at the expense of the civilian government.

Aside from these critical events, the Japanese military were materially assisted in their rise to power by civilian ideologists: Kita Ikki, Ōkawa Shūmei, and a rabid expansionist, Mori Kaku. The first two shared in common the conviction that the military leadership was absolutely essential to the success of any program for national reconstruction. The politician, Mori, unwilling to relinquish civilian control of the government and hand it over entirely to the military, nevertheless hoped to obtain Army backing in order to institute a new political order.

In short, it was the crisis of the early thirties that brought the army's influence to the fore of Japan's politics and, once secure in power, the army saw to it that the atmosphere of crisis continued. Yet it was patently a question of time before Japan would come face to face with a concert of superior powers which could not allow her to continue expanding at the expense of her neighbors. When this critical moment arrived, the Japanese military dared not back down lest they suffer loss of prestige in the eyes of their own people. Therein lies the root of the greatest tragedy ever to befall the nation.

The present study relies heavily upon the dossiers of the Tokyo War Crimes Trials. Equally significant have been certain diaries, memoirs, and autobiographies published in Japan since 1950—for example, works by Wakatsuki, Shidehara, Shigemitsu, Ugaki,

Okada, and Harada, all of whom figured prominently in the politics of the period. In many instances the data contained in these more recent sources have made it possible for me to fill in gaps and reconstruct the development by key incidents in a new light.

It was inevitable that in the process the roles and responsibilities of a number of individuals and groups should be re-evaluated, in particular Mori Kaku, a man comparatively little known in the West, who paved the way for the armed occupation of Manchuria and the eventual collapse of party government in Japan. Attention has also been paid to developments in the early stages when the Japanese army was beginning to act independently of the civilian government, a phase especially relevant to a study of military-civilian relationships and a topic of great interest at the present time. I should mention that the present work was undertaken without the benefit of literature emanating from Chinese sources or a visit to Japan. Hence I would be the first to admit its limitations. However, it is my modest hope that the story I have developed here will help especially those who cannot read Japanese to understand the crises Japan faced in the early thirties and their effect on the course of world history in the decade that followed.

The Hepburn system of romanization has been used to transcribe Japanese words and the Wade-Giles system of romanization for Chinese words. However, the transcription of Chinese geographical names follows the spelling in the Chinese Postal Atlas. In citing oriental names, family names are generally given first, except when the individuals are better known by their Western given names.

The present publication is an outgrowth of a doctoral dissertation presented to Yale University; I am indebted in one way or another to each member of the graduate faculty at Yale with whom I studied international relations. The over-all discipline I received from them provided a framework within which the complex relationships between two oriental nations could be worked out.

I would, however, like to take this occasion to acknowledge my particular gratitude to Arnold Wolfers, now with The Johns Hopkins University; and to Walter R. Sharp, Samuel Flagg Bemis, Hajo Holborn, and Frederick C. Barghoorn, all of Yale. The idea of making a study of the rise of the Japanese military in conjunction with the invasion of Manchuria came to me while I was taking a course in the government and politics of Eastern Asia given by David N. Rowe. I am deeply grateful for the wise counsel I received from him in the course of completing my thesis. Were it not for unflagging encouragement and moral support from Chitoshi Yanaga throughout these years, I would probably never have reached the point of undertaking the present study. Few students have owed so much to their teacher for patient guidance, thoughtful suggestions, and generous assistance.

I owe a great deal also to Warren Tsuneishi of the Yale University Library staff for innumerable suggestions and the unstinting help he provided to materially improve my manuscript. Osamu Shimizu, Andrew Kuroda, Katsuyo L. Takeshita, Shōjō Honda, and Hisao Matsumoto have been most helpful at the Library of Congress, where I spent many hours. I have received encouragement from Dean Ernest S. Griffith and William C. Cromwell of the School of International Service of the American University. I am deeply grateful to David Horne and Marian Neal Ash of the Yale University Press for their moral support and the hours of time and effort they have put in to edit my manuscript with thought and care. Finally, I would like to thank my wife, Chiyo, for her attention to details and quiet patience in retyping the drafts many times between her household chores and regular working hours at a busy office.

T. Y.

Washington, D. C.
February 1963

CONTENTS

MAPS

SHORT TITLES

Aoki, *The Pacific War*—Aoki Tokuzō, *Taiheiyō Sensō Zenshi* (History of Events Leading to the Pacific War), *1*, Tokyo, 1953

Asahi, *Taiheiyō*—Asahi Shinbun-sha, *Taiheiyō Sensō e no Michi* (The Road to the Pacific War), *1, 2,* Tokyo, 1962

Hanaya, *Himerareta Shōwashi*—Hanaya Tadashi, "Manshū Jihen wa Kōshite Keikaku Sareta" (This is how the Manchurian Incident was Planned), *Himerareta Shōwashi,* Supplement to *Chisei,* December 1956

Harada Diary—Harada Kumao, *Saionji-kō to Seikyoku* (Prince Saionji and Political Developments), *1, 2,* Tokyo, 1950

Hirano, *Manshū*—Hirano Reiji, *Manshū no Inbōsha* (A Conspirator in Manchuria), Tokyo, 1959

IMTFE—International Military Tribunal for the Far East
International Prosecution Section Document, Tokyo, 1949
Judgment, Tokyo, 1948
Proceedings, Tokyo, 1948

Iwabuchi, *Military Cliques*—Iwabuchi Tatsuo, *Gunbatsu no Keifu* (The Lineage of Military Cliques), Tokyo, 1948

Kinoshita, *Japanese Fascism*—Kinoshita Hanji, *Nihon Fashizumu-shi* (History of Japanese Fascism), *1,* Tokyo, 1949

Kiyozawa, *May 15, 1932 Incident*—Kiyozawa Retsu, "Go-ichi-go Jiken no Shakaiteki Konkyo" (Social Origin of the May 15, 1932 Incident), *Kaizō, 15* 1933

Lytton Report—League of Nations, *Appeal by the Chinese Government: Report by the Commission of Enquiry,* Geneva, 1932

Maruyama, *Contemporary Politics*—Maruyama Masao, *Gendai Seiji no Shisō to Kōdō* (Thoughts and Actions Underlying Contemporary Politics), *1,* Tokyo, 1958

Morishima, *Conspiracy*—Morishima Morito, *Inbō, Ansatsu, Guntō* (Conspiracy, Assassination, and the Sword), Tokyo, 1950

Okada Memoirs—Okada Keisuke, *Okada Keisuke Kaikoroku* (Okada Memoirs), Tokyo, 1950

Shidehara Kijūrō—Shidehara Heiwa Zaidan, *Shidehara Kijūrō,* Tokyo, 1955

Shidehara Memoirs—Shidehara Kijūrō, *Gaikō Gojūnen* (Fifty Years of Diplomacy), Tokyo, 1951

Shigemitsu Memoirs—Shigemitsu Mamoru, *Gaikō Kaisōroku* (A Diplomatic Memoir), Tokyo, 1953

Suzuki, *Himerareta Shōwashi*—Suzuki Teiichi, "Hokubatsu to Shō: Tanaka Mitsuyaku" (The Northern Expedition and Chiang Kai-shek: Tanaka's Secret Agreement), *Himerareta Shōwashi,* Supplement to *Chisei,* December 1956

Tanaka Giichi Denki—Takakura Tetsuichi, ed., *Tanaka Giichi Denki* (The Biography of Tanaka Giichi), Tokyo, 1960

Toyoshima, *Himerareta Shōwashi*—Toyoshima Fusatarō, "Chōsengun Ekkyō Shingeki su" (Japan's Korea Army Crosses the Border and Advances), *Himerareta Shōwashi,* Supplement to *Chisei,* December 1956

Ugaki Diary—Ugaki Kazushige, *Ugaki Nikki* (Ugaki Diary), Tokyo, 1954

Ugaki Memoirs—Ugaki Kazushige, *Shōrai Seidan* (Refreshing Discourse at Shōrai Villa: A Memoir), Tokyo, 1951

Usui, *Himerareta Shōwashi*—Usui Katsumi, "Chō Sakurin Bakushi no Shinsō" (The Truth Regarding the Assassination by Bombing of Chang Tso-lin), *Himerareta Shōwashi,* Supplement to *Chisei,* December 1956

Uyehara Checklist—Cecil H. Uyehara, comp., *Checklist of Archives in the Japanese Ministry of Foreign Affairs, Tokyo, Japan, 1868–1945,* Washington, 1954

Wakatsuki Memoirs—Wakatsuki Reijirō, *Kofūan Kaikoroku* (Memoirs of Kofūan [Wakatsuki's pseudonym]), Tokyo, 1950

Yamada, *National Income*—Yamada Yūzō, *Nihon Kokumin Shotoku Suikei Shiryō* (Statistical Estimates of Japan's National Income), Tokyo, 1951

CONSPIRACY AT MUKDEN
The Rise of the Japanese Military

1.
THE MUKDEN INCIDENT, I

On the Scene

The date was September 19, 1931. The residents of Mukden were puzzled by the unaccustomed sight of Japanese sentries standing guard at street intersections that Saturday morning. To be sure, they had heard the loud booming of guns the preceding night, but only the overly cautious had taken special note of them. Training maneuvers by the Japanese railway guards[1] had been going on nightly for almost a week, and the residents had become accustomed to the clatter of machine-gun fire. Hardly a soul knew that on the night before an actual skirmish between Chinese and Japanese troops had taken place; still less did anyone suspect that the skirmish was swiftly developing into an occupation of Manchuria by the Kwantung Army of Imperial Japan.

1. These so-called railway guards were detailed to protect a zone extending the length of the South Manchuria Railway and wider than the tracks by a few yards, as well as some fifteen municipalities known as Japanese railway towns, situated on the railroad from Dairen to Changchun and from Antung to Mukden. For locations, functions, and legal status of the guards see below, pp. 130–31.

From December 1929, when the Nationalist flag was unfurled in Manchuria, to the outbreak of the Mukden Incident in September 1931, the Three Eastern Provinces—Liaoning, Kirin, and Heilungkiang—were nominally under the Nanking government, but Chang Hsueh-liang, a local warlord, held de facto control. Nevertheless, Chang had to defer to the Japanese in a number of important matters because of the extensive rights which Japan had acquired in these provinces. These included the leasehold

According to the Japanese version,[2] on the night of September 18 a small guard detachment under First Lieutenant Kawamoto Suemori was patrolling the tracks of the South Manchuria Railway just to the north of Mukden when a loud explosion was heard. The detachment about-faced and marched, at double time, approximately two hundred yards to the north. There, where the ends of two rails were joined, they picked up a fragment of rail and two pieces of wood from a railroad tie.[3] The official Japanese report said that "the end of each rail had been cleanly severed, creating a gap in the line of thirty-one inches."[4] At this point the patrol was fired upon from the fields to the east of the track. The Japanese troops, quickly deploying and returning fire, pursued the attackers, only to encounter more fire from a contingent estimated at about three to four hundred men. Fearing encirclement, Lieutenant Kawamoto sought reinforcement from

---

on the Kwantung Province and railroad, mining, and commercial rights. However, there was a great deal of controversy over the rights Japan insisted she had acquired in Manchuria and Inner Mongolia under Article Four of the Twenty-One Demands. Chinese authorities were determined not to honor the terms of this article, which Japan had extracted from China under exceptional circumstances in 1915. Any concession to the Japanese demand would have meant flying in the face of the strong "rights recovery" movement flourishing in China at the time. Although the Japanese repeatedly protested to Chang Hsueh-liang, he avoided direct negotiations with them and discreetly referred them to Nanking as the duly constituted government of China. This diversionary tactic, as subsequent events bore out, taxed the patience of the Japanese government and especially of the direct actionists of the Kwangtung Army.

2. League of Nations, *Appeal by the Chinese Government: Report by the Commission of Enquiry* (Geneva, 1932), pp. 67–69 (hereafter referred to as the *Lytton Report*).

3. These three objects constituted the entire evidence of the explosion. They were held in the custody of Kwantung Army headquarters. Mori Shōzō, *Senpū Nijūnen* (Twenty Turbulent Years) (Tokyo, 1955), p. 53.

4. *Lytton Report,* pp. 67–68. In a written report which Minami Jirō, the Minister of War, brought to the extraordinary meeting of the cabinet on the morning of September 21, it was stated that Chinese soldiers invaded the railway zone and attempted to destroy the track. Shidehara Kijūrō, *Gaikō Gojūnen* (Fifty Years of Diplomacy) (Tokyo, 1951), p. 172 (hereafter referred to as *Shidehara Memoirs*).

the Third Company, which was engaged in night maneuvers some 1,500 yards to the north.

It was about this time that the men heard the roar of an approaching train from Changchun. Fearful of a derailment, the Japanese patrol broke off the engagement and tried to stop the train by placing detonators on the rails. Unheeded, the express sped by at full speed. In cautiously phrased language, the Japanese report later observed that "when the express reached the site of explosion, it was seen to sway and incline to one side; but it recovered and passed on without stopping." It was reliably reported on the night of the explosion that the train had arrived at Mukden on schedule at 10:30 P.M., and by calculating backward Lieutenant Kawamoto concluded that the explosion had occurred at about 10 P.M.

The Third Company under Captain Kawashima Tadashi arrived on the scene at about 10:50 P.M. Meanwhile, Lieutenant Colonel Shimamoto Masaichi at battalion headquarters in Mukden had ordered the First and Fourth Companies to rush to the aid of the forces already on the scene and had sent a hurried call to the Second Company at Fushun, about twenty-five miles due east.

Shortly after midnight the company from Mukden arrived at the scene of the skirmish, increasing the strength of the Japanese troops to approximately 500 men, an insignificant force when compared to the estimated 10,000 Chinese soldiers quartered at the North Barracks in Mukden. Nevertheless, Shimamoto ordered an attack on the barracks, believing, as he later recalled, that offense was the best defense.

When the Japanese troops reached the North Barracks, about 250 yards from the railroad tracks, the area was "aglitter with electric lights."[5] The Third Company spearheaded the attack by breaching the left wing of the west wall. The First Company attacked the right wing and the Fourth Company the center portion of the same wall. At 5 A.M., after two cannon shells had demol-

5. *Lytton Report.* For a more graphic record of the engagement at the North Barracks, see Map 1.

ished the gate to the south wall, a detachment under Lieutenant Noda poured through the gap. Although the Chinese soldiers resisted fiercely, in the face of Noda's flanking attack they yielded ground; by 6 o'clock the North Barracks was completely in Japanese hands, and the defenders were retreating via the east gate northeastward toward the village of Erhtaitze.

The Chinese maintained that the Japanese attack on the North Barracks was unjustified.[6] According to a report by an officer named Liu, a train of three or four coaches without the usual type of locomotive stopped to the northwest of the barracks at 9 P.M. At 10 there was a loud explosion followed by rifle fire. At 10:30 the roar of distant artillery was heard coming from the southwest and northwest. A general attack on the southwest corner of the barracks came at about 11, and the Japanese effected an entry into the compound half an hour later.

By midnight live shells were bursting within the barracks. The main body of Chinese troops evacuated the grounds, building by building, without offering resistance. The only exception was the 620th Regiment, whose path of retreat was cut off at the eastern exit by the Japanese troops. It was here, according to the Chinese account, that their heaviest casualties were sustained.

In Mukden at 10:30 P.M. Colonel Hirata Yukihiro heard from Colonel Shimamoto of the bombing incident and of the latter's intention to rush to the site with reinforcements. At 11:30 Colonel Hirata led his troops in an attack on the walled city in Mukden, capturing it by 3:40 the following morning. He encountered resistance only from the Chinese police, of whom seventy-five were slain. The staff of the Second Division and a part of the Sixteenth Regiment arrived shortly after 5 A.M. from Liaoyang, and the arsenal and airfield located to the east of the walled city were captured at 7:30. The East Barracks three to four miles northeast of the city was occupied by 1 P.M. Thus within fifteen hours all important military installations in and about Mukden were completely in the hands of the Japanese army.

During the same night Chinese troops at Antung, Yingkow,

6. Ibid., pp. 69–70.

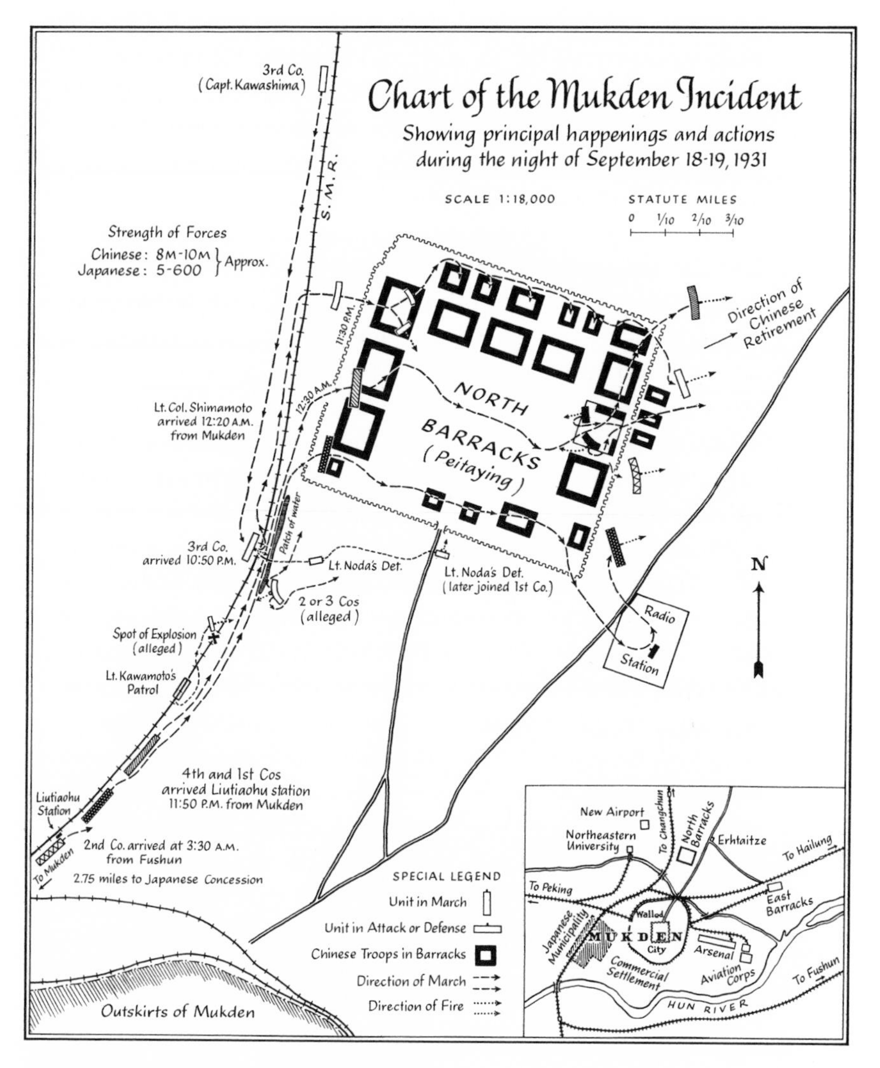

Replica of Map No. 6, *Lytton Report*.

Liaoyang, and other smaller towns were overcome and disarmed without resistance. The attack on Changchun, the northern terminus of the South Manchuria Railway, began on the night of September 18 and the city was occupied by 3 P.M. the following day. Kirin, approximately seventy miles to the east, was captured on the 21st without a shot.

The League of Nations' Lytton Commission, sent to investigate the Japanese irruption in Manchuria, made these observations: First, on the night of September 18–19 the Japanese, by their own admission, executed "with swiftness and precision" a plan that had been laid out in advance of the incident. Secondly, there was no proof that the Chinese had plans to attack the Japanese troops or molest the persons or property of Japanese nationals. Instead, it was the Chinese who were taken by surprise. The Japanese themselves corroborated this fact by stating that the barracks area was "aglitter with electric lights." Thirdly, the damage done to the rails by the explosion on the night of September 18 was minimal—the southbound express from Changchun passed over the affected portion of the railroad without mishap and arrived in Mukden on time. Fourthly, the military actions by the Japanese troops on the night of September 18 could therefore not be regarded as acts of legitimate self-defense.

The Commission made the reservation that "it does not exclude the hypothesis that the officers on the spot may have thought they were acting in self-defense,"[7] and the evidence seems to show that this was indeed the case.[8]

In Tokyo

The first news of the hostilities at Liutiaohu[1] reached the Japanese Ministry of War in Tokyo at 2 A.M., September 19. At 10:30 A.M. the cabinet met in extraordinary session, and Pre-

7. Ibid., p. 71.
8. See below, pp. 159–64.
1. The precise location at which the bombing of the railroad took place.

mier Wakatsuki Reijirō asked General Minami Jirō, the Minister of War:

> Did the incident break out because the Chinese troops destroyed the rail and opened fire on the Japanese guards? Was it truthfully an act of legitimate self-defense? If, on the contrary, it turns out to be an act of conspiracy by the Japanese army, what do you propose to do about our nation's standing in the world? . . . Whatever may have caused the incident, I will immediately instruct the commanding officer of the Kwantung Army not to enlarge the theater of conflict nor to bombard and occupy government buildings and fortifications.[2]

Though reportedly caught off guard, Foreign Minister Shidehara Kijūrō entertained no illusions about the real objectives of the extremists of the Kwantung Army[3] and immediately recognized the gravity of the situation.

A top-secret telegram from Hayashi, the Consul General at Mukden, the same morning confirmed Shidehara's misgivings:

> In view of the fact that there were several requests from the Chinese side to settle the incident amicably, I telephoned Staff Officer Itagaki. I explained to him that Japan and China had not yet formally declared the existence of a state of war. Moreover, the Chinese stated that they would adhere strictly to the principle

2. Harada Kumao, *Saionji-kō to Seikyoku* (Prince Saionji and Political Developments), *2* (Tokyo, 1950), 62 (hereafter referred to as *Harada Diary*). Author's translation.

3. The group included Colonel Itagaki Seishirō, Lieutenant Colonel Ishihara Kanji, Major Hanaya Tadashi, Captain Imada Juntarō, and a few others. "I had a series of forewarnings prior to the sudden outbreak of the Liutiaohu Incident," wrote Shidehara in his memoirs, citing a succession of presaging events. *Shidehara Memoirs,* p. 170. For a detailed treatment of the point see below, pp. 152–54.

> of non-resistance. They also stressed the importance of not aggravating the situation at this juncture and of seeking a settlement through diplomatic channels. Itagaki replied that the prestige of the Japanese nation and army was at stake. Efforts would be made to protect foreign residents, but the Chinese army would have to be dealt with, since it was they who opened the attack first. As Itagaki showed no sign of heeding my advice, all I could do was to repeat the same message over and over to him.[4]

At the emergency cabinet meeting Shidehara insisted, over the War Minister's objections, that the scope of military operations be kept to a minimum as long as possible. Minami had good reason to object since he was confronted with a serious tactical problem. In his own words:

> Since the army strongly advocated sending reinforcements for operational reasons, it took some time before its argument could be overcome and the cabinet could decide on a non-aggressive policy. The army's greatest concern was whether or not the small Kwantung Army, in the presence of 250,000 Chinese troops, could protect 200,000 Japanese and 1,000,000 Korean residents

4. International Military Tribunal for the Far East, *Proceedings* (Tokyo, 1948), pp. 15,734–35 (hereafter referred to as IMTFE, *Proceedings*). It is a moot question whether Shidehara read this telegram before he attended the cabinet meeting at 10:30 the same morning. Shidehara's account is further corroborated by the following passage in a memoir by a consular official stationed in Mukden: "During the night of September 18–19, Dr. Chao Chin-po, the supreme advisor of the Three Eastern Provinces, pleaded repeatedly on the telephone, 'The Chinese side will adhere to nonresistance; will the Japanese forces cease attack immediately.' After each call from Dr. Chao, the Consul General or myself [a Consul] transmitted the message to Itagaki, but without any response." Morishima Morito, *Inbō, Ansatsu, Guntō* (Conspiracy, Assassination, and the Sword) (Tokyo, 1950), p. 53 (hereafter referred to as Morishima, *Conspiracy*). Author's translation.

> and the long railway lines. If the Massacre of Nikolaevsk of 1920 had been repeated, the army would have been charged with dereliction of duty.[5]

Shidehara finally extracted from Minami assurances that "the events would not be permitted to expand beyond the present point." At 12:20 P.M. the Prime Minister announced to press reporters the cabinet's decision to adhere to nonaggression. The Minister of War transmitted the decision to General Honjō Shigeru, Commander of the Kwantung Army.[6] Later the same afternoon the Chief of the General Staff, General Kanaya Hanzō, sent an identical instruction of General Honjō. The latter action, however, was made in the name of the supreme command, thereby bringing all subsequent military operations in Manchuria technically under the command of the Chief of the General Staff.

Immediately after the cabinet meeting the Minister of War, the Chief of the General Staff, and General Mutō Nobuyoshi, Inspector General of Education—the so-called Big Three of the army—met to deliberate on a future course of action. Curiously, their decision contradicted that which the cabinet had reached only a short time before. After the meeting, Minami told press reporters that the Army need not consult the cabinet about measures to be taken with respect to exigencies which may arise in the future, but will leave the matter to the discretion of the commanding officer of the Kwantung Army.[7]

This decision was tantamount to giving the Kwantung Army free rein to occupy the remainder of Manchuria at top speed. For, after the Mukden Incident, Honjō, the Commanding General, and Miyake Mitsuharu, his Chief of Staff, were virtually

5. IMTFE, *Proceedings*, pp. 19,780–81.

6. One writer states that Minami's directive went so far as to prescribe a status quo ante bellum—that the Japanese army withdraw to its original stations within the railway zone. Matsumura Hidesugu, *Miyakezaka* (Tokyo, 1952), p. 41.

7. Tatsuji Takeuchi, *War and Diplomacy in the Japanese Empire* (New York, 1935), p. 351.

powerless to check the expansionist ambitions of their extremist subordinates, who planned and executed simultaneous attacks on strategic cities in South Manchuria, occupying them in short order. Once the deed was accomplished, Honjō could hardly pull back his army in retreat. Increasingly, Honjō and his chief of staff came to be treated as puppets, dancing to the expansionist tune played by their ostensible subordinates.[8]

8. Morishima, *Conspiracy,* p. 63. *Harada Diary, 2,* 77.

2.
PORTENTS OF CRISIS

Resignation of the Wakatsuki Cabinet

It is clear today that the Mukden Incident could not have erupted at a more inopportune time for the government in Tokyo. Beset by economic difficulties and lacking in positive leadership, its power was at a low ebb, and it could hardly afford a further weakening of its authority. Yet this was precisely what happened when the Kwantung Army continued to expand in Manchuria in defiance of a contrary policy laid down by the cabinet.

How did Wakatsuki's government come to be caught in such a predicament? For the answer we must turn back to the latter half of the twenties and trace Japan's prior attempts to expand her sphere of influence in the mainland of Asia, studying this expansion within the context of her internal difficulties.[1]

Wakatsuki was no stranger to troubles from extremist quarters. In the spring of 1927, fully two and a half years before the Wall Street crash, Japan was confronted with a domestic financial

1. In the words of a perceptive scholar of Japan's recent history: "Japanese expansion on the Asiatic continent and in the Pacific has so held the interest of most Western writers that little attention has been paid to the internal struggle within Japan. Yet the key to the expansionism lies in these struggles. It is only by careful study and analysis of Japan's internal history that the events abroad may be understood." R. J. Wald, "The Young Officers Movement in Japan, ca. 1925–37: Ideology and Action" (Unpublished doctoral dissertation, University of California at Berkeley, 1949).

crisis. Thirty-five banks, including the Bank of Taiwan, one of the largest in Japan, closed their doors. At this juncture the ultra-nationalists and expansionists—proponents of the so-called "positive policy" and avowed foes of Foreign Minister Shidehara's conciliatory policy toward China[2]—capitalized on the bank crisis to administer the finishing blow to Wakatsuki's first government.

The crisis developed in March 1927 when the Bank of Japan notified the Bank of Formosa that it could no longer honor the notes of the Suzuki Company which the Bank of Formosa was unloading in large quantities. In desperation, the Bank of Formosa turned for help to Kataoka Kenkichi, Minister of Finance. Since the government could not very well let down a bank with semiofficial status, it sought to advance a loan of 200 million yen by means of an emergency imperial ordinance. Such an ordinance, however, had to be approved by the Privy Council before it could take effect, and Itō Miyoji, as chairman of the Reviewing Committee of the Council, used his influence to block it. Confronted with the failure of one of Japan's important banking institutions and the ensuing chaos in domestic finance, the Wakatsuki government was left with no choice but to resign.

The stormy petrels of the positive school had been incensed because Shidehara's diplomacy was cued to Anglo-American leadership in the post-World War I period and was conducted within the framework of the League of Nations and the Washington Conference. It sought to reach international agreement by means of negotiation and persuasion rather than direct action. This meant that the Shidehara school treated Manchuria as an integral part of Chinese territory. As demonstrated during the Nanking Incident of March 1927, it did not take the position that

2. Vociferous members of this group included Itō Miyoji and Hiranuma Kiichirō of the Privy Council, and Mori Kaku and Yamamoto Jōtarō of the Seiyūkai. Mori, in particular, worked closely with the extremists in the army, but it was Itō who was largely instrumental in bringing about the collapse of the Wakatsuki government.

the Japanese residents in China were entitled to special protection by Japan's military forces.

The ultranationalists and the expansionists denounced the Minseitō party for Shidehara's weak China policy. Not only was the policy criticized as weak and unrealistic, it was scorned as downright unpatriotic. The extremists of the Seiyūkai party joined the chorus of opposition and criticized Shidehara for having gone too far in observing the rights of China and of the nations of the West to the detriment of Japan's vital interests.

While the overriding task of the succeeding cabinet, headed by Baron Tanaka Giichi, should have been to create a semblance of order in domestic finance as quickly as possible, it made its debut on April 20, 1927, as a matter of political expediency, with a new look on the diplomatic front—a positive or get-tough policy in China. In the words of Admiral Yamamoto Gonbei, "China was Tanaka's only talking point in politics."[3]

Determined to effect a démarche in China policy when he was named Premier, Tanaka also assumed the post of Minister of Foreign Affairs. According to General Suzuki Teiichi,[4] "In those days Premier Tanaka used to turn to younger men and complain about the weak diplomacy which the Minister of Foreign Affairs was conducting under Wakatsuki. He said that he would personally assume the post of Minister of Foreign Affairs and with the

3. Baba Tsunego, *Gendai Jinbutsu Hyōron* (Character Sketches of Contemporary Figures) (Tokyo, 1930), p. 42. Author's translation.

4. Suzuki was a close friend of Mori Kaku, Tanaka's chief lieutenant. Suzuki and Mori first met in Hankow in the spring of 1926 when the latter visited the Wuhan government with Matsuoka Yōsuke and Yamamoto Jōtarō. From April 1941 to July 1944 Suzuki held the important cabinet post of president of the Cabinet Planning Board under the second and third Konoe governments and under the Tōjō government. He received a life sentence from the Tokyo War Crimes Tribunal in November 1948. See Suzuki Teiichi, "Hokubatsu to Shō: Tanaka Mitsuyaku" (The Northern Expedition and Chiang Kai-shek: Tanaka's Secret Agreement), in *Himerareta Shōwashi* (Hidden History of the Shōwa Era), Supplement to *Chisei* (December 1956), p. 24 (hereafter referred to as Suzuki, *Himerareta Shōwashi*).

aid of a resolute and capable man thoroughly overhaul and rebuild the ministry."[5]

Tanaka's Private Diplomacy with Chang Tso-lin

Tanaka's articulate concern for an immediate solution of Chinese problems stemmed in large measure from his belief that he could thereby forestall the activities of extremists clamoring for a hard policy toward China. In the latter part of April 1927, shortly after he became Premier, he summoned Colonel Machino Takema, an advisor to Marshal Chang Tso-lin (independent ruler of Manchuria) for well over a decade,[1] and confided his plan to steal a march on these elements: "The real reason for my assuming the premiership at this time is to settle the Chinese problems—that is to say, the outstanding issues pertaining to Manchuria. Manchuria is Japan's lifeline. If we should allow the Manchurian issues to keep on drifting, they would give rise to such a controversy at home that eventually the situation would get out of hand. This would lead to a war. That I want to avoid."[2]

Tanaka then asked Machino to undertake preliminary nego-

5. Yamaura Kanichi, *Mori Kaku* (Tokyo, 1940), p. 580.

1. There were in Manchuria, among old China hands from Japan, certain army officers of active or reserve status, like Lieutenant General Matsui Nanao, Lieutenant Colonel Machino Takema, Major Giga Nobuya, and Colonel Doihara Kenji, who enjoyed access to the Marshal. Although nominally his advisers, they were in fact observers for the Japanese army. They also acted as go-betweens for Japanese business interests, such as the Ōkura combine, which sought concessions in Manchuria. On the other hand, inasmuch as these Japanese officers had to deal directly with Chang Tso-lin, they were more sympathetic about his problems and, at the same time, were more aware of the growing hostile sentiment of the resident Chinese in Manchuria toward the Japanese. These sentiments, however, were not shared by the staff officers of the Kwantung Army who were advocates of military action out of sheer exasperation. Included in this group were Major General Saitō Tsune, the Chief of Staff, Colonels Kōmoto Daisaku and Itagaki Seishirō, and Lieutenant Colonel Ishihara Kanji. They were critical of these so-called advisers because the latter were generally exploiting their connection with the Marshal to promote the interests of some specific business group rather than to enhance the over-all prestige and influence of Japan in Manchuria.

2. The quotations and the facts cited are based on an article by Shin-

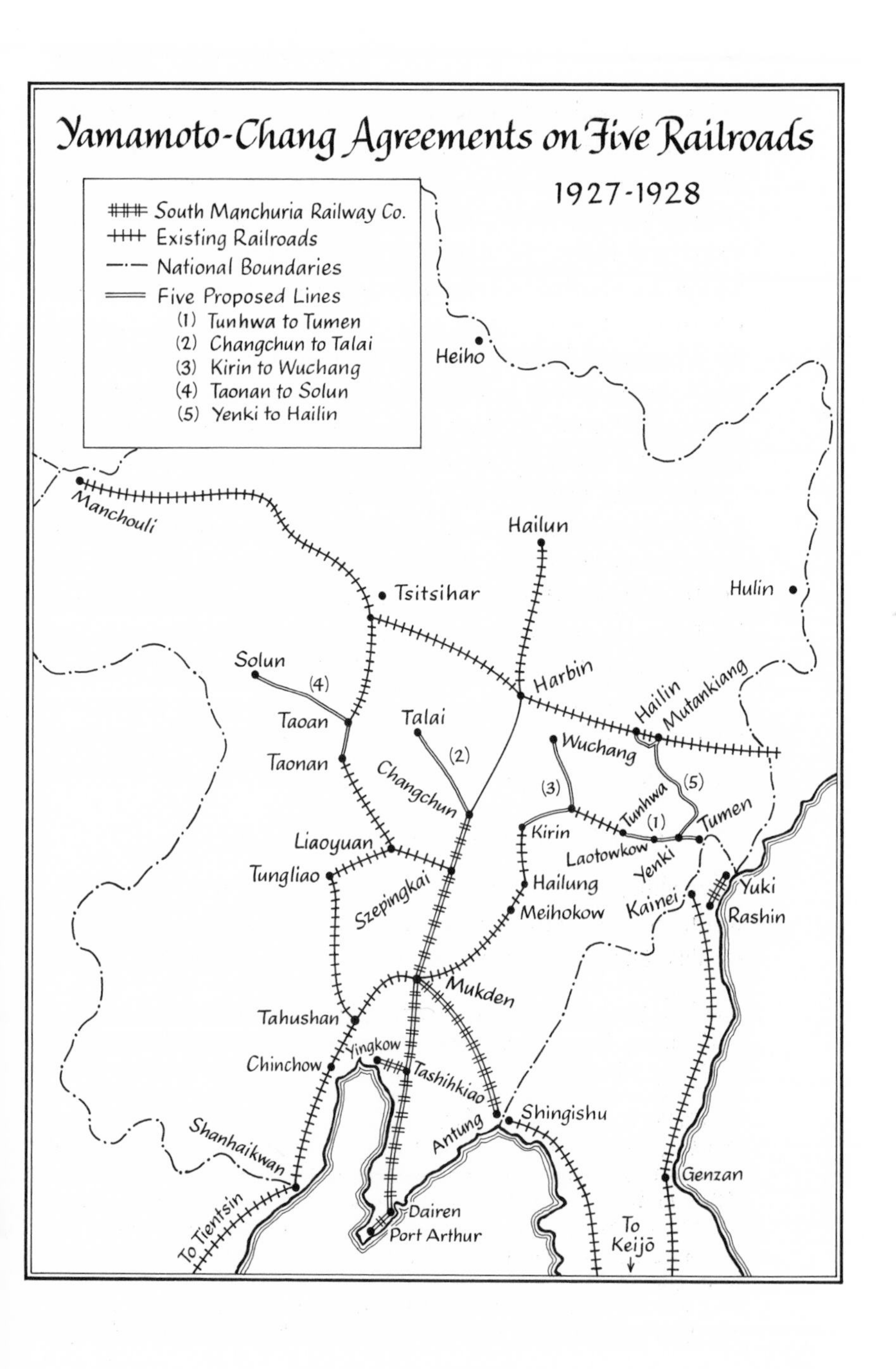
Yamamoto-Chang Agreements on Five Railroads
1927-1928
South Manchuria Railway Co.
Existing Railroads
National Boundaries
Five Proposed Lines
(1) Tunhwa to Tumen
(2) Changchun to Talai
(3) Kirin to Wuchang
(4) Taonan to Solun
(5) Yenki to Hailin
Heiho
Manchouli
Hailun
Tsitsihar
Hulin
Solun
(4)
Harbin
Taoan
Talai
Hailin
Mutankiang
Wuchang
(2)
Taonan
Changchun
(3)
(5)
Tunhwa
Kirin
(1)
Tumen
Liaoyuan
Laotowkow
Yenki
Tungliao
Hailung
Yuki
Szepingkai
Meihokow
Kainei
Rashin
Mukden
Tahushan
Yingkow
Chinchow
Tashihkiao
Shingishu
Antung
Shanhaikwan
Genzan
To Tientsin
Dairen
Port Arthur
To Keijō

tiations for railroad loans to be made to Chang Tso-lin. His proposal was that Japan should finance the construction or the development of five railways between Tunhwa and Tumen, Changchun and Talai, Kirin and Wuchang, Taonan and Solun, and Yenki and Hailin. In addition, Tanaka instructed Machino to inform the Marshal of Japan's willingness to finance the outright purchase of Russia's share in the Chinese Eastern Railway and the Changchun-Harbin Railway in order that the two railways might be operated jointly under Sino-Japanese partnership. Tanaka continued, "If these plans can be carried out, I can maintain order at home and we shall probably get by without a war."[3]

That same night Tanaka summoned Yamamoto Jōtarō and, following Machino's advice, asked him to assume the presidency of the South Manchuria Railway Company, which the latter did in July of the same year. Tanaka repeated to Yamamoto his proposals for the railroad loans to be made to Chang Tso-lin.[4] The two parted company with a firm understanding that the matter of railroad negotiations was to be kept a strict secret among the three men. Machino returned to Peking and began to negotiate vigorously with Chang Tso-lin.

The Other Arm of Tanaka's China Policy

Meanwhile, for his right-hand man Tanaka appointed Mori Kaku to the post of Parliamentary Vice Minister of Foreign Affairs. By this time Mori had already made a name for himself among

myō Takeo, "Shōwa Seiji Hisshi—Chō Sakurin Bakusatsu" (Secret History of the Shōwa Era—The Bombing of Chang Tso-lin), *Chūō Kōron* (April 1954), pp. 190–201. Author's translation.

3. Ibid., Asahi Shinbun-sha, *Taiheiyō Sensō e no Michi* (The Road to the Pacific War) *1* (Tokyo, 1962), 294–97, Supplement, pp. 2–3 (hereafter interests, such as the Ōkura combine which sought concessions in Man-referred to as Asahi, *Taiheiyō*). See Peter S. H. Tang, *Russian and Soviet Policy in Manchuria and Outer Mongolia, 1911–1931,* (Durham, 1959), pp. 35–51, 208–234 for the origin of the Chinese Eastern Railway and the undeclared Sino-Soviet war which was waged in 1929 over the question of its control.

4. For the details of the Yamamoto-Chang railroad negotiations see Takakura Tetsuichi, ed., *Tanaka Giichi Denki* (The Biography of Tanaka

his colleagues as a fighter. His original ambition had been to reorient Japan's China policy by first bringing Japan's domestic politics under his control; to accomplish this he had aspired to the post of Parliamentary Vice Minister of Home Affairs but had been thwarted in achieving this goal by a fellow member of the party.

Upon assuming his post in the Foreign Office, Mori summoned the ranking officers of the ministry and told them bluntly that he intended to get tough with China. They were dumfounded. Heretofore, the post of Parliamentary Vice Minister of Foreign Affairs, unlike that of Permanent Vice Minister of Foreign Affairs, had been strictly a political office of minor importance: the Parliamentary Vice Minister neither had access to classified materials nor was expected to take part in important decision-making conferences.[1] But Mori, as soon became evident, was in fact the Minister of Foreign Affairs.

About the time Tanaka was forming his cabinet, a two-pronged drive launched the previous summer by the Nationalist-Communist armies from Canton against the northern warlords was well under way.[2] Japanese expansionists both in and out of the Seiyūkai had viewed this advance with alarm, since the success of the Northern Expedition could very well hasten the unification of China under the aegis of either the Nationalists or the

---

Giichi) 2 (Tokyo, 1960), 678–88 (hereafter referred to as *Tanaka Giichi Denki*).

1. See Ishii Itarō, *Gaikōkan no Isshō* (Life Story of a Diplomat) (Tokyo, 1950), pp. 140–41, for Mori's overbearing conduct as Parliamentary Vice Minister of Foreign Affairs. When Premier Tanaka assumed concurrently the post of Foreign Minister he told Debuchi, Permanent Vice Minister of foreign Affairs, "Don't discuss important matters with Mori. Whether they concern the work [of the Foreign Office] or its fiscal policy, go right ahead and do as you think best." *Tanaka Giichi Denki, 2,* 643–44, based on account given by Debuchi Katsuji. Author's translation.

2. For accounts of the Nationalist expedition against the northern warlords and the ensuing intraparty struggle between the Wuhan and the Nanking regimes, see H. F. MacNair, *China in Revolution* (Chicago, 1931), pp. 61–64, 108–26; Paul M. A. Linebarger, *Government in Republican China* (New York, 1938), pp. 54–55, 105–07; Yamaura, *Mori Kaku,* pp. 606–07.

Communists with the resultant diminishing of Japan's influence there and eventually in Manchuria.[3] Therefore, when Foreign Minister Shidehara had refrained from joining forces with the Western powers in retaliating against antiforeign outrages in the Nanking Incident of March 24, the Seiyūkai, then the out-party, had joined the opposition chorus in a scathing attack on the Minseitō's timidity in China.

Meanwhile the Fengtien (Mukden) Armies of Chang Tso-lin, which had pulled back to the vicinity of Peking after their defeat by the Nationalist forces on the banks of the Yangtze River, regrouped and began a new advance. In March they crossed the Yellow River and drove southward through the province of Honan.

In the latter part of April, Wuhan troops under Tang Shen-chih marched northward from Hankow to engage the Fengtien Armies. At the scene of impending clash between the two armies Feng Yu-hsiang, in league with Yen Hsi-shan, thrust his reconstituted Northwest Army from Shensi into the plains of Honan.

In the ensuing encounters between the Fengtien and the Wuhan forces near Chumatien from May 21 to 28, heavy losses were sustained by both sides. Chang Tso-lin was again forced to retreat toward Peking. Now Feng wedged his army between

3. Cf. Yamaura, *Mori Kaku,* pp. 530, 534–39, regarding a three-week trip made by Mori, Yamamoto Jōtarō, and Matsuoka Yōsuke, all three prominent party members of the Seiyūkai, to visit Michael Borodin, Eugene Chen, and other notables of the Wuhan government in late February and early March of 1927. Upon his return to Tokyo, Mori delivered an extremely pessimistic speech at a luncheon given by a businessmen's club, the Kōjunsha, on April 1 predicting that enterprises in China would suffer as a result of the upsurge of nationalistic sentiment and the penetration of Soviet influence. Mori and his group were not, however, the first Japanese emissaries to visit the Wuhan government. Suzuki Teiichi, a Japanese army officer, had been earlier dispatched by General Ugaki Kazushige, Minister of War in Wakatsuki's cabinet, in December 1926 to Hankow, where he saw Borodin and later was to encounter Mori. Suzuki then proceeded to Kiukiang, met Chiang Kai-shek, and finally returned to Tokyo in May 1927 to report his findings to Premier Tanaka. Suzuki, *Himerareta Shōwashi,* pp. 23–24.

the two weakened forces and, after taking Chenchow, established himself in Kaifeng. Yen Hsi-shan, whose alignment had been somewhat in doubt till then, openly sided with Chiang Kai-shek.

Thus in late May 1927 the situation was fluid, and the fate of North China and ultimately of Manchuria seemed to hang in the balance. In view of the impending battle between the opposing forces, Mori argued that the Tanaka government must send troops to Shantung to protect the life and property of Japanese residents if the Seiyūkai were to keep face.

Initially, opposition to the expedition was voiced from within the government, especially the army, lest it precipitate an untoward incident.[4] Tanaka was himself reluctant and suggested that a mere token force of two battalions be sent from Tientsin to Tsingtao. Mori persisted, however, and singlehandedly turned the cabinet decision in favor of the expedition.

Saitō, the Consul General at Tsinan, pleaded most urgently against the sending of troops, which he felt would do more harm than good. He pointed out that the cabinet decision to dispatch an expeditionary force was based on erroneous information given by General Shirakawa Yoshinori, Minister of War. Despite Saitō's last-minute telegram, some 2,200 Japanese troops from Manchuria landed at Tsingtao on May 30.

From Peking, Chang Tso-lin protested that "Japan's action not only departs from [accepted practices in the] comity of nations but violates China's sovereignty, arousing the enmity of the Chinese people. Her actions only aggravate the situation."[5] The Nanking government followed with a protest of similar purport.

It is appalling to realize that this was a one-man venture. Mori's persistence can be gathered from his defiant tone: "If Tanaka will not assent to sending the expeditionary force, I'll make him resign from the presidency of the Seiyūkai."[6] Because

4. Yamaura, *Mori Kaku,* p. 608. Asahi, *Taiheiyō, 1,* 288–89.

5. Ibid., p. 609. Author's translation.

6. Ibid. The following episode is indicative of the peculiarly vulnerable position of Tanaka in relation to Mori. According to Matsuoka Shunzō, Mori's fellow member of the Seiyūkai, "On the day Yokota Sennosuke

of Mori's close ties with the army, he is said to have brought pressure to bear upon the members of the General Staff as well, for it was reported that Major General Araki Sadao, Chief of the Division of Strategy, and his subordinates, Obata Toshio and Suzuki Teiichi, carried out the mobilization order with utmost reluctance.[7]

Though Tanaka, despite misgivings, gave in to Mori in sending troops to Shantung, the Premier sought in other ways to preserve Chang Tso-lin as a pro-Japanese ally in Manchuria. Once again, for example, he resorted to private diplomacy by dispatching General Yamanashi Hanzō to Peking in the summer of 1927 to visit the Marshal.[8] Yamanashi pleaded with Chang Tso-lin to pull back to Mukden and secure his position there behind the assured support of the Japanese army. Tanaka hoped that, if Marshal Chang were to give up Peking without a struggle, the Nationalists would be satisfied with the attainment of their primary goal—the seizure of Peking—and there would be less likeli-

---

[the incumbent president of the Seiyūkai] died, Mori, Kasuga Toshibumi, and I happened to meet at Yokota's residence. Tanaka was also there; so we walked over to his side to tell him that since Yokota was dead, we were switching our support to him and made a toast to that effect. Then Mori and Kasuga turned to Tanaka and said, 'Hereafter we want you to listen to whatever we have to say.' Tanaka assented. Mori then turned to me and said in a defiant tone, 'You are Tanaka's subordinate, but I am no pliant servant of Tanaka. He is the one who is going to take orders from me.' " Ibid., p. 494. Author's translation. For a perceptive description of Tanaka as a politician, see Scalapino, *Democracy and the Party Movement in Prewar Japan,* p. 232.

7. Yamaura Kanichi, "Bōshō Mori Kaku" (Mori Kaku, The Arch-Schemer), *Fūun Jinbutsu Tokuhon* (Review of the Men of the Hour), Supplement to *Bungei Shunju, 33,* no. 12 (1955), 64.

8. Although Shigemitsu Mamoru in his *Shōwa no Dōran* (Political Disturbances of the Shōwa Period, *1* (Tokyo, 1952), 34, indicates that Premier Tanaka was responsible for General Yamanashi's mission to Peking, Suzuki in *Himerareta Shōwashi,* p. 24, states that he sent Yamanashi to Chang Tso-lin in Peking. While one can only wonder how a lieutenant colonel could have ordered a full general on assignment, there is a hint that Suzuki may well have been the originator of the idea.

hood of their pushing on into Manchuria to fill the vacuum left by the defeat of Marshal Chang's army.

Chang, however, was extremely reluctant to abandon Peking, largely because it symbolized prestige. He retorted defiantly that it was he who was waging Japan's war against the Communist hordes, even to the extent of advancing against them. Therefore he was frankly puzzled as to why Japan should ask him to pull his punches; in his eyes this was tantamount to siding with the Nationalists, who had fallen under Communist influence. To this, General Yamanashi had no ready answer, and he returned to Tokyo to report on Chang's obdurate attitude.

The Second Eastern Regions Conference[1]

While the Chinese people were still smarting from the incursion of the Japanese expeditionary forces into Shantung, Mori set afoot even more aggressive moves with respect to Manchuria by persuading Tanaka to summon a second Eastern Regions Conference. The Premier was unenthusiastic from the outset, for he had his own secret plans.[2]

Unlike the first Eastern Regions Conference summoned by Premier Hara Kei as a consultative body, the second assembly of ranking diplomatic officials and military officers from China, Manchuria, and the Kwantung Territory met primarily to be informed about and agree to the Seiyūkai's reinvigorated China policy and the means to implement it. Suzuki Teiichi tells what

1. Premier Hara Kei convened the first Eastern Regions Conference in May 1921. It was a consultative conference in which ranking officials, civil and military, reported to Tokyo from their overseas posts on the Asiatic continent to participate in the formulation of Japan's over-all policy in China and Manchuria.

2. See above, pp. 14–16. Although Ugaki fails to give reasons for Tanaka's lukewarm attitude toward summoning the Eastern Regions Conference, see Ugaki Kazushige, *Shōrai Seidan* (Refreshing Discourse at Shōrai Villa: A Memoir) (Tokyo, 1951), p. 316 (hereafter referred to as *Ugaki Memoirs*).

Mori Kaku, this slight but energetic expansionist, was trying to do:[3]

> About the time of the second Eastern Regions Conference, when I was with the General Staff, I met Mori at his request. His main argument was that the Chinese problem would not be solved unless the politicians and the military united. Mori's idea underlying the Eastern Regions Conference was that Japan would take upon herself the task of maintaining peace and order in Manchuria. I replied that I went along with him but that I would like to add some observations of my own. Mori asked me to put them into writing.
>
> In summary my views were that since the resumption of Sino-Russian relations in 1924, Russia had openly engaged in spreading communism in China. I was convinced by 1927 that this could not go on. Unless Japan waged war, she would find it difficult to solve her continental problems.[4] Thinking that at least the military ought to be prepared for such a contingency, I took the matter up with the younger officers of the General Staff and the Ministry of War. In this group were Isihara Kanji and Kōmoto Daisaku.[5]
>
> My object was to unify their ideas with respect to Japan's course on the continent. The consensus was to cut Manchuria off from China proper and bring it under Japan's political control. This meant that

3. Yamaura, *Mori Kaku,* pp. 599–601. Author's translation.

4. In the original text there is an expurgated portion, represented by four blank spaces, as follows: "ippen ( ) ( ) ( ) ( ) na kere ba tairiku mondai no kaiketsu wa konnan da." It seems highly plausible that the four letters omitted were (sen) (sō) (o) (shi), i.e. to wage war. Yamaura, *Mori Kaku,* p. 599.

5. Colonel Kōmoto was later responsible for the death of Marshal Chang Tso-lin in 1928. Soon afterward he was retired from active status but remained in Manchuria and maintained close contact with the expansionist elements of the Kwantung Army. Ishihara was the guiding mind behind the plot to engineer the Mukden Incident on September 18, 1931.

> Japan's whole policy—domestic, foreign, and military—must be directed toward the attainment of this single objective.
>
> We knew that the execution of the plan called for circumspection and finesse, since it was obvious that no minister in Tanaka's cabinet would support such a plan. I then went to see Mori. He suggested that we see Yoshida Shigeru, the Consul General of Mukden, who happened to be in Tokyo at the time. Yoshida thought that, since the United States would be the difficulty, Saitō Hiroshi[6] would be the man to consult. It was, therefore, Saitō who took my draft and revised it into a more presentable form.

It soon became apparent that the undisguised object of the second Eastern Regions Conference, which took place from June 27 to July 7, 1927, was to hammer out a course of action precisely as outlined by Suzuki—viz., Japanese seizure of Manchuria.

It is true that various other problems were dealt with. A fund was appropriated to assist Japanese residents in the Yangtze Valley, where they were suffering from the effects of the anti-Japanese campaign. There was some discussion of the large unsecured loans made to China. Mori subjected to searching scrutiny the role the South Manchuria Railway Company had played in the past, blaming the rapid deterioration of Japan's influence in Manchuria on the fact that the company had failed to perform its role as the vanguard of Japanese imperialism in Manchuria and Mongolia. He made a five-point proposal that would have stripped the company of two of its essential functions—its right to develop the natural resources of Manchuria and Inner Mongolia and its authority to administer the areas immediately adjoining the railway zone. That portion of the proposal was not accepted.[7]

6. Japan's Ambassador to the United States.
7. See below, pp. 29–31.

At this point there is a large gap in the records of the conference, and one may surmise that Mori ordered the portion of the proceedings dealing with his drastic proposals for Manchuria and Mongolia stricken from the records.[8] But from other sources we can piece together a fairly coherent picture of what these proposals embodied.

A clue lies in the eight-point program that Premier Tanaka announced on the final day of the conference. China took a grave view of these disquieting statements because they departed radically from Shidehara's policies. The most significant were 5, 6, 7, and 8:

> 5. It is clear that lawless elements in China will from time to time disrupt the peace, causing unfortunate international incidents. It is expected that the Chinese regime and the awakened people will surpress these rebellious elements and restore peace and order. However, Japan will have no choice other than resort to measures of self-defense should Japan's rights and interests or the life and property of the Japanese residents be jeopardized.
>
> Moreover, in order to impress on the Chinese the nature of Japan's rights, Japan must act against those elements who wantonly instigate anti-Japanese campaigns and the boycott of Japanese goods by spreading false rumors.
>
> 6. Since Manchuria and Mongolia and particularly the Three Eastern Provinces [Heilungkiang, Kirin, and Liaoning] affect in the gravest way Japan's existence as a nation, Japan feels responsible for the maintenance of peace and the economic development of these areas.
>
> 7. Japan must count on the efforts of the people

8. For details of the conference see Yamaura, *Mori Kaku*, pp. 575–601; also under "Tōhō Kaigi" in "Papers Recovered from the Estate of the Late

> of these three provinces for the maintenance of peace and order there. She will support any regime deemed capable of fostering political stability, which would also respect Japan's special interests.
>
> 8. Should the spreading of the civil war into Manchuria and Mongolia jeopardize Japan's special rights and privileges, Japan must be ready to deal swiftly with any faction threatening her rights so that these regions may be maintained as safe and suitable areas for development by local and foreign residents.[9]

Mori appears to have had four main points. First, the Tanaka government would not hesitate to send troops into China proper, Manchuria, or Inner Mongolia to protect the rights, interests, life, and property of the Japanese residents or to quell anti-Japanese activities. He was saying that Japan was ready to intervene by force in the domestic affairs of China when she thought such a move was warranted. Secondly, since Manchuria and Inner Mongolia were of utmost importance to Japan's security, she would insist that peace and order be maintained in these regions. Thirdly, Japan would back a regime indigenous to the Three Eastern Provinces if it would respect Japan's special interests. Fourthly, Japan was ready to isolate Manchuria and Inner Mongolia from China proper and set up a puppet regime if the Nationalists should alter the special status of these regions.

There is a clue to the momentous import of Mori's proposals in an exchange between Premier Tanaka and Lieutenant General Mutō Nobuyoshi, commanding officer of the Kwantung Army, on the first day of the conference. General Mutō said to Tanaka,

---

Matsumoto Tadao, Parliamentary Vice Minister," designated as PVM 41 in Cecil H. Uyehara, comp., *Checklist of Archives in the Japanese Ministry of Foreign Affairs, Tokyo, Japan, 1868–1945* (Washington, 1954), p. 109 (hereafter referred to as *Uyehara Checklist; Tanaka Giichi Denki, 2,* 644–62; and Asahi, *Taiheiyō, 1,* 289–91.

9. Modified from Yamaura, *Mori Kaku,* pp. 592–93. Author's translation.

"Although this is not a pleasant prospect, Japan must be prepared to face a world war if such a drastic program is to be carried out. To begin with, America will not tolerate it. If America will not acquiesce, neither will England nor the rest of the powers. Are you prepared to cope with America and the eventuality of a world war?" Tanaka replied, "I am prepared to face the consequences." Mutō repeated, "You are sure you will not waver later on, are you?" "I am all set to face the worst." Mutō said, "If the Government is so determined, I have nothing else to add. We shall wait for the order to come and simply carry it out." Thereafter, Mutō did not utter a word throughout the whole conference.[10]

The Dairen Conferences[1]

The landing of the second contingent[2] of Japanese forces in Shantung in July, following closely on the heels of the Eastern Regions Conference, aroused the ire of the Chinese people. This

10. Ibid., pp. 636–37. Author's translation.

1. A collective designation for the series of meetings, held as a sequel to the Eastern Regions Conference, between Mori and Japanese officials in Manchuria and the Kwantung Territory. The meetings were held on successive days in Mukden, Dairen, and Port Arthur, August 13–15, 1927. One author alleges that the so-called Tanaka Memorial drew upon the decisions rumored to have been reached at the Dairen Conferences. Cf. Ozawa Eiichi, Takai Hiroshi, and Oda Yasumasa, *Shiryō Nihonshi* (A Source History of Japan) (Tokyo, 1958), p. 346. On the other hand, Chinese delegates to the League attributed to Tanaka the authorship of an alleged confidential memorial to the throne of July 25, 1927. Japan has denied the attribution (and at the same time has never quite succeeded in proving that it was a forgery), but her military actions in Manchuria, Inner Mongolia, and China after 1931 offer striking parallels to the proposals made in the memorial. However, J. W. Ballantine in the Tokyo Trials declared he found no evidence to substantiate the Chinese charges. For further details see Samuel F. Bemis, *A Diplomatic History of the United States* (New York, 1951), p. 809, n. 1; also Morishima, *Conspiracy,* pp. 7–8; Shigemitsu, *Shōwa no Dōran, 1,* 33. Shigemitsu and Morishima, as members of the Foreign Office, made an exhaustive investigation to discover the true author of the alleged memorial. Both men deny its authenticity.

2. After Chiang Kai-shek's troops successfully occupied the southern

move, it seemed evident, was an implementation of Tanaka's "positive" policy. In China itself the boycotting of Japanese goods quickly gathered momentum[3] and in Manchuria a similar movement gained headway.[4] Irate Japanese residents of Manchuria countered by calling a mass meeting and demanding resolute action by their home government. They sent representatives to Tokyo to arouse and enlist support both in and out of the government.[5]

In Mukden, meanwhile, Consul General Yoshida was pushing negotiations with the Chinese authorities in accordance with the decision reached at the Eastern Regions Conference; but little could be expected in such a hostile atmosphere. Simultaneously, Japan's Minister to China, Yoshizawa Kenkichi, was negotiating with Chang Tso-lin in Peking. He was embarrassed when he was told by the wily Yang Yu-ting (a powerful political figure in the Mukden government and second only to the Marshal) of the talks already in progress between Chang Tso-lin and

---

part of Shantung Province in early July 1927, former subordinates of Chou Hsien-jen in Kiaochow shifted their allegiance to the Nationalists, thereby cutting off railway connections between Tsinan and Tsingtao. This isolated some 2,000 Japanese residents in Tsinan, a potential war zone. Tanaka then obtained imperial sanction on July 6 to move inland to Tsinan Japanese troops stationed in Tsingtao, after which he rushed the Eighth Brigade in Dairen to Tsingtao as replacements. In late August, however, Tanaka ordered the evacuation of Japanese troops from Tsinan, because the Northern Expedition had come to a halt after Chiang's relinquishment of his military command to facilitate rapprochement between the Nanking and Wuhan regimes.

3. The Central Headquarters of the Nationalist party (Wuhan), in a circular telegram of June 8, 1927, publicized its decision to boycott Japanese goods. The Shanghai League of Economic Boycott against Japan passed a resolution on July 2 calling for cessation of transactions with Japanese banks.

4. During the month of August 1927 there were many displays of anti-Japanese sentiment throughout Manchuria. The Mukden Chamber of Commerce at its general meeting on August 7 ordered a boycott of Japanese goods. On August 16 the first anti-Japanese mass meeting was held in Mukden.

5. Yamaura, *Mori Kaku,* p. 601. Free translation by author.

Yamamoto Jōtarō,[6] president of the South Manchuria Railway Company. Yoshizawa sent a scorching telegram to Tanaka, not knowing that Yamamoto had earlier received secret instructions from Tanaka.

Mori had been waiting impatiently in Tokyo, hoping to receive word of progress in the talks being held in Mukden and Peking between Chinese and Japanese officials. When a month passed without tangible result, he hastened to the continent to learn firsthand the sources of the difficulties. There he held a series of conferences with staff members of the Peking legation and the Consulate General of Mukden and with executives of the South Manchuria Railway Company.

That Tanaka was only a skeptical bystander to Mori's latest move is evident in a statement Tanaka made to press reporters on August 17, 1927: "Although I am told that the follow-up conference to the Eastern Regions Conference in Tokyo is currently convening in Dairen, I say that deciding on a rigid course of action vis-à-vis a nation such as China whose domestic situation is constantly in a state of flux is simply not feasible. Our government is taking the position that we negotiate with Chang Tso-lin so long as he prevails in the north and likewise with Chiang Kai-shek so long as he is in control of the south."[7]

Mori proposed that ineffective approaches to the solution of Manchurian problems be discarded and new lines of attack devised. Spheres of operation were to be staked out more distinctly, so that each team comprehended the task it was to perform. The South Manchuria Railway Company would continue to handle railroad problems while Yoshida, as the Consul General at Mukden, would deal with local issues in Manchuria. Negotiations covering outstanding questions on Manchuria and Inner Mongolia were to be conducted in Peking between Chang Tso-lin and Yoshizawa.

These so-called outstanding questions pertained to the rights

6. See above, pp. 14–16.
7. Author's free translation from *Tanaka Giichi Denki, 2,* 740.

and privileges Japan claimed to have acquired in Manchuria and Inner Mongolia under Group II of the Twenty-one Demands of May 25, 1915.[8] Yoshizawa's proposed broad agenda touched upon the following points.

1. The extension of the leases of Port Arthur, Dairen, South Manchuria Railway, and Antung-Mukden Railway to ninety-nine years
2. The right of Japanese nationals to lease land for commercial, manufacturing, and agricultural enterprises, and to reside and travel
3. The right of Japanese nationals to undertake joint enterprises with Chinese nationals
4. Suitable localities in eastern Inner Mongolia to be opened to foreigners for trade and residence
5. The right to prospect and extract mineral resources
6. The prior right of Japanese nationals to invest in railroad building in South Manchuria and eastern Inner Mongolia
7. Prior right of Japanese nationals to be employed as advisers or instructors in political, financial, military, and police matters
8. Speedy revision of the Kirin-Changchun Railway Loan Agreement

The Chinese government had consistently questioned the validity of these agreements, since it had been forced to conclude them under duress. That the United States frowned upon the treaties, and the world in general disapproved of Japan's action, strengthened China's moral position and made her all the more reluctant to continue them. Moreover, Japan was flying in the face of the rights recovery movement of the late twenties, where-

8. Yamaura, *Mori Kaku*, pp. 588–90, 602. H. F. MacNair and Donald F. Lach, *Modern Far Eastern International Relations* (New York, 1950), p. 184.

by China sought wholesale abrogation of the rights the powers had extracted from her by means of unequal treaties.[9]

Of particular significance was the temper of the Dairen Conferences. The consensus among the participants was that the time had come for Japan to apply coercive measures. The impatient went so far as to demand immediate occupation of Manchuria, foreshadowing the abortive attempt made less than a year later, in May 1928.[10] But what seemed like a well-coordinated two-pronged drive on the Chinese at Peking and Mukden met rebuffs from unexpected quarters.

When Yamamoto Jōtarō learned at the Dairen Conferences of the drastic measures Mori was proposing, he rushed back to Tokyo to report to Tanaka on the progress he was making in negotiating directly with Chang Tso-lin. Yamamoto then invited to his residence Mori and other key figures of the Foreign Office, including Debuchi Katsuji, Vice Minister of Foreign Affairs, Kimura Eiichi, Chief of the Asia Bureau, and Uehara Etsujirō, parliamentary councilor, and informed them of the private negotiation in which he was engaged with Chang Tso-lin in Peking. Yamamoto pleaded that the decisions reached at the Dairen Conferences would only undo favorable concessions he had extracted from the Marshal on five railroads, of which Chang had already formally approved two.[11] Although indignant, Mori, Yoshizawa, and the staff of the Foreign Office had to drop their plans. The incident again pointed up Tanaka's ineptness in formulating a well-coordinated China policy, as well as the excessive influence which Mori was attempting to exert over Tanaka's foreign policy.

Upon returning to Mukden, Yoshida promptly changed tack. Assuming that it was within the competency of the officials on the spot to implement the policies decided at the Eastern Regions and Dairen Conferences, he threatened to abrogate the Pact of

9. For additional information see *Foreign Relations* (Washington, 1915), pp. 197–204; and MacNair and Lach, *Modern Far Eastern International Relations,* pp. 183–97.

10. See below, pp. 37–40.

11. See Morishima, *Conspiracy,* p. 13. Asahi, *Taiheiyō, 1,* 457 n.

1909, which enabled the Peking-Mukden railroad to cross the rails of the South Manchuria Railway Company and reach Chang's arsenal within Mukden's city walls. An arsenal deprived of its spur tracks would have materially weakened Chang's hand.

This time Yoshida encountered opposition from the headquarters of the Kwantung Army: he was bluntly told that it was premature to apply extreme measures. Since no diplomatic move could hope to attain its objective in Manchuria without the backing of the Kwantung Army, he had no way out but to feign illness and withdraw to Tokyo. Reportedly the rebuff was intended purely as a personal affront to Yoshida, whose caustic tongue had incurred the ill feelings of highly placed officials in Port Arthur.

Having narrowly prevented Mori from performing what he called a "surgical operation" on Manchuria, Yamamoto and Machino had all the more reason for continuing their negotiations in Peking with renewed vigor. They sensed that time was running out. Only after a concentrated effort was Machino successful in overcoming the Marshal's initial reluctance and paving the way for the final stage of the negotiations. In November, Yamamoto visited Peking and at last obtained the formal approval of Chang Tso-lin and Yang Yu-ting on two of the railways. Machino returned to Tokyo the same month to report to Tanaka on the progress of the negotiations. In February 1928 Chang and Yamamoto concluded an agreement, which they decided to announce formally in July.

As part of the pact, parcels of land were to be attached to each railway zone. In addition to financing the development of the railroads, under the nominal designation of rent Japan agreed to pay a total of ten million yen in two installments. The first five million was to be paid in July when the agreement was announced and the balance when construction was actually begun. However, on the initiative of Machino the date of the initial payment was advanced, and a draft for five million yen was paid in February 1928.

Why did Marshal Chang accede, though reluctantly, to a

portion of the Japanese demands? There is no question that the Marshal was in critical need of up-to-date arms for his troops. In November 1927 it was only a question of time before the Nationalist Army resumed its northward march. Chiang Kai-shek was homeward bound from Japan to take over military command.[12] In the severe fighting around Chumatien in May 1927 Marshal Chang had had a foretaste of the superiority of disciplined and well-equipped Nationalist troops. Thus Japan was obliged to advance the date of the initial payment if the Marshal were to block the Nationalist troops from surging into Manchuria.

Also working in favor of Japan's railroad designs in Manchuria were Marshal Chang's suspicion and dislike of the Russians and his preoccupation with eliminating Soviet influence in Manchuria—attitudes that resulted from the Karakhan-Koo Agreement of May 1924, whereby the Soviets succeeded in restoring the old Tsarist rights over the Chinese Eastern Railway.[13] Chang Tso-lin, as independent ruler of Manchuria, flatly refused to recognize this agreement. Later the same year, however, when the Soviets threatened his rear by massing their troops along the northern borders during his crucial struggle with Wu Pei-fu, Chang Tso-lin had to accede. On September 20, 1924, the Marshal concluded a special convention with Ambassador Leo Karakhan in Mukden confirming the Karakhan-Koo Agreement, although with some modifications.

At the time, the Marshal demanded and secured from the Soviets as quid pro quo an arms understanding and assurance that they would not molest his rear during the Shanhaikwan battle against Wu Pei-fu in October 1924. The understanding was not made effective until the following spring, when the Marshal was in need of fresh arms to liquidate the enemy positions around Peking. Then, however, his effort to obtain arms from

12. See below, p. 33.

13. See MacNair and Lach, *Modern Far Eastern International Relations,* pp. 264–66; also Putnam Weale (Bertram Lenox Simpson), *Why China Sees Red* (New York, 1925), pp. 92–93.

the Soviets met with an open rebuff. He was so enraged that he hastily sanctioned the construction by Japan of the Taonanfu-Tsitsihar Railway, which, by intersecting the Chinese Eastern Railway, would have driven a wedge into the Russian sphere in Manchuria. The tension between the Marshal and the Soviets continued to mount; in early 1926 Chang ordered the arrest of M. Ivanov-Rinov, the director-general of the Chinese Eastern Railway, though he was later released. Thus there was historical reason to presume that Chang's railway concessions to Japan may in part have stemmed from the Marshal's desire to check the penetration of Soviet political and economic influence into Manchuria.

The Tsinan Incident

In September 1927, Japanese troops were evacuated from Shantung. Only eight months later, in May 1928, Tanaka's cabinet was again saddled with the responsibility of safeguarding Japanese residents in that area. In mid-March Chiang Kai-shek, now fully restored to power and in league with Feng Yu-hsiang and Yen Hsi-shan,[1] had resumed a general offensive against Chang Tso-lin and the remnants of the northern warlords. By mid-April a combined force of some quarter of a million troops was deployed in a semicircle ready to converge on Tsinan. Residing in and about the city were 2,000 Japanese; an additional 17,000 lived along the Shantung railway or in the city of Tsingtao.[2]

Details of the second Japanese expedition and the unfortunate collision with the Nationalist forces that ensued has been ade-

1. In the previous summer the Northern Expedition came to a stop when, in order to make possible the rapprochement between the Nanking and Wuhan governments, Chiang went into voluntary exile and visited Japan. It was during his sojourn there that he held a conversation with Tanaka and Mori at Hakone. In this interlude the Wuhan government purged itself of communist elements.

2. Japanese residents in Shantung and Hopeh were distributed as follows: Tsinan, 2,233; Tientsin, 6,746; Peking, 1,586; Tsingtao, 13,621. Figures are derived from *Tanaka Giichi Denki, 2,* 621.

quately dealt with in a number of well-known works.[3] Our primary concern is to understand the circumstance which prompted the Tanaka government to send the second expeditionary force to Shantung despite the unpopularity of the first.

This time also there was bitter opposition from both houses of the Diet, and Tanaka and the army were opposed to sending troops. Moreover, Tanaka was reluctant to go back on the understanding he had reached with Chiang the previous October at Hakone. He had agreed that Japan would recognize the Nationalist revolution and the unified China which emerged as a result of it, one proviso being that the party dissociate itself from its Communist elements. Chiang, in return, recognized Japan's rights and vested interests in Manchuria.[4]

Mori also had participated in the Hakone conversations, but he now insisted that troops be sent to the trouble spot again. He argued that the Seiyūkai must live up to the public statement it had made at the time of the first expedition, when the Japanese troops were evacuated—that in the future it would be under obligation to send troops to China whenever a disturbance threatened the life or property of Japanese residents there.[5] One

3. Takeuchi, *War and Diplomacy in the Japanese Empire,* pp. 248–61. Chitoshi Yanaga, *Japan since Perry* (New York, 1949), pp. 455–56. MacNair and Lach, *Modern Far Eastern International Relations,* p. 307. MacNair, *China in Revolution,* pp. 130–34. The Incident was triggered by the firing of a gun by Japan's Special Service Agent as Chinese and Japanese troops confronted each other in Tsinan. Nezu Masashi, *Dai Nihon Teikoku no Hōkai* (Collapse of Imperial Japan) *1* (Tokyo, 1961), 91.

4. For the mutual understanding achieved at Hakone see Yamaura, *Mori Kaku,* pp. 614–15; Shigemitsu, *Shōwa no Dōran, 1,* 34–35; Suzuki, *Himerareta Shōwashi,* pp. 24–25, *Tanaka Giichi Denki, 2,* 741–47. One writer contends that it was not Tanaka but Lieutenant General Matsui Iwane who met Chiang Kai-shek at Hakone to pave the way for a subsequent meeting between Chiang and Tanaka at the latter's residence in Tokyo on November 5, 1927. This writer states that Tanaka's appointment book does not mention the date or place of the alleged meeting, nor does it even place Tanaka at Hakone during October. Cf. *Tanaka Giichi Denki, 2,* 741, 828–29. However, the question is not where these two men met but whether they actually reached a firm understanding. Mr. Takakura, the editor of *Tanaka Giichi Denki,* does not clarify this point.

5. Yamaura, *Mori Kaku,* pp. 610–11.

author believes it was a part of Mori's vote-getting tactics.[6] Mori contended that, although the Nationalist troops might not require attention, there was the possibility that the retreating army of Chang Tso-lin might molest Japanese residents.

After the sharp Sino-Japanese clash of arms at Tsinan, it took almost a year of painstaking negotiation between the representatives of the two governments before the incident was amicably settled. However, the resentment of the Chinese people did not subside so easily; it persisted for years and plagued the relations between the two countries.

It is essential to point out that Shigemitsu Mamoru, Japan's principal negotiator, encountered difficulties on two fronts. The inflexible attitude of Mori gave him as much as, or even more trouble than, the demands made by the Chinese representatives. Seldom does one come across passages like the following from Shigemitsu's diplomatic memoirs, which portray Mori's intentions toward China in such startling fashion:

> It was decided that I should proceed to Shanghai to find a way out of the present impasse in the Japanese-Chinese negotiations. On February 18 [1929] the leading officials of the Foreign Office met to deliberate over the instructions which were to guide my negotiations. Present at the meeting were Yoshida Shigeru, Vice Minister of Foreign Affairs; Mori Kaku, Parliamentary Vice Minister of Foreign Affairs; Uehara Etsujirō, a Parliamentary Councilor; Arita Hachirō, Chief of the Asia Bureau; and myself.
>
> What I recall vividly to this day was Mori's attitude. Since Tanaka held the portfolio of Foreign Minister concurrently with the premiership, Mori took the attitude that he was to run the Foreign Office. Moreover, with respect to China, Mori entertained ideas which were at variance with all others. That day Mori

6. See Itō Masanori, *Gunbatsu Kōbōshi* (The History of the Rise and Fall of the Military), *2* (Tokyo, 1958), 133–34.

said to me in an overbearing tone of voice, "To begin with, it's all wrong to try to reach a settlement over an incident like the one at Tsinan. We have gotten ourselves into troubles like today's because Yoshizawa [Minister to China] tried to reach a settlement. You must be prepared to make little of turning places like Shanghai into shambles. When you go to Shanghai this time, you must bear in mind not to be lulled into a conciliatory attitude. Negotiations of this sort must be dashed to pieces."

Yoshida and Arita listened in amazement. Mori was babbling beyond the bounds of reason. Since I was warned beforehand by Tani Masayuki of Mori's disquieting attitude, I managed to gloss over the situation by replying, "Your point of view is well taken." Mori's idea was diametrically opposite to the briefing I had received from Premier Tanaka, who had given me instructions in his capacity as Minister of Foreign Affairs. It seemed as if Mori was already in league with the extremists of the army and was itching to create disorder in China in order that they might capitalize on the confusion to extend Japan's influence there.[7]

The Attempt on Chang's Troops at Shanhaikwan and Other Plots

After the Sino-Japanese clash at Tsinan, the Nationalist troops bypassed the city and resumed their northward march toward Peking. In the face of the advance of the better disciplined Nationalists, Marshal Chang's forces beat a hasty retreat across the northern plains toward the capital city, and by the middle of May 1928 its fall appeared imminent.

At this critical juncture Yamamoto Jōtarō, president of the

7. Shigemitsu Mamoru, *Gaikō Kaisōroku* (A Diplomatic Memoir) (Tokyo, 1953), pp. 65–66 (hereafter referred to as *Shigemitsu Memoirs*). Author's translation.

South Manchuria Railway Company, again arrived in Peking to press Chang Tso-lin to sign the particulars of the railway agreements to which Chang had grudgingly assented the previous fall.[1] In this exigency, Yamamoto finally extracted from the Marshal approval for Japan to engage in further development and construction of railroads between Kirin and Kainei and between Changchun and Dairen.

Concurrently, however, an even bitterer pill was being prescribed for Marshal Chang in Tokyo. As a result of the cabinet meeting of May 16, a decision was reached to issue warnings to both Chang Tso-lin and the government in Nanking, declaring that the Japanese government would take appropriate and effective measures to maintain peace and order in Manchuria in the event that hostilities reached the Peking-Tientsin area and threatened the peace of Manchuria.[2]

It was close to midnight on May 18 when Yoshizawa Kenkichi, Japanese Minister to China, called on Marshal Chang to deliver this warning and elaborate its purport. The gist of Yoshizawa's advice was that Chang should withdraw into Manchuria before he was defeated by the Nationalists; otherwise the Kwantung Army would block the passage of both Chang's retreating troops and the pursuing Nationalist forces at Shanhaikwan and disarm them. This was in fact an ultimatum. Chang, visibly perturbed, is said to have retorted, "Even if I have to give up my life, I do not want Feng Yu-hsiang in Peking."[3]

As a preliminary to armed intervention in China, Japan's Kwantung Army on May 18 shifted its headquarters from Port Arthur to Mukden.[4] At this point, at the instigation of C. T. Wang of the Nanking government, Washington sent a reminder

1. The account of Chang Tso-lin's last days in Peking are drawn from Yamaura, *Mori Kaku,* pp. 631–32, and Usui Katsumi, "Chō Sakurin Bakushi no Shinsō" (The Truth Regarding the Assassination by Bombing of Chang Tso-lin), *Himerareta Shōwashi,* pp. 28–29 (hereafter referred to as Usui, *Himerareta Shōwashi*).

2. This is referred to as the "Notification of May 18th," *Himerareta Shōwashi,* p. 29. Author's translation.

3. Ibid.

4. *Tanaka Giichi Denki, 2,* 943–44.

to Tokyo cautioning the Japanese government to apprise the United States in advance if it intended to take any action in Manchuria.

Beginning on May 20, another Eastern Regions Conference, meeting in emergency sessions, spent five days in fruitless debates. Those who had been given to bluffing at the second conference, in the preceeding summer, were unnerved by the surprise thrust from Washington. Confusion reigned over the question of how to answer it. Mori, who as usual was the chairman, insisted that no choice remained but to proceed according to the predetermined plan.

General Araki, recalling the hectic days, said, "Everyone had different ideas; no one agreed; we were just going around in circles wasting precious time. If they were going to waver at this late stage of the game, why did those men assent to the proposals when they were first presented at the Eastern Regions Conference?"[5]

Meanwhile, the Kwantung Army, poised for instant action in Manchuria, was becoming more and more impatient and began harassing Tokyo with queries. The acute sense of frustration coupled with an awareness of imminent action is recorded by Major General Saitō Tsune, Chief of Staff of the Kwantung Army. The following are excerpts from his diary:

> Mukden, May 21:
>
> On the assumption that the Imperial Order [to mobilize] decreed at 9 A.M. in Tokyo would become effective at 12 noon here, I advised my subordinates to that effect and at 12 summoned them. But the orders did not come through. I am beginning to think that in all likelihood the plans of the Army Command have been disrupted by some plot. . . .
>
> Waited all night but the orders never arrived. The

5. Yamaura, *Mori Kaku,* p. 634. Author's translation.

Kwantung Army, bursting with spirit, is piqued by the government's indecision.

Mukden, May 22:

At 10 A.M. moved Command Headquarters to the top of the Tōtaku Building. At 3:47 P.M. the Commander in Chief [Lieutenant General Muraoka Chōtarō] arrived [from Port Arthur] on schedule and immediately occupied the temporary headquarters. . . . I sense a growing warlike mood spreading about us.

Mukden, May 23:

A Colonel Tashiro, Chief of the China Section of the General Staff Office, arrived from Tokyo to brief us on the government's position. According to him, Chang Tso-lin is not to be pressed to relinquish his status . . . although the manifest policy of the government is that both the Northern and the Southern Armies are to be disarmed alike; in practice, however, the Commanding General of the Kwantung Army is authorized to use discretion and treat the Northern Army more leniently.

The Kwantung Army in Mukden, expecting mobilization orders at any moment, is in a state of animated suspense. Feeling of antagonism toward the indecisive Tokyo government is daily mounting. Even Peking is buzzing with rumors of the Kwantung Army's pending expedition to Chinchow and the forcible seizure of the Peking-Mukden Railway.[6]

On May 25, Mori forced a decision in Tokyo to carry out his predetermined plan. The decision was taken to Premier Tanaka, then at his villa near Kamakura, for final approval. That evening,

6. Usui, *Himerareta Shōwashi,* p. 32. Author's translation.

as he strolled along the beach accompanied by two men—Arita Hachirō of the Foreign Office and General Abe Nobuyuki, who had conveyed the decision made earlier in the day in Tokyo—Tanaka made up his mind. Mori's plan had to be brought to a halt. There was to be no occupation of Manchuria.[7]

General Abe and Arita were back in Tokyo the following morning. Mori was first dumfounded and then indignant. His main concern now became how to placate activists within the ranks of the Kwantung Army, who had been fretting for action. But he did not quite succeed; within ten days Marshal Chang Tso-lin was to meet an untimely death at the hands of a certain highly placed officer of that same army.[8]

Although the Kwantung Army was bent on taking Manchuria, Tanaka was not ready to risk a war with the United States. His sudden abandonment of Mori's so-called predetermined plan marked the parting of ways for the two men. A handful of activists within the Kwantung Army, however, did not give up easily; and it sought to do by indirection what Tanaka had directly prohibited by his refusal to sanction the Mori plan. This plot, as described by Admiral Okada Keisuke in his memoirs, involved the imposition of a barrier to the northward retreat of Chang Tso-lin's troops, so that the Kwantung Army could move easily into the ensuing vacuum. The plot was to be sprung when and if Chang Tso-lin were defeated in the northern plains of China by the Nationalist Army and had to withdraw to Manchuria. At a preliminary meeting between the representatives of the army, navy, and Foreign Office, an army representative proposed blocking Chang Tso-lin's retreat by landing a division at Shanhaikwan, after which the Kwantung Army would have an easy task in occupying Manchuria.

7. About this time at a cabinet meeting, General Shirakawa Yoshinori, Minister of War, also undertook to persuade Tanaka that action be taken to retire Chang Tso-lin from public life, but Tanaka steadfastly refused to accede to Shirakawa's proposal. Shidehara Heiwa Zaidan, *Shidehara Kijūrō* (Tokyo, 1955), p. 361 (hereafter referred to as *Shidehara Kijūrō*).

8. See below, pp. 45–51.

Rear Admiral Yonai Mitsumasa, who represented the Office of Naval Operations at the preliminary meeting, flatly refused to be a party to such a proposal and returned to report what was afoot to Admiral Suzuki Kantarō, Chief of Naval Operations. In turn, Admiral Suzuki asked Admiral Okada, who was then the Minister of the Navy, to shelve such a proposal if the army introduced it at a cabinet meeting.

As anticipated, the very next day the army brought up the plan at the cabinet meeting, and, when it looked as if the proposal might go through unopposed, Okada pointed out that sending an expeditionary force to the Peking-Tientsin area constituted a violation of a time-honored treaty[9] and that Japan must be prepared to go to war against America and England if she chose to violate it. In astonishment Premier Tanaka naïvely remarked, "So there is such a treaty? Well, then the whole venture will have to be called off."[10]

It should be noted that, about the same time the army was proposing in Tokyo that Chang's retreating troops be blocked at Shanhaikwan, the Kwantung Army was on the verge of advancing on Chinchow of its own accord. This action was halted only at the last minute by an imperial edict.[11]

Assassination of Chang Tso-lin[1]

We now direct our attention to Mukden, the new focal point of crisis in view of the imminent return of Chang Tso-lin to his former seat of power. By late May, Chang's retreating troops were swarming into the walled city at five to ten thousand a day.

9. Admiral Okada was probably referring to the Nine-Power Pact, although he does not so specify.

10. Okada Keisuke, *Okada Keisuke Kaikoroku* (Okada Memoirs) (Tokyo, 1950), pp. 34–35 (hereafter referred to as *Okada Memoirs*).

11. Morishima, *Conspiracy,* p. 20.

1. I am indebted to Hirano Reiji's *Manshū no Inbōsha* (A Conspirator in Manchuria) (Tokyo, 1959), pp. 75–91 (hereafter referred to as Hirano, *Manshū*), for the general sequence and development of the narrative in this chapter. For passages freely rendered into English from the pages

Adding to the existing confusion was the influx of 50,000 fresh men from the northern province of Heilungkiang under the command of General Wu Chun-sheng. This state of affairs only contributed to the heightening of the sense of insecurity among the Japanese residents, who were already harassed by the mounting incidence of unfriendly acts toward them. In some cases it was the Japanese adventurers themselves who tried to incite mobs into touching off anti-Japanese incidents to give the Japanese army in the area a pretext to go into action. The fact was that the Kwantung Army, with a view to moving south toward Shanhaikwan to intercept Chang's army, had requested and had been provided with a mixed brigade from Korea to protect Japanese residents in Mukden during its absence from that city.

It was during this explosive situation that a coded cable from Tokyo Headquarters—representing Premier Tanaka's veto of Mori's desperate move—reached the temporary headquarters of the Kwantung Army early on May 26, ordering the army to "suspend completely previously decided plan [of action]."[2] The staff officers were crestfallen. According to Hirano, "Colonel

---

above, acknowledgments are made in the foregoing footnotes. Other pertinent sources for the story in this chapter are *Tanaka Giichi Denki, 2,* 947–51; Usui, *Himerareta Shōwashi;* pp. 26–38; Itō, *Gunbatsu Kōbōshi, 2,* 136–39; Mori, *Senpū Nijūnen,* pp. 11–18; Machino Takema, "Chō Sakurin Bakushi no Zengo" (Events Preceding and Following Chang Tso-lin's Death from Bombing), *Chūō Kōron* (September 1949), pp. 72–80; and Kōmoto Daisaku, "Watakushi ga Chō Sakurin o Koroshita" (I killed Chang Tso-lin), *Bungei Shunju* (December 1954), pp. 194–201. There are indications that Hirano's account has drawn upon the facts contained in Colonel Kōmoto's own article. In his writings, Kōmoto expresses resentment toward the ineptness of Japanese military advisers attached to Chang Tso-lin. Since the facts of the secret Chang-Yamamoto railroad negotiations were then known to the Kwantung Army and the members of the Foreign Office, it is hardly conceivable that Kōmoto was unaware of them. Years later Machino speculated that Kōmoto and his fellow conspirators may have decided to dispose of Chang Tso-lin before the railway agreements were announced in July, lest their thunder be stolen. See Shinmyō, "Shōwa Seiji Hisshi—Chō Sakurin Bakusatsu," *Chūō Kōron* (April 1954), p. 196.

2. "Kitei hōshin zenmenteki ni chūshi seyo," Hirano, *Manshū,* p. 75. Author's free translation.

Kōmoto clutched the telegram in his hand and bit his lip. . . . Commander Muraoka [Chōtarō] and Chief of Staff Saitō [Tsune] hardly spoke the rest of the day. Even normally voluble Ishihara and easy-going Itagaki were silent."[3]

Kōmoto decided to go to Tokyo to confront Mori, determined to find out for himself why the original plan[4] to disarm Chang Tso-lin's retreating troops had been abandoned. He was also intent on calling on Army Headquarters to seek some means whereby the heavy flow of Chang Tso-lin's troops into Mukden could be prevented. Failing this, he wanted assurance that Headquarters would send substantial reinforcements, so that the combat strength of the Kwantung Army would reach some semblance of parity with that of Chang Tso-lin's force. Kōmoto confided his plans to Araki Gorō, major general in command of Chang Hsueh-liang's bodyguard, and asked if Araki could maintain order for a month until he returned from Tokyo. Araki assured him that his Chinese troops were just as reliable as the Japanese regulars.[5]

On the following day, May 27, Kōmoto revealed his plans to Colonel Itagaki Seishirō and to Lieutenant Colonel Ishihara Kanji, subordinate members of his staff. The two readily agreed to Kōmoto's plans. Since it was Itagaki and Ishihara who later engineered the Mukden Incident, the meeting of minds at this stage is a matter of extreme significance. It would seem that Itagaki and Ishihara were responsible for keeping alive the idea of bringing Manchuria and Mongolia under the direct control of the Kwantung Army—an idea that fired the imagination of the men at least three years prior to the Mukden Incident.[6] How-

3. Ibid. Author's free translation.

4. Colonel Kōmoto was quite aware of Mori's original plans, since he had attended the Eastern Regions Conference held in Tokyo from June 27 to July 7, 1927, as an aide to General Mutō. At the conference, Kōmoto had sided with Mori, asserting emphatically that Japan's problems in Manchuria "could no longer be solved by feeble diplomatic protests." Hirano, p. 71.

5. Ibid., p. 77.

6. It is possible that if Colonel Kōmoto had remained on active duty

ever, Muraoka Chōtarō, the commanding general, while not opposed to Kōmoto's trip, counseled postponement because the situation in Mukden just then was fluid and critical.

Meanwhile, in North China, in order to meet the three-pronged drive launched by the Nationalists, Chang Tso-lin marched his troops southward. The result was that some 200,000 men confronted each other on fronts extending over 100 miles in what had every appearance of being a decisive encounter.

The Northern Army initiated a general offensive on the 27th but was soon forced to retreat in the face of a determined counteroffensive by the superior southern armies. On the 30th the Northern Army withdrew northward beyond the line of the Liuli River and thereafter deliberately avoided any decisive encounter; Chang Tso-lin was determined to keep his army intact. On June 2 in somewhat of an anticlimax, Chang Tso-lin, by means of a circulating telegram, let it be known that he intended to withdraw his forces into Manchuria, thereby sparing the residents in and about Peking from the ravages of war.

---

after the death of Chang Tso-lin, he could have been the principal architect of the Mukden Incident. There was a meeting of minds among Kōmoto, Itagaki, and Ishihara, and the three often dined together at Japanese restaurants in Dairen to discuss their secret plans on how to effect Japan's colonial policy in Manchuria. Hirano, p. 66.

Hirano relates the following incident, which reveals Kōmoto's obsession with the idea of continental expansion: "One day Kōmoto baited General Mutō about staging an insurrection. Mutō said, 'That is not a light matter; just what do you have in mind?' Kōmoto replied, 'My proposition is to blast the Yalu River Bridge and so enable the Kwantung Army to become independent of the central authority. Subsequently we shall establish a small independent state separate from Japan and China. In the face of this fait accompli our actions would not be censurable by the government in Tokyo, nor would the United States and England be in a position to lodge complaints with Japan. After that it would be up to the newly founded nation to make the best of the situation. Too, we shall be able to head off the spread of communism, which is in the process of subverting China and eventually Japan.' Kōmoto stared intently at General Mutō's face but the General dared not utter a word." Since Hirano attributes a liberal amount of Kōmoto's thinking to Ishihara's ideas, it may be said that the notion of engineering the Manchurian Incident and eventually establishing a puppet state was already envisaged by Kōmoto, Itagaki, and Ishihara about 1928. Hirano, *Manshū,* pp. 67–68. Author's free translation.

The admission of defeat by Chang Tso-lin was taken as a signal for instant action by the anti-Chang elements in the Kwantung Army. In Mukden one day Kōmoto unexpectedly caught sight of Lieutenant Colonel Takeshita Yoshiharu, a military attaché from Harbin, emerging from Muraoka's office.[7] Kōmoto, somewhat puzzled, sensed that something was afoot behind his back because issuance of travel orders for military attachés was normally part of his duties. He bade Takeshita to come into his office.

There Kōmoto, by deftly alternating cajolery and browbeating, forced Takeshita to divulge the fact that he was under orders from General Muraoka to proceed to Peking, engage an assassin, and dispose of Marshal Chang Tso-lin. Kōmoto convinced Takeshita that Peking was not the proper place for such a bold undertaking, since it would be directly under the watchful eyes of the world. Takeshita was reluctantly prevailed upon to transfer his assignment to Kōmoto. Takeshita was then entrusted with the task of proceeding to Peking and identifying from there the train the Marshal would board. Finally, Kōmoto cautioned Takeshita to keep their understanding a secret from Itagaki and Ishihara and, of course, from General Muraoka.

There followed a period of intense activity. Kōmoto summoned First Lieutenant Kanda Yasunosuke, commanding a company attached to the 20th Engineers Regiment, and ordered him to study the terrain around the railroad bridge over the Chuliu River near Mukden. He reported back that the area was under such tight guard that even reconnoitering posed a problem.

Kōmoto then suggested an alternative site near Huangkutun, where the tracks of the South Manchuria Railway passed over the Peking-Mukden Railway. This time Lieutenant Kanda returned with a more heartening report stating that only Japanese railway guards patrolled the area and that Chinese guards were

7. The story of the encounter between Kōmoto and Takeshita is taken from Hirano, pp. 79–81.

not posted there. Thereupon, Kōmoto gave Kanda detailed instructions.

Along about this time an officer commanding the Independent Railroad Guard, a Major Tōmiya,[8] was also determined on a certain course of action to be taken in view of the imminent return of Marshal Chang to Mukden. As Lieutenant Kanda began to frequent the zone patrolled by the railway guards, he was spotted by Tōmiya, who recognized the guiding mind of Lieutenant Colonel Kōmoto at work behind Kanda's clandestine activities.

Major Tōmiya thereupon went to Lieutenant Colonel Kōmoto and reminded him that he was intruding upon his area of responsibility. Kōmoto declared in veiled language that on the crucial day the responsibility of patrolling the site of the railroad overpass would no longer rest with Tōmiya because Kōmoto would see to it that the area was placed under the joint patrol of the Kwantung Army and the troops of Chang Tso-lin. Therefore, were an accident to occur at the site, Kōmoto insisted that he and he alone would be held accountable for having allowed the Chinese to share in the patrol duties. Tōmiya, realizing the futility of resisting Kōmoto, consented to cast his lot with Kōmoto's plot. Thereupon the two confided to each other the details of their plans.

Kōmoto entrusted the execution of the plot entirely to Tōmiya and turned over to him the necessary funds. The following day Tōmiya and Lieutenant Kanda began the task of installing the explosives. A handful of enlisted men from the engineer corps transported cement bags packed with explosives to the site of the railway overpass. Lieutenant Sugano, a demolition expert, deftly installed the detonator, and the explosives were ready to be triggered at any time.

To camouflage the crime, Kōmoto engaged Adachi Takamori,

8. The encounter between Kōmoto and Tōmiya follows the account in Hirano, pp. 83–85. For Tōmiya's version of this conspiracy see Morishima, *Conspiracy*, p. 23.

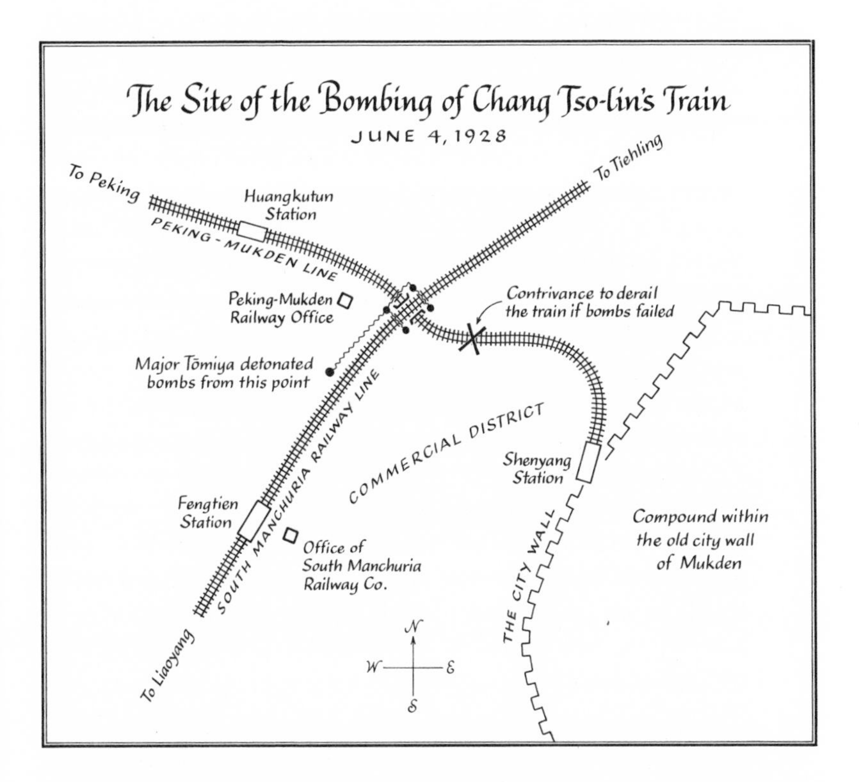

Note: The approximate location from which Major Tōmiya detonated the bomb is based on a diagram in Ozaki, *Rikugun o Ugokashita Hitobito,* p. 107. For a variant version, see Asahi, *Taiheiyō, 1,* 307, where the location of the lever to actuate the bomb appears on the Commercial District side of the tracks approximately 200 yards from the point at which the Peking-Mukden Railway goes under the tracks of the South Manchuria Railway.

an adventurer, to line up three henchmen of Liu Tsai-ming[9] to be used as decoys. The three men were told to come to the sentry box on a designated day to get their instructions.

In the meantime, at Peking, working closely with Lieutenant Colonel Takeshita, Captain Tanaka Ryūkichi kept close check on the schedule and composition of trains departing for Mukden. Just to make sure, these trains were spotted again by observers detailed at key points such as Shanhaikwan and Chinchow along the Peking-Mukden Railway.[10] From about June 1 Kōmoto and his fellow conspirators waited daily for the all-important signal.

While these men were biding their time, Marshal Chang's security guard had reason to be apprehensive of the security of the railway overpass at Huangkutun. First Lieutenant Chin of the gendarmes called upon Major Mitani, a squad leader of the Japanese gendarmery in Mukden, and sought the latter's permission to post Chinese sentries in the vicinity of the overpass and the embankments. Initially Mitani rejected Chin's proposal, but in the end the two agreed to share the responsibility—that is to say, the Japanese would assume the responsibility of guarding the overpass while the Chinese would do likewise with the area beneath.[11]

9. Liu Tsai-ming was an underling of Kuo Sung-ling, who was executed for leading an insurrection against Chang Tso-lin in 1925. See Hirano, p. 86. Kōmoto detailed Captain Ozaki Yoshiharu with his detachment to stand by at a point beyond the railroad crossing (see Map 3). Had the bombs failed, it was so devised that the train would be derailed at this point and Ozaki was to direct his detachment to rush into the train and attack the Marshal. Ozaki Yoshiharu, *Rikugun o Ugokashita Hitobito* (Figures Who Wielded Influence in the Army) (Odawara, 1960), pp. 105–110.

10. Usui, *Himerareta Shōwashi,* p. 35.

11. Ibid., pp. 35–36. There are indications that Marshal Chang was informed by his agent in Tokyo of the plot to bomb his train. When he discussed this report with Colonel Machino, the latter assured the Marshal that he would personally accompany him, thereby implying that the report was groundless. A. Vespa, *Secret Agent of Japan: A Handbook to Japanese Imperialism* (London, 1938), p. 16.

Apparently, Kōmoto also had his moments of doubt. After he received the signal that the Marshal's train had left Peking, Kōmoto called on

The heavily guarded train bearing the Marshal left Peking at 1:15 A.M. on June 4. Accompanying him as members of his cortege were General Wu Chun-sheng, Colonel Machino, Major Giga, and Chang Ying-huai, the director general of transportation. Machino got off the train at Tientsin with Premier P'an Han to proceed to Techou, where the two were to meet Chang Tsung-ch'ang, the leftist military leader of Shantung. The latter had indicated to the Marshal that he would, on his own, try to hold off the Southern Army.[12] Nevertheless, it is only natural that Machino's action aroused the suspicion that he knew in advance of the plot to assassinate the Marshal. But if, let us say, someone had tipped him off at the last minute, it is inconceivable that Machino would have knowingly allowed Chang Tso-lin to go to his death. This would have meant the complete negation of the railroad negotiations over which he had labored for months. Moreover, as stated earlier, Machino and Giga were at odds with Kōmoto, Itagaki, and Ishihara; thus, there was every reason for Kōmoto and his group to keep their plot concealed from Machino and Giga.

On the morning of the 4th, Shenyang Station and the adjoining compound were surrounded with a heavy cordon of military guards. At 5:20 A.M. the air suddenly became tense upon receipt of the report that the Marshal's train had just passed Huangkutun.

Aboard the train a game of mah-jongg had just broken up. Chang Ying-huai, Wu Chun-sheng, and Major Giga hurriedly returned to their quarters toward the rear of the train. The Marshal was alone, still seated at the mah-jongg table, when with a thunderous roar his car blew up. He was struck in the

---

Captain Ozaki and asked if the venture ought not be called off. Kōmoto was apprehensive lest the plot be exposed because the bombing might have to take place in daylight. Ozaki objected. Subsequently, he regretted doing so, for had he concurred with Kōmoto history might have followed a different course. Ozaki, *Rikugun o Ugokashita Hitobito,* p. 39.

12. Machino, "Chō Sakurin Bakushi no Zengo," Chūō Kōron (April 1949), p. 79.

nose by a fragment of steel apparently just as he was about to duck under the table. He lay unconscious.[13]

A press officer rushed through the wreckage to the Marshal's side and directed soldiers standing in a state of confusion to carry the Marshal into a nearby linen factory, whence he was surreptitiously transported by truck to a hospital within the city walls of Mukden, where he died.

For several weeks Tsang Shih-yi, commandant in charge of maintenance of public peace in Mukden, cleverly concealed Chang Tso-lin's death by fabricating stories about his progress toward recovery. But the truth eventually came out. Of the three henchmen engaged by Adachi Takamori, two were bayoneted by Japanese guards, but the third escaped to report the whole incident to Chang Hsueh-liang, the Marshal's son.[14]

Premier Tanaka was utterly dismayed. General Ugaki Kazushige, who happened to be visiting Tanaka when he received the telegram, reported that Tanaka sighed, "What fools! They [the Kwantung Army] behave like children. They have no idea what the parent has to go through."[15]

As a matter of fact, Colonel Kōmoto's plan went beyond the mere removal of Chang. In the wake of Chang's death, Kōmoto ordered Captain Ozaki, his subordinate, to demand that Headquarters mobilize the Kwantung Army and engage Chang's troops. The proposal was rejected by Lieutenant General Saitō Tsune, Chief of Staff of the Army.[16] Kōmoto had hoped that during the ensuing confusion the Army could set up a new political order in Manchuria.

After the bombing of Chang's train, acts of terrorism—among them the bombing of meeting halls of Japanese residents in Mukden—were perpetrated by agents of the Kwantung Army.

13. Based on Hirano, p. 89. For a somewhat different version cf. Paul S. Dull, "The Assassination of Chang Tso-lin," *Far Eastern Quarterly, 11* (1952), 456.

14. Morishima, *Conspiracy,* pp. 21–22.

15. *Ugaki Memoirs,* p. 317.

16. Itō *Gunbatsu Kōbōshi, 2,* 137–38.

Subsequently, the Army prodded the Consulate General with repeated telephone calls asking whether the consular police force alone could afford adequate protection for the residents. By discreetly declining the Army's offer to mobilize, the Consulate General narrowly averted an incident at Mukden at this earlier date. In 1931, however, the Army did not bother to consult the Consulate General. It went into action without heeding the Consulate General's repeated pleas to cease fire.[17]

The Aftermath

There was a lapse of several weeks following the death of the Marshal before his son, Chang Hsueh-liang, cautiously made his way back to Mukden from his hideout in Chinchow to face a highly fluid political situation in the Three Eastern Provinces. The question of who was to step into the Marshal's shoes was yet to be settled. Informed sources guessed that Yang Yu-ting, the Old Marshal's Chief of Staff, or Chang Tso-hsiang, the provincial governor of Kirin, was just as likely to succeed the Marshal as his own son.

Premier Tanaka's formula for ameliorating the crisis was to install Chang Hsueh-liang as nominal ruler under the tutelage of Yang Yu-ting. There were others, like Yamamoto, president of the South Manchuria Railway Company, Hayashi, Consul General of Mukden, and Colonel Machino, military adviser to the late Marshal, who supported Tanaka's proposal.[1]

A smaller but no less influential group of individuals, among them General Muraoka, Commanding General of the Kwantung Army, and Matsuoka Yōsuke, vice president of the South Manchuria Railway Company, however, were bitterly opposed to Yang Yu-ting's assuming any role in the new regime. A third faction, including the Ōkura interests and General Matsui Nanao, another military adviser to the late Marshal, favored grooming

17. Morishima, *Conspiracy,* p. 24. Asahi, *Taiheiyō, 1,* 309.

1. *Tanaka Giichi Denki, 2,* 958–59; Hirano, *Manshū,* p. 91; Morishima, *Conspiracy,* pp. 30–31.

Yang Yu-ting for the role of future ruler of the Three Eastern Provinces. Thus, to summarize briefly, the consensus in the Kwantung Army and among the higher circles in the Japanese government was to name Chang Hsueh-liang as the ruler of Manchuria; the precise status of Yang Yu-ting remained the center of heated controversy.

As for Chang Hsueh-liang himself, he was forced to turn to the Japanese early in the summer of 1928, despite his deep-seated aversion toward and mistrust of them, because they offered the only way to safety in the face of the southern armies and opposition within Manchuria itself.[2] He was careful not to offend the Japanese, lest some of the extremists in the Kwantung Army decide to take matters into their own hands; at the same time he was spared from becoming a complete tool of the Japanese because they themselves were split into factions, each group bitterly determined to be the sole sponsor of the Young Marshal.

While Chang Hsueh-liang held the Japanese at bay and at the same time deftly utilized Japan's military presence to maintain his position in Manchuria, he had to contend with a third force—namely the South—whose alignment with his adversaries in Manchuria could upset the uneasy equilibrium. Thus the Young Marshal was fully aware that Yang Yu-ting or Chang Tso-hsiang might negotiate a compromise with the Nanking government behind his back. Were this to happen, Kirin Province for certain, and perhaps Heilungkiang too, would have sided with the Nationalists, leaving Chang Hsueh-liang a puppet clutched in the arms of the Kwantung Army. This was an end he sought to avoid at all cost, since he well knew that his political

2. In describing the sequence of events and the actions of Chang Hsueh-liang immediately after the death of Chang Tso-lin, the author is indebted to an exceedingly perceptive article by Akira Iriye on the complex interplay of forces which culminated in the final raising of the Nationalist flag in Manchuria on December 29, 1928. See "Chang Hsueh-liang and the Japanese," *Journal of Asian Studies, 20* (1960), 33–43; also Asahi, *Taiheiyō, 1,* 311–17.

future would be doomed once he was cast in the role of a collaborator.

Nevertheless, Chang Hsueh-liang dared not openly seek rapprochement with the South, for several reasons. First, the Seventeen-Member Peace Preservation Committee, of which he was a member, was sharply divided between those who were for casting their lot with the Nationalists at an early date and those who were opposed on the ground that the time was not yet ripe; the latter felt that, rather than toss precaution to the winds, efforts should be made to get along with the Japanese, at least until such time as the political status of the Three Eastern Provinces could be clarified. Chang Hsueh-liang's tactics of temporizing indicate that until about the middle of July he sided with the latter group; at least his actions had the practical result of maintaining the status quo.

For even were Chang Hsueh-liang to side with the former faction and respond to the overtures made from the South, it would gain him little, since at this time the authority of the Nanking government was still confined to the lower reaches of the Yangtze River and to the regions just north of it. Moreover, the militarists who had rallied around the Nanking government in support of the Northern Expedition were far from being in accord on the future status of the Three Eastern Provinces.

In the meantime, however, it became increasingly evident to Chang Hsueh-liang that public sentiment in the Three Eastern Provinces was steadily growing in favor of union with the South. By the middle of July he had to admit to Hayashi, the Japanese Consul General at Mukden, that he was powerless to resist it.[3] Also, Chang saw an opportunity to strike a political bargain with Chiang Kai-shek. Thus, on the understanding that Jehol would be incorporated as a fourth province in Manchuria and that the Nationalist government would not intervene in its internal affairs, the Nanking and Mukden governments agreed that the Nationalist flag should be raised in Manchuria about July 22.

3. Ibid., p. 36.

Meanwhile, earlier in July, Hayashi had received a lengthy telegram from Premier Tanaka declaring that, although Japan could view with equanimity the hoisting of the Nationalist flag in Manchuria, she could not remain passive if branches of the Kuomintang were established in the Three Eastern Provinces, since it would then be well-nigh impossible to forestall the flow of the political influence of the South into Manchuria.[4]

Thus, despite repeated prodding from Premier Tanaka and Mori Kaku that Hayashi start negotiating with the Young Marshal on matters of railroad construction which Yamamoto and the Old Marshal had agreed to in Peking, and on Japan's commercial rights in Manchuria, Hayashi discreetly delayed, waiting for better days, and concentrated on winning Chang to the side of Japan.[5] Hayashi directed his efforts entirely to dissuading the Young Marshal from reaching an accord with the South.

It is not entirely inconceivable that in these informal talks between Hayashi and Chang during the earlier weeks of July, Hayashi may have hinted at worse things in store if Chang were overly hasty about reaching an agreement with the Nanking government. However, when on July 19 the Nationalist government notified the Japanese government of the abrogation of the existing Sino-Japanese commercial treaty, Hayashi on the same day formally warned Chang Hsueh-liang against raising the Nationalist flag in Manchuria. Thus we note that on July 21 the Young Marshal informed Hayashi that efforts in this direction would be abandoned for the time being, and at the same time he wired the Nanking government: "It is regrettable that, because of Japanese intervention, negotiation toward reaching an accord has fallen into abeyance. However, there has been no change in my own attitude toward seeking eventual peaceful unification of China."[6] This was probably not the only reason.

4. *Tanaka Giichi Denki, 2,* 960–62.

5. Morishima, *Conspiracy,* p. 36.

6. *Tanaka Giichi Denki, 2,* 962. Author's translation. On October 19, 1928, at Keio University in Tokyo, Shidehara delivered a lecture on the

The Seventeen-Member Peace Preservation Committee was still sharply divided between those who advocated immediate agreement with the Nationalists and those who advocated gradualism. Thus, the Young Marshal probably deemed it wiser to temporize for the time being until the emergent political development in the Three Eastern Provinces became more settled. Although the Peace Preservation Committee at its meeting on August 10 decided to postpone talks with the Nationalists for a period of three months, by the middle of the same month the Young Marshal was again engaged in negotiations with Chiang Kai-shek and other key members of the Kuomintang government.

On the other hand several developments forced the Tanaka government to revert to a more conciliatory attitude toward the regimes in Mukden and Nanking. The formal warning which Consul General Hayashi had delivered to the Young Marshal on July 7 only heightened anti-Japanese sentiment throughout China and added impetus to the economic boycott. Elsewhere it excited the suspicions of the Western powers, thereby weakening the Seiyūkai's position because of the criticism to which it was subjected by the opposition party. Moreover, on October 8 Tanaka learned with certainty that Japanese army officers were responsible for the death of Chang Tso-lin, placing Japan, at least in Tanaka's own thinking, in a morally indefensible position.[7] Inevitably his government was forced to modify its demands on China, abandon the positive approach adopted by Mori Kaku at the Eastern Regions Conference, and retreat to

"Essentials of Japanese Diplomacy and its Guiding Principles." In his talk, he took to task the Tanaka government's inept meddling in the internal affairs of China. Shidehara reproached the government and said that Japan's interference in the rapprochement between the Nanking and the Mukden regimes for a mere three months accomplished nothing in the interest of Japan. Moreover, it was an unwarranted assumption that Japan should take it upon herself to safeguard both the local and foreign residents in Manchuria, a territory which was without question a part of China. *Shidehara Kijūrō,* pp. 372–74.

7. Ibid., pp. 964–65. Also see p. 1030 for a description of the agony that Tanaka suffered.

a policy much closer to that of the opposition party under Shidehara—the protection of Japan's treaty rights and interests. In this process, too, the site of negotiations on matters of Japanese rights with the Chinese authorities tended more and more to be moved away from Mukden, where it was under the watchful eyes of the Kwantung Army, to Nanking, where Minister Yoshizawa was in residence.

By the fall of 1928 the adherents of early recognition of the Nanking regime were definitely in the ascendant, and Chang Hsueh-liang could no longer postpone the crucial decision. The Kuomintang, moreover, had appointed him a member of the State Council at Nanking, and he was assured that the key officials of the Three Eastern Provinces would be appointed by the Mukden regime. These developments, together with a compromise on the composition of the political council of Jehol, laid the setting for the rapprochement between the Nanking government and the Mukden regime. On December 29 the blue and white revolutionary flag of the Nationalist government was raised throughout the Manchurian provinces.

This time the Tanaka government did not panic, for it was reconciled to accepting the inevitable. Nevertheless, it could not escape the criticism that the incident represented a new low in Japanese prestige in China. In retrospect, it can be stated that Japan had only her inept officers like Kōmoto and his fellow plotters to blame. Naïvely these activists believed that the removal of Chang-Tso-lin would miraculously bring about an improvement in the over-all situation in Manchuria, to the benefit of Japan.[8]

Moreover, a factor which probably contributed just as much to the fiasco was the mistaken notion shared by the members of the staff of the Kwantung Army that orphaned and inexperienced Chang Hsueh-liang could be readily won over and made into

8. See Hanaya Tadashi, "Manshū Jihen wa Kōshite Keikaku Sareta" (This is how the Manchurian Incident was Planned), *Himerareta Shōwashi,* p. 42 (hereafter referred to as Hanaya, *Himerareta Shōwashi*).

a pliant servant of Japan.[9] As matters turned out, the officers and dignitaries from Japan who called on Chang Hsueh-liang were led astray by his suave manners, grossly underrating his firm determination not to give in to Japanese demands.[10]

Finally, some key officials in the Tanaka government—Mori Kaku in particular[11]—and the majority of the Japanese military simply refused to face up to the realities of the rights recovery movement, which was sweeping the whole of China in the wake of Nationalist victory in the South. The overriding political fact of the day was that no Chinese leader could hope to remain in power by defying this fiery expression of national sentiment even if it meant losing the support of the Kwantung Army or arousing the enmity of the Japanese people.

Tanaka Resigns[1]

Shirakawa, Minister of War, at first refused to believe that Japanese officers were responsible for the death of Marshal Chang, but in view of persistent rumors he sent Miné, command-

9. As a means of paving the way for Japan's dominance over Manchuria and Inner Mongolia, Kōmoto advocated the removal of Chang Tso-lin. Once this was accomplished it would be easy to win over the "inexperienced" Chang Hsueh-liang. See Mori, *Senpū Nijūnen,* pp. 13–14; *Tanaka Giichi Denki, 2,* 956–57.

10. For a rather impressionistic yet perceptive thumbnail sketch of Chang Hsueh-liang see Morishima, *Conspiracy,* pp. 27–29. The author emphatically refutes the thesis that Chang Hsueh-liang's rapprochement with the Nanking government was motivated solely by the desire to safeguard his status. Chang was sympathetic to the objectives of the Nationalist party and possessed a genuine desire to back the drive against foreign domination of China under the rights recovery movement.

11. See Nashimoto Yūhei, *Chūgoku no naka no Nihonjin* (Japanese in China), *1* (Tokyo, 1958), pp. 56–57. Matsuoka Yōsuke, vice president of the South Manchuria Railway Company, bitterly poured out his invectives against Mori Kaku for his ill-starred Tsinan military venture, Matsuoka accused Mori of being a "cancerous growth" in the Japanese government and denounced him for being overeager to bring fame to himself.

1. For the dilemma in which Tanaka was caught see Paul S. Dull, "The Assassination of Chang Tso-lin," *Far Eastern Quarterly, 11* (1952), 457–63.

ing general of the gendarmery, as an undercover investigator to Mukden. It was only after Shirakawa had read Miné's full findings that he was convinced that a Japanese officer was implicated; he reported the fact to Premier Tanaka on October 8. By this time some four months had elapsed since the crime had been committed, and Tanaka was compelled to take the position that the offenders should be brought to trial and punished.

There is little doubt that Tanaka was prompted by Prince Saionji, who summoned the Premier and advised him to be firm,[2] saying that the truth would come out no matter how hard the government of Japan tried to conceal it. If it became plain that the guilty party was a Japanese military man, he must be punished without delay. Only by so doing could the government uphold discipline within the ranks of the military and her status of honor and respect among the nations of the world. In the long run this too would enable the Chinese to maintain friendly feelings toward Japan. Also it would reflect favorably upon the military background of the Premier and the prestige of the Seiyūkai party. When Tanaka vacillated by saying that he would look into the matter after the coronation,[3] Saionji urged him at least to report the incident to the Emperor right away.

But this was quite contrary to the opinion held by executive members of the Seiyūkai. They took the position that under no circumstances should the culprit be punished, because this would be an open admission of Japan's guilt. After all, the crime was committed by members of the Emperor's own troops. How could the Emperor, in name the Commander in Chief, maintain face in the presence of foreign diplomats? They thought that Prince Saionji was wholly in the wrong, and presently there developed a strong movement to whitewash the whole incident.

In the face of strong opposition from within his party, Tanaka was extremely reluctant to take resolute action; but in the end he was prevailed upon, by Saionji's repeated urging, to report the

2. *Harada Diary, 1,* 3–4. *Okada Memoirs,* p. 38.
3. Held in Kyoto, November 10, 1928.

incident to the Emperor. At an audience, Tanaka stated that it appeared likely that the offending party was a Japanese army officer and that he should be brought to trial before a military tribunal. The Emperor responded tersely, "Military discipline must be maintained with rigor."[4] Tanaka pledged that His Majesty's wishes would be carried out.

But Tanaka discovered that it was well-nigh impossible to hold a trial by court-martial. Not only were ranking army officers violently opposed to it, but objections were voiced even from the members of his own cabinet. The Seiyūkai was exerting utmost pressure on Tanaka to prevent him from conducting a trial.[5]

For instance on October 23, at the second meeting of the "Special Committee to Investigate the Death of Chang Tso-lin," Ōba, an administrative official of the Kwantung Territorial Government, testified that Itō Kenjirō and Staff Officer Kōmoto were the principal offenders. The meeting was thrown into such a turmoil that Mori suspended it for the day.[6] Even more alarming was the growing resentment of the general populace against holding the trial. Tension reached a point so critical that some feared outbreaks of violence.

Tanaka was left with no choice but to bow to public sentiment and accept the formula suggested by the Minister of War, who proposed that the offenders be punished by administrative action. General Muraoka and Colonel Kōmoto were now charged with dereliction of duty, the specific charge being failure to post railroad guards at a zone requiring protection. By disposing of the case in this way, General Muraoka would not even be suspected of being implicated in the plot; it would be believed that he was being punished solely because of his position as Commanding General of the Kwantung Army.

4. *Harada Diary, 1,* 5. Author's translation.

5. For Tanaka's earnest efforts to court-martial Colonel Kōmoto and his losing battle against overwhelming odds, see Shinmyō, *Chūō Kōron,* (April 1954), pp. 197–99.

6. Kurihara Ken, *Tennō* (The Emperor) (Tokyo, 1955), p. 42.

The Emperor was displeased when Tanaka reported to the throne the change in the mode of bringing the offenders to account. No sooner did Tanaka finish reading the memorial than the Emperor charged, "You are contradicting what you said the last time." Mortified, Tanaka replied, "I shall further explain the various matters to Your Majesty." "There is no need for further explanation," the Emperor retorted, and retired into the inner chamber. Later Tanaka sought another audience, but the Grand Chamberlain, Suzuki Kantarō, said apologetically, "I shall convey your wishes to His Majesty, but I am afraid that it will be useless."[7]

Tanaka returned to his office crestfallen, firmly resolved to resign. Although some members of the Seiyūkai objected, this time he stuck to his decision. Shortly thereafter he died of heart failure. There were rumors that he had committed suicide, but this was not true.[8]

A new cabinet was formed under Premier Hamaguchi of the Minseitō party, and Shidehara returned as Foreign Minister.

Though Tanaka passed from the scene quietly, his indecisive handling of the death of Marshal Chang reaped the whirlwind,[9] marking as it did the beginning of the army's domination of Japan. The army had already defied the Premier and had even dared to ignore the imperial will.

7. See *Okada Memoirs,* pp. 40–41. Author's translation. Years later the Emperor reportedly expressed misgivings about having been too harsh with Tanaka (Kurihara, *Tennō,* p. 46).

8. For details of Tanaka's dying hours see *Tanaka Giichi Denki, 2,* 1052–53.

9. Koizumi Sakutarō, Tanaka's contemporary, once observed, "Tanaka has taken over the government but has not accomplished a thing that he set out to do. Instead, he has been made to do everything he has not wanted to do" Baba, *Gendai Jinbutsu Hyōron,* p. 183. Author's translation.

3.
TENSIONS WITHIN JAPAN

Dissension over the London Naval Agreement

In January 1930, delegations representing Great Britain, the United States, Japan, France, and Italy met in London to negotiate an agreement governing the specifications and total tonnage of cruisers (of 10,000 tons and less), destroyers, and submarines. Although the five powers had reached an agreement on capital ships and aircraft carriers at the Washington Conference in 1922, subsequent efforts at Geneva in 1927 to reach an accord on various auxiliary ships had failed, owing to Anglo-American differences.

As 1929 drew to a close, these two nations were willing to try again with Japan, Italy, and France also participating. Because of the acute financial depression gripping these countries, each had good reason to try to head off a possible armament race in the auxiliary class.

The London Naval Conference has already been studied in great detail by a number of scholars,[1] and here we shall recount

1. The fullest account is to be found in E. L. Woodward and Rohan Butler, eds., *Documents on British Foreign Policy,* 1919–39, Second Series, *I* (London, 1930). Also see Vol. 1 of *Foreign Relations* (Washington, 1930). For the controversy which raged within the Japanese government over the ratification of the treaty see the detailed treatment by Takeuchi, *War and Diplomacy in the Japanese Empire,* pp. 283–336; and Aoki Tokuzō, *Taiheiyō Sensō Zenshi* (History of Events Leading to the Pacific War), *I* (Tokyo, 1953), 3–101 (hereafter referred to as Aoki, *The Pacific War*). The author is greatly indebted to this work in recounting the events up to April 2, 1930.

only salient facts relating to protests which the Japanese Naval General Staff lodged against the deliberate actions of their own government.[2] This account should show in sharp relief the growing split in Japan's ruling circles during a period of declining Japanese influence in China. We shall examine in particular the growing dissatisfaction of the Japanese military and the ultranationalists with the Minseitō government, particularly Shidehara, because of its insistence on conducting its foreign relations in accordance with anticipated responses from the leading powers of the West.

The very fact that the government was able to prevail over the forces of reaction in the Privy Council only by threatening to invoke the authority of the Emperor so incensed reactionary elements that, in the words of one observer, "The sentiment evoked and the resentment stirred up in connection with the London Naval Treaty were echoed and re-echoed in subsequent years by arousing public opinion against the political parties, politicians, and liberals."[3]

In the late summer of 1929, Japanese Naval Officers, and especially members of the "fleet clique,"[4] viewed any naval limitation conference with grave misgivings. Still rankling in their hearts was the memory of the Washington Naval Conference, particularly the unpopular settlement forced on Japan with respect to the capital ship ratio of 5:5:3. Inferiority in capital

2. Perhaps the most significant Japanese work on the London Naval Conference is virtually the entire first volume of *Harada Diary*. See also the memoirs of Wakatsuki Reijirō, Japan's Chief Delegate to the Conference, entitled Kofūan Kaikoroku (Memoirs of Kofūan [Wakatsuki's pseudonym] hereafter referred to as *Wakatsuki Memoirs*) (Tokyo, 1950), pp. 332–66; *Shidehara Memoirs*, pp. 120–45; *Okada Memoirs*, pp. 42–74; *Shidehara Kijūrō*, pp. 403–26; Yatsugi Kazuo, *Shōwa Jinbutsu Hiroku* (Inside Stories of Personalities of the Shōwa Era) (Tokyo, 1954), pp. 63–99; and *Uyehara Checklist*, pp. 205–06.

3. Yanaga, *Japan since Perry*, p. 466.

4. Generally speaking, this group consisted of younger naval officers who espoused the cause of Japan's expansion while decrying the treaties which fettered Japan's freedom of action in the Far East. The so-called "shore clique" was comprised mostly of the old guards of the navy who believed in Japan's abiding by treaty obligations.

ships vis-à-vis Great Britain and the United States had thus become Japan's lot. Admiral Katō Kanji, Chief of the Naval General Staff, was speaking not only for himself when he brushed aside an offer to represent Japan as one of the delegates to the London Conference by saying that his job was to wage war, not to take part in a conference to end wars.[5]

The Japanese Admiralty was quite aware of the difficult nature of the forthcoming negotiations and therefore undertook to be prepared well in advance of the opening of the conference. Early in October a preparatory committee of experts met to examine and discuss technical questions pertaining to arms reduction. Thus, by October 7, the same day on which the Japanese Embassy in London received from the British government the invitation to the Naval Limitation Conference, the Japanese Admiralty sent one of its vice admirals to Prince Saionji, the last of the surviving Elder Statesmen, to explain and secure his understanding and support of the Admiralty's position.

The position from which the Admiralty was firmly resolved that it would not retreat was spelled out in the so-called "three fundamental claims," which were regarded as being "adequate for defensive, but not for offensive purposes." First of the desiderata was that Japan would be allowed to possess in the class of 10,000-ton cruisers mounting eight-inch guns an aggregate tonnage equivalent to 70 per cent of that of either the United States or Great Britain, whichever had the greater tonnage. Secondly, Japan would be permitted to retain intact her then-current tonnage, 79,000 tons, of undersea craft. Thirdly, the aggregate tonnage of auxiliary ships, excepting the 10,000-ton class cruisers and undersea craft already mentioned, should be 70 per cent of that of the United States or Great Britain.

The London Naval Conference opened on January 21, 1931. For the first six weeks, negotiations centered around proposals submitted by Japan; but progress was slow as the United States and Great Britain voiced various exceptions. Finally, as a matter of expediency, it was proposed and accepted that Senator David

5. Mori, *Senpū Nijūnen,* p. 21.

A. Reed and Matsudaira Tsuneo, Japanese Ambassador to England, should enter into private conversations. From these talks emerged a compromise proposal. Actually, Matsudaira conducted his negotiations with Reed without benefit of Japanese naval experts and without consulting Admiral Takarabe, Minister of the Navy and a member of the delegation.[6] Nevertheless, Takarabe initialed the draft proposal, which was wired to Tokyo for instructions. A convincingly clear explanation is still wanting as to why Takarabe did not refuse to initial this document because it was obvious both to him and to Wakatsuki that the terms embodied in the proposal would not be acceptable to naval leaders in Tokyo. One can only surmise that after protracted negotiations they did not wish to bear the onus of responsibility for contributing to the collapse of the conference.

The gist of the Matsudaira-Reed compromise was that Japan's tonnage in auxiliary ships of all classes was to be 69.75 per cent of that of the United States or of Great Britain. In aggregate tonnage this would have been short of Japan's proposal by 1,290 tons, a difference of seemingly minor importance. However, the draft proposal contained an additional provision restricting Japan's cruisers in the 10,000-ton class mounting eight-inch guns to 60 per cent of that of the United States or Great Britain. With respect to undersea craft, the proposal stipulated that the three powers would maintain parity at 52,700 tons. This would have meant a reduction by one-third of the tonnage which Japan then possessed in this class of ships. Were she to assume that the replacement age of these ships would be agreed upon at thirteen years, she would not be able to build a single undersea craft until 1936. She feared that during this period existing facilities and the technical skill required to build these highly specialized craft would fall into obsolescence.

Another source of disappointment to Japan was her inability

6. Takeuchi, *War and Diplomacy in the Japanese Empire,* p. 293. According to Wakatsuki, Takarabe and the naval officers objected strenuously and declared that they would submit a protest to the home government. Yatsugi, *Shōwa Jinbutsu Hiroku,* p. 88.

to come to terms with the United States on retaining excessive tonnage in undersea craft by accepting a reduction in other forms of auxiliary ships. Although Japan had hoped that this difference could be made up by reducing the tonnage of her light cruisers and destroyers, the draft proposal called on Japan to reduce her over-all tonnage in the 10,000-ton cruiser class.[7]

Despite the fact that Wakatsuki, the Chief Delegate, had grave misgivings concerning the reception of the draft proposal by the navy—it obviously represented a distinct departure from the three fundamental claims—he transmitted it to his home government, stating that it was beyond his power to extract any further concessions from the United States. In Tokyo the Foreign Office advocated immediate acceptance of the draft proposal in the interest of promoting more stable and friendly relationships with the other nations. The navy, however, was disturbed and highly resentful. Admiral Katō, Chief of the Naval General Staff and Vice Admiral Suetsugu Nobumasa, Katō's immediate subordinate, vigorously opposed the proposal. Siding with the two admirals were a number of young naval officers, retired military officers, and many civilians representing right-wing elements.

During the critical weeks that followed, the tactics employed by the Office of the Naval General Staff lacked decisiveness. Actions taken by Katō and Suetsugu can at best be characterized as ineffectual holding operations. On March 17 Suetsugu indicated his opposition to the draft proposal by publishing it in the press. Again on the 22nd he was about to release his views to the press when he was restrained from doing so. Nevertheless, several Tokyo papers did manage to report on the suppressed news. Meanwhile, on the 19th, Admiral Katō called on Premier Hamaguchi Osayuki and emphasized that the navy would not give ground unless an agreement could be reached on effective security measures, in which case the three fundamental claims could be modified.

On the 22nd, the leaders of the navy met in order to prepare

7. Aoki, *The Pacific War, I*, 8.

a strongly united front since it had become apparent that Hamaguchi was unwilling to take any stand that might jeopardize the success of the London Conference. The consensus of the naval leaders was that the draft proposal was unacceptable because it did not reflect the strategic requirements of the Japanese navy as determined by professional naval personnel; moreover, it was suggested that a compromise, such as the Matsudaira-Reed proposal, should be resorted to only as a last measure. Representations were made by the naval leaders that the Premier should clarify to this group the government's thinking as soon as it had drawn up its instructions. Finally, the group drew up its own set of proposals to be incorporated into the instructions to be sent to London. The so-called naval proposals, for reasons unknown, ended in a conciliatory tone by conceding that, even were their proposals to be rejected, the navy would abide by the decision of the government.

The three desiderata outlined above were drawn up in a memo and, after review by the Board of Admirals of the Navy and the Supreme War Council, were presented to Foreign Minister Shidehara and Premier Hamaguchi on the 25th. Despite these actions, the naval men remained ill at ease and on the 27th sent two admirals, Okada and Katō, to see the Premier and again to make representations. Hamaguchi candidly admitted that although he was the Administrative Minister of the Navy in the absence of Admiral Takarabe, the issue of disarmament must be viewed as a broader question affecting the peace of the world and the welfare of the nation as a whole. He went on to say that reduction in naval armament was necessary to lighten the financial burden on the people and also to insure that a costly naval armament race would not ensue in the wake of the collapse of this conference. Thus, Hamaguchi made it clear that he intended to accept the draft proposal Wakatsuki had submitted.

Katō denied that the breakup of the conference would touch off a naval building race. Moreover, he charged that agreements affecting naval combat strength were the primary concern of the supreme command; if the government were to conclude a treaty independently of the Chief of the Naval General Staff, it would raise a grave constitutional issue.

Meanwhile, the Ministry of Foreign Affairs had completed the draft of instructions to be sent back to London. Thus, on the night of March 31, high officials of the Foreign Office met with the leading members of the Admiralty in order to brief the latter on the substance of the instructions prior to the cabinet session to be held on April 1. Very little was accomplished at this gathering, however, because Admiral Suetsugu persisted in reiterating the naval side of the argument. Therefore, early the following morning Hamaguchi invited Admirals Okada, Katō, and Yamanashi to the Premier's residence where they were shown the draft of the instructions. While Okada responded in a conciliatory tone, since it was his role as an insider to mitigate the intransigency of the naval diehards, Katō stuck to his argument that acceptance of the draft proposal would impair Japan's naval strategy.

With less than an hour remaining before the cabinet assembled, Okada and Yamanashi withdrew to the residence of the Minister of the Navy to confer hastily with the representatives of the Admiralty. For reasons which would soon be obvious, Katō absented himself from this gathering.[8] Yamanashi read the instructions prepared by the Foreign Office. Several revisions of a minor nature were suggested, but no one present objected to either the substance of the instructions or the precipitate manner in which the approval of the instructions was being obtained. Then Yamanashi read off three times the memo[9] which the naval men had prepared to be presented to the cabinet that morning. It was accepted without revision. The general tone of the meeting tends to indicate that the naval leaders were resigned to the fact that

8. Some two months later in June, Katō regretted the fact that he had failed to take a positive stand on April 1. Aoki, *1*, 51.

9. The text of this memo so far has not been located. However, it was most likely couched in conciliatory tones and called for some means of compensating for the concession made in the 10,000-ton class of cruisers.

their opposition would be futile, and therefore in return for their cooperative attitude they felt they could extract concessions from the government to maintain naval strength by some other means.

The crucial cabinet meeting was held later the same morning. Foreign Minister Shidehara opened the session with an explanation of how the struggle for a month and a half on the part of Japanese delegates to have the United States accept Japan's proposals had resulted in a stalemate because both the British and the American delegates had insisted on making extensive changes to Japan's proposal, and how the deadlock had finally been broken and a compromise reached by means of informal discussions between Ambassador Matsudaira and Senator Reed. Shidehara pleaded that the instructions, which were based on the draft proposal, be accepted since the latter was an end product of a laborious negotiation and no further concession could be expected from the United States. The fact was that Wakatsuki was determined to tender his resignation if the government suggested a major change in the draft proposal or called for further concessions of a far-reaching nature.[10]

Yamanashi, repeating the familiar theme, deplored the downward revision in tonnage of the cruisers of the 10,000-ton class and of undersea craft but accepted the instructions, stating that the navy was left with no choice. He did, however, request that in return for the navy's submitting to the will of the Premier and the Foreign Office the government redirect the 700 million yen realized from reduction in tonnage of cruisers toward increasing the strength of the navy through other means, such as naval aviation. The Premier and the Minister of Finance assured Yamanashi that full consideration would be given to this request. Thereupon Hamaguchi reported the action of the cabinet to the Emperor that afternoon and received his sanction, and Shidehara sent the instructions to Wakatsuki in London.

Admiral Katō, in the meantime, having realized the futility of trying to reason with Premier Hamaguchi, was determined to

10. Yatsugi, *Shōwa Jinbutsu Hiroku,* p. 88.

block the instructions and sought an audience with the Emperor on the morning of April 1, but he was told that His Majesty's calendar for the day was filled;[11] he waited until the following day and made a direct appeal to the throne on the morning of April 2. Details of this address, classified as top military secret, have not been disclosed. Aoki, without giving his sources, mentions that Katō protested that a substantial reduction of Japan's naval armament according to the American proposal would gravely alter the strategic plans based on the national defense policy which Emperor Taishō had sanctioned in 1923.[12]

On the same day that Admiral Katō made his direct appeal to the Emperor, there were other developments which bespoke the troubles yet to come. On the afternoon of April 2 Premier Hamaguchi invited Yabuki, Parliamentary Vice Minister of the Navy, and Vice Admiral Suetsugu, Vice Chief of the Naval General Staff, to his residence for a frank exchange of opinion. That Hamaguchi made no headway with Suetsugu is apparent from the interview which the latter subsequently held with news reporters. Suetsugu disclosed that he had remained adamant in the face of Hamaguchi's pleas and had told the Premier that the navy could not be expected to alter on short notice a long-standing policy based on years of experience, study, and sacrifice.[13]

When the agreement was finally ready for signing in London, Katō, still smarting under the reverse inflicted upon him and his staff at the hands of the government, sent an official protest in the form of a memorial to the throne to Admiral Yamanashi, Vice Minister of the Navy. When Admiral Okada questioned his motives, Katō replied that he wished to resign before the agreement was signed. However, dissuaded by Okada from doing so,

11. Mori Kaku summoned Harada and asked point-blank if he had had any part in preventing Admiral Katō from making a direct appeal to the throne on April 1 before Premier Hamaguchi made his report on instructions to be sent to London. *Harada Diary, 1,* 64.

12. Aoki, *The Pacific War, 1,* 15. The nature of this policy is not known.

13. *Tokyo Asahi,* April 3, 1930.

Katō then asked that this memorial be kept in custody until it could be shown to Admiral Takarabe on his return from London.

In this memorial, which Katō later tendered to Takarabe, Katō insisted that there must be direct communications between the throne and the Naval General Staff if the national defense policy were to have continuity and be divorced from the vagaries of politics. Article 12 of the Constitution, together with Article 55, empowered the Emperor, with the advice of the Minister of the Navy, to determine questions of naval organization and the standing fleet; Katō argued that a sound decision could not be made unless the Naval General Staff, with the advice and consent of the Emperor, had in advance determined the over-all strategic requirements of the empire.[14] Insofar as the London Naval Agreement called for a change in the composition of Japan's naval fleets, it stood to affect their combat strength. Therefore, this was a domain of utmost concern to the Naval General Staff. Moreover, observed Katō, the London Agreement limited the size of auxiliary fleets in terms of tonnage, but did not set a ceiling in terms of allowable expenditures. This lack of precision made the task of carrying out the new agreement difficult for those who were charged with that responsibility.

Thus, concluded Katō, Article 12, which gave primacy to the government in matters of military organization, was inseparably linked with Article 11, which gave primacy to the supreme command in matters affecting strategy, and the two should not be regarded as constituting separate entities. Those who deliberately memorialized the Emperor on matters of grave importance to the nation, such as the level of armaments in peacetime, without consulting the Naval General Staff, were bound to err—as had hap-

14. Article 11: The Emperor has the supreme command of the army and navy. Article 12: The Emperor determines the organization and peace standing of the army and navy. Article 55: The respective ministers of state shall give their advice to the Emperor, and be responsible for it. All laws, imperial ordinances, and imperial rescripts of whatever kind that relate to the affairs of state, require the countersignature of a minister of state.

pened when the government dispatched the final instruction to the delegation in London.[15]

Takarabe rejected Katō's memorial, stating that the right to interpret the Constitution did not belong to the military,[16] and that he had therefore no right to make a direct appeal to the throne on these matters.

It was well toward the end of April, along about the time that the 58th Diet Session convened, that the smoldering dispute between the government and the Naval General Staff flared into the open. The government's action in forcibly railroading the London Naval Agreement through was labeled "a violation of the imperial prerogative of supreme command"—a sanctimonious phrase coined by the navy at this time as a protest against the government's encroachment upon what it considered to be its prerogative.[17] This phrase was subsequently employed frequently by the military to escape government censure for its arbitrary actions. Admiral Katō probably meant either ignoring the views of the Chief of the Naval General Staff or entering into an international agreement relevant to national defense without his prior consent.[18]

15. Aoki, *The Pacific War, 1,* 33–34. Aoki cites the fact that Regulation No. 7 in the *Procedures of Mutual Consultation on Matters pertaining to Administrative Matters* of the Ministry of the Navy prescribed that the Minister of the Navy reach an accord with the Chief of the Naval General Staff when the former was making decisions on matters pertaining to the state of naval preparedness or increase or decrease in the naval strength. Ibid., p. 42. For helpful background accounts of the Naval General Staff, see Arthur E. Tiedman, "The Hamaguchi Cabinet, First Phase, July, 1929–February, 1930: A Study in Japanese Parliamentary Government," dissertation (Columbia University, 1960), pp. 26–29; especially footnote 1 on p. 26.

16. Aoki, *1,* 52.

17. Prof. Nakano and others have based the independence of the supreme command on the establishment of the General Staff Office by Imperial Ordinance of December 5, 1878. Nakano Tomio, *Tōsuiken no Dokuritsu* (The Independence of Supreme Command) (Tokyo, 1934), pp. 360 ff.

18. Admiral Okada continued, "If this were to be the case, hereafter no one would ever accept the post of ambassador plenipotentiary. As a min-

The struggle between the government and the Naval General Staff to determine who had the final say in matters of armament developed into a legal battle over the interpretation and relative merits of Articles 11 and 12 of the Japanese Constitution. Jurists of the new school like Professor Minobe, who championed the cause of constitutional government, argued that, first of all, the power to determine the strength and composition of the military establishments in time of peace stemmed from the Emperor's prerogative over affairs of state and not from the prerogative of supreme command. Secondly, they contended that the cabinet had a voice in military matters, as seen in Prince Itō's commentary on Article 12, which read in part, "It is true that this power is to be exercised with the advice of responsible ministers."[19] These jurists insisted that "responsible ministers" meant every member of the cabinet who was answerable to the Diet for administrative decisions, which was tantamount to saying that in peacetime the authority to determine the strength and organization of the armed services rested, to a considerable extent, in the cabinet.

However, the jurists of the new school lifted Itō's passage out of context. The balance of the sentence read, "still, like the imperial military command, it nevertheless belongs to the sover-

---

ister of state, it is the function of the Minister of the Navy to represent the admiralty. The Naval General Staff may approach the Minister of the Navy, but it is not within his power to deal directly with the government. It would be a grave matter if, upon the objection of the Chief of General Staff, treaties were to be blocked. Katō is being used as a cat's-paw by conspirators who are trying to prevent the ratification of this treaty by invoking the sanctity of the supreme command. We really have a problem on hand. In the end I suppose Katō will have to resign." *Harada Diary, 1,* 62–63. Author's free translation. With respect to the inconsistent behavior of Katō, Harada observed that Katō stayed in line when he was not being goaded by Suetsugu; but that he acted up as soon as Suetsugu clamored for action. Thus, while Suetsugu was apparently the man behind Katō, Suetsugu in turn seems to have been under the influence of Hiranuma Kiichirō, a member of the Privy Council. Ibid.

19. Quoted in Kenneth W. Colegrove, *Militarism in Japan* (Boston, World Peace Foundation, 1936), p. 18.

eign power of the Emperor, and no interference in it by the Diet should be allowed." Jurists of the old ultranationalistic school—like Professors Hozumi Yatsuka and Uesugi Shinkichi—took this to mean that "responsible ministers" in Article 12 referred only to the Ministers of War and the Navy and did not include civilian cabinet officials.

Precedent was in favor of the latter school. Prior to the promulgation of the Meiji Constitution, the Emperor was free to issue military orders without the countersignature of a minister. Insofar as this procedure had not been abrogated by subsequent enactments, the practice prevailing prior to the promulgation of the Constitution was still valid.[20] In actual practice, the General Staffs made decisions on matters pertaining to national defense and dispositions of troops, and the Ministers of War and the Navy were informed of the fact later. That this practice was not confined to Japan is seen in Quincy Wright's observation that "on certain occasions the military or naval authorities [of France] have taken action on their own responsibility, and the cabinet, confronted by a fait accompli, has had to endorse it." Incidents of this nature have occurred in France despite the fact that, unlike the Japanese Constitution, "the French Constitution is based upon parliamentary sovereignty with full cabinet responsibility to the parliament and the subordination of the military to the civilian cabinet."[21]

Perhaps the most convincing argument in favor of the Naval General Staff was advanced at a much later date. The defense counsel for the young naval officers who were implicated in the May 15 Incident of 1932[22] maintained that the instructions for

20. Soejima Giichi, *Nihon Teikoku Kenpō Ron* (Principles of the Constitutional Law of Japan), p. 667, cited in Tomio Nakano, *The Ordinance Power of the Japanese Emperor* (Baltimore, 1923), p. 157.

21. This quotation and the one immediately preceding were taken from Takeuchi, *War and Diplomacy in the Japanese Empire,* p. xviii.

22. On this day a mixed group of about 40 men including young naval officers, cadets from the Military Academy, and youths of peasant background participated in a coup d'état referred to as the "Five-One-Five

the Japanese delegation to the London Naval Conference were based on the draft memorial which the Chief of the Naval General Staff had submitted to the throne. Accordingly, any proposal to modify these original instructions ought to have gone through the same procedure; i.e. after the Chief of the Naval General Staff had memorialized the Emperor with regard to changes in the instructions, the government ought to have waited for imperial approval before wiring back its consent to the delegates in London.[23]

En route home from the conference, Admiral Takarabe, Minister of the Navy, acting on advice from Hamaguchi, deliberately delayed his arrival in Tokyo in order to avoid facing the hostile Diet.[24] As was bound to happen, however, on May 29 at the meeting of the Supreme War Council, Takarabe and Katō clashed head on. The acrimonious debate that ensued lasted more than three hours. The following month Katō resigned, on the ground that he had no confidence that an adequate defense plan could be worked out on the basis of the London Naval Treaty.

The row between the Minister of the Navy and the Chief of the Naval General Staff was fraught with dire consequences. For one thing, it marked the beginning of a factional strife between the "shore duty" and "fleet" groups. The former stood for abiding by the terms of the treaty and were represented by Admirals Yamamoto, Kiyoura, Saitō, and Okada—the old guard of the

---

Incident." A contingent broke into the residence of Premier Inukai and assassinated him while others attacked the Bank of Japan, the Metropolitan Police Office, and the headquarters of the Seiyūkai party. Their stated object was to effect the "Shōwa Restoration" by putting an end to the parliamentary form of government, which they charged was corrupt and compromised Japan's position in disarmament conferences. Since their plans did not go beyond tearing down the existing form of government, it was not surprising that the coup failed. Nevertheless, this incident sounded the knell for party government, with the result that the military eventually dominated the affairs of government in Japan.

23. Kiyose Ichirō, "Go-ichi-go Jiken no Bengo ni Tachite" (In Defense of the May 15 Incident), *Kaizō* (November 1933), pp. 283–91.

24. See Aoki, *The Pacific War, 1,* 29–30.

Japanese navy. The latter group, often referred to as the "anti-treaty" faction, was composed of young officers who were in touch with the Araki-Mazaki faction of the army. It was the extremists of the fleet group who on May 15, 1932, staged an abortive coup and assassinated Premier Inukai.

When the London Treaty reached the Privy Council for ratification in September, the issue of the supreme command came to a head, for the Council was dominated by staunch supporters of the Naval General Staff.

Itō Miyoji was unrelenting in employing obstructive tactics. As chairman of the Treaty Examination Committee, he packed his committee with members of the Privy Council openly hostile to the London Treaty and deliberately omitted members qualified in matters of foreign relations, such as Viscount Ishii Kikujirō, dean of Japan's diplomatic corps, who was known to have favored the success of the London Naval Conference. As a means of embarrassing the government, the committee took the position that Admiral Katō should be permitted to testify before the Council. It also demanded access to data submitted to the Emperor on Japan's naval strength.

Premier Hamaguchi brooked no opposition from the Privy Council and stoutly rejected all its proposals. Moreover, he made known his firm intention to effect a shakeup in the personnel of the Council by appealing directly to the throne if the body persisted in making trouble. The most tangible clue to Hamaguchi's boldness in his dealings with the Council is to be found in his diary under the date of March 27, 1930:

> This day I had an audience with the Emperor. I undertook to outline to His Majesty the issues in the disarmament talks and their development to the present. I stated the government's intention to do its utmost to reach an accord in these matters. I withdrew from the audience chamber awed and inspired by his gracious words and was conveying the gist of the audience

> to the Grand Chamberlain in the anteroom when he was summoned by the Emperor. After a while, the Grand Chamberlain returned with further wishes from His Majesty. From this moment my mind was made up about the Naval Conference.[25]

That the Emperor was determined to bring the London Conference to a successful conclusion is corroborated by Admiral Okada. In the latter part of January 1930, as the fate of the conference hung in the balance, Okada met with Makino, Lord Keeper of the Privy Seal, who said to Okada, "For the sake of Japan, the conference must not be allowed to break up or our nation will be in trouble." Okada sensed that Makino was conveying the Emperor's wish.[26]

Hamaguchi's hand was further strengthened by the vigorous backing of Prince Saionji, whose prestige was second only to that of the Emperor. While the London Conference was still in progress, Saionji remarked to Harada, "It would be a grave matter if, as the result of our naval delegation's vociferous opposition, the conference collapsed and Japan were to be blamed for it. If any of the delegates should give Wakatsuki trouble, I want him to send them home and remain behind by himself to bring the conference to a successful conclusion."[27] On another occasion, when Saionji heard Admiral Saitō Makoto express deep concern for the progress of the London Conference, the Prince remarked, "Saitō will be rendering infinitely greater service to Japan by lending his support now to bring the Naval Conference to a successful conclusion than by serving ten years in Korea as a Governor General."[28] Aside from Saionji and Makino, moral support came from others who were close to the throne. Suzuki Kantarō,

25. Kurihara, *Tennō,* p. 50. Author's translation.
26. *Okada Memoirs,* p. 44. Author's translation.
27. *Harada Diary, 1,* 20. Author's translation.
28. Ibid., *1,* 23–24. Author's translation.

the Grand Chamberlain, took it upon himself to dissuade Prince Fushimi from siding with Katō. Furthermore, he exerted his influence to moderate Katō's demands. Highly significant was the vital role played by Admiral Okada, who utilized to the limit the role played by personal ties in Japanese group relations. Not only was he the senior of Admiral Katō in the navy, but the two came from the same prefecture—Fukui—and local loyalties are a vital tie in Japanese politics. As much as Katō may have fretted, in the end he had to bow to Okada. In regard to Okada's exceptional performance in placating Katō, Wakatsuki speculated in his memoirs, "Might it not have been Okada's distinguished service at the time of the London Conference which brought him to Saionji's attention, and later prompted the Prince to recommend Okada to premiership?"[29]

Two additional factors contributed to the unprecedented victory achieved by the Hamaguchi government. The general election of February 20 resulted in an overwhelming victory for the Minseitō, giving Hamaguchi absolute control over the Lower House of the Diet. The government also enjoyed a measure of popular support from segments of the informed public as well as from the liberal press, which recently had changed its stand. This was an unexpected development, since throughout the conference the press of Japan had been united in support of the navy.[30]

Quick to sense its vulnerable position, the Privy Council backed down, and the reversal came so unexpectedly and swiftly that a comedy of errors ensued for the opposition party. The Seiyūkai saw in the protracted duel between the government and the Privy Council a fair chance of unseating the Hamaguchi cabinet. Unaware of the Council's impending change of policy, Inukai, president of the party, at a mass meeting on September 16 denounced the Minseitō's violation of the supreme command and pledged his party's undivided support of the Privy Council.

29. *Wakatsuki Memoirs,* p. 366. Author's translation.

30. Takeuchi, *War and Diplomacy in the Japanese Empire,* pp. 303–05.

The next day Inukai suffered loss of face when the Council suddenly reversed its stand and gave unconditional approval to the London Naval Treaty.

At least momentarily, the ratification of the treaty meant a resounding victory for the cabinet over the navy and the Privy Council. Indeed, the prestige of the Naval General Staff sank to the lowest point ever reached. Those given to hasty conclusions thought that the event heralded at long last the dawn of responsible government in Japan. Yet the triumph of parliamentary government was far from assured. It has been observed already that the supremacy of the Diet over other governmental bodies had not been established in theory or practice. Hamaguchi did not dare, even in the flush of victory, to state the constitutional grounds on which his government assumed responsibility for the London Naval Treaty. "To have done so would have been to assert cabinet superiority in state affairs, not only over the naval advisers, but also over the army advisers. Such treatment would have resulted in aligning the army, even more powerful than the navy, against the cabinet; and the cabinet could not face the risk."[31] An episode which followed less than five months later testified eloquently to the shaky basis of the Minseitō government, as will be seen below.

Hamaguchi's vigorous stand released such a torrent of reaction from his opponents that in the long run the cause of parliamentary government suffered a disastrous blow—from which it was unable to recover until after Japan's defeat in 1945. And for his temporary success Hamaguchi personally had to pay dearly: on the morning of November 14, just as he was boarding a westbound train from Tokyo, he was shot and wounded by a young "patriot" named Sagoya Tomeo. The would-be assassin was a member of the Aikoku-sha, an ultranationalist organization that vehemently denounced communism and advocated a positive policy on the continent.

31. Introduction by Quincy Wright in Takeuchi, *War and Diplomacy in the Japanese Empire*, p. xviii.

It has been stated that "assassination is an index of the gap between the driving political impulses of men and the limit for their attainment set up by the existing political forms."[32] In the case of Japan in the early thirties, the rising counterelites were the ultranationalists, of whom Sagoya was a partisan. This group had not attained anywhere near the power necessary to challenge the rule of the government in power. Sagoya was driven by desperation to assault the head of the government, and the effect of his action on its control structure was minimal, but its impact upon the public could hardly be overestimated.

Finally, the most significant effect of the London Naval Agreement was the fact that it forced the hands of the extremists. How did this come about? By virtue of this treaty, Japan had to be content with a navy which could not engage the American fleet in Far Eastern waters.[33] With respect to Manchuria and Inner Mongolia, it meant that Japan had to conduct herself in a manner that would be agreeable to the United States. Such a prospect was hardly to the liking of the continental expansionists, especially those of the Kwantung Army, who considered it their mission to bring these areas under the firm control of Japan. They were already restive, some even desperate, because of the rapid inroads which the Nationalist government was making into the Three Eastern Provinces then under the aegis of Chang Hsueh-liang. To add to this there was the ever-present fear of the Soviet Union to the north. Also, the fact that the attempt to take over Manchuria in 1928 had been quashed only heightened the sense of urgency and frustration among the activists of the Kwantung Army and impelled them to resort to a desperate course of action the following year—the explosion that came to be known as the Mukden Incident.

32. Max Lerner in *Encyclopedia of Social Science, 2* (New York, 1930), 271–75.

33. Satō Kenryō, *Tōjō Hideki to Taiheiyō Sensō* (Tōjō and the Pacific War) (Tokyo, 1960), pp. 164–65.

After the Conference

While Hamaguchi was convalescing from the bullet wound, it fell to Shidehara to face the Fifty-Ninth Session of the Diet as Acting Premier. The treatment accorded him by the opposition party in the Lower House was anything but cordial; for the Seiyūkai it was humiliating enough to be soundly defeated in the general elections without having to put up with an Acting Premier who was not even a member of the Minseitō he was representing.[1] Mori and his associates bitterly assailed the Minseitō for lifting the embargo on gold and ascribed to it the continuing economic ills. Their real target of attack, however, was the London Naval Treaty, which they pointed out as another example of Shidehara's weak-kneed diplomacy. Outnumbered and outmaneuvered by the Minseitō, Mori and the extremists of the Seiyūkai were ready to resort to any tactic to wrest control of the government from the party in power.

A rare opportunity presented itself on February 3, 1931, in an incident popularly referred to as "Acting Premier Shidehara's slip of the tongue." On this day, Nakajima Chikuhei, a newly elected Seiyūkai member of the Lower House, in an interpellation of Shidehara at a meeting of the budget committee, asked how he could reconcile statements made by Admiral Abo Kiyokazu, the newly appointed Minister of the Navy, with those of Shidehara and Hamaguchi. He charged that, although Premier Hamaguchi and Foreign Minister Shidehara had assured the Fifty-Eighth Session of the Diet that the terms of the London Naval Treaty did not endanger Japan's national defense, subsequently Admiral Abo had testified at a budget meeting of the Lower House that the Japanese navy could not carry out its strategic program if it abided by the terms of the London Naval Treaty.

Shidehara replied blandly that the treaty could not harm Japan because it was approved by the Emperor. Mori, who was seated

1. As a career diplomat, Shidehara was not affiliated with any political party, although his policies were closely identified with those of the Minseitō.

in the rear of the room that day as a spectator, suddenly rose to his feet and shouted, "Shidehara, retract that! Retract that!" implying that Shidehara was using the throne to shield a grave diplomatic blunder, for the Meiji Constitution decreed that the person of Emperor was sacred and inviolable. The other members of the Seiyūkai were caught unawares. As if roused from a bad dream they stood up, only then sensing that something grave was afoot. For the following three quarters of an hour the House was in an uproar. Members of the Seiyūkai, including the executives, stormed the dais shouting, "This is no ordinary slip of the tongue! Resign, all of you!" Referring to the wild melee, the press dubbed the incident the "mud-slinging contest."

After two days of recess, the General Budget Committee reconvened, only to be summarily adjourned on account of the bitter feeling which still persisted. As Shidehara and Adachi Kenzō, Minister of Home Affairs, left the committee room protected by a cordon of guards, Shidehara was again surrounded by a hostile crowd, which hurled abusive language at him.[2] One of the lobbyists for the Minseitō crashed a desk nameplate through a glass pane to distract the attention of the unruly mob. This only aggravated the tension. When the fragments of glass showered upon the heads of the Seiyūkai lobbyists, a free-for-all ensued in which two members of the Diet and several scores of lobbyists were injured. Amidst the confusion, Shidehara was spirited away by the guards. According to the bylaws, the budget had to be in by February 11. The Seiyūkai's strategy was to block passage of the budget by obstructing the progress of the meeting, thereby forcing the Minseitō cabinet to resign.

The fracas between the two parties was settled finally at the

2. According to Shidehara's own account, as he left the Budget Committee's room, a suspicious-looking character who was crouched by the side of a radiator reached for the cuffs of his trousers trying to trip him. Shidehara kicked the man on the forehead with the heel of a shoe causing blood to streak down his face. The man staggered and fell backward. Had Shidehara tripped and fallen, he is certain he would have been trampled to death by the angry crowd surging out of the committee room. *Shidehara Memoirs,* p. 133.

highest level, between Adachi and President Inukai. After accord was reached, Inukai summoned Mori to his residence and made him accede to the terms of interparty compromise.

Mori's strategem went a great deal farther than obstruction. Yamaura had reason to believe that Mori entertained a secret plan for a *putsch* in conjunction with action by certain members of the army. Their plot was to surround the Diet with antiparliamentary forces and cause a collapse of the cabinet, after which a wholesale reform of the government was to follow, presumably with General Ugaki as Premier. Shidehara's conciliatory policy would be swept aside to bring the Manchurian problems to a quick settlement. If this were not Mori's plan, Yamaura asks, "Why should Mori issue a secret order to the party members to desist from criticizing General Ugaki, Minister of War?"[3] Actually, Ugaki was vulnerable to attack since he made no effort to reject the Minseitō platform, one of the planks of which was to reduce army expenditures. Yamaura implies that Mori may have been playing with the idea of grooming Ugaki for the premiership should the army coup d'état come off successfully. There is a flaw in Yamaura's theory, however: since Mori identified himself closely with General Araki and the young officers of the Kōdō-ha, who were at odds with General Ugaki, it seems unlikely that he would have forsaken Araki to back another general whose views were not consonant with his.

The fracas, coming as it did eight months before the Mukden Incident—a deliberate act of defiance of the central authority by the Kwantung Army—was but a symptom in the syndrome of a nation whose body politic was gravely afflicted. It was quite clear, as indicated in the following chapters, that between the mounting domestic economic crisis and the relentless attack on the government by Mori and the extremists of the right, representative government in Japan was on the verge of collapse. Moreover, the intransigency of the extremists in demanding a positive solution of the Manchurian problems made peaceful

3. Yamaura, *Mori Kaku,* pp. 681–82.

adjustment of her relation with China or the world in general problematical.

The March Plot

Months before the outbreak of hostilities in Manchuria in September 1931, restive elements of the military were planning to stage a coup d'état to take over control of the civil government in Tokyo. Once more they were thwarted, this time because of a change of heart of some of the would-be participants. Our primary concern in the abortive coup—known as the March Plot[1]—is not so much with uncovering its mechanism as in identifying the elements working for and against the conspiracy. Generally speaking, stresses in a society—whether social, political, or economic—terminating in violent action result from a sense of insecurity and inadequacy.[2] Although the actions of malcontents may be quelled temporarily, as long as the basic insecurity exists it must be presumed that the tensions will persist. Our second concern, therefore, is to observe the new direction in which the revolutionary force moved after its initial attempt had been thwarted.

The March Plot was a conspiracy to set up a military government around the person of General Ugaki, then Minister of War. The extent to which General Ugaki was personally involved in the plot remains a mystery to this day. So tight was the censorship clamped on the abortive coup that it was a year before news-

1. See R. Storry, *The Double Patriots* (Boston, 1957), pp. 57–65, for an account of the same incident. My account of the March Plot, the Manchurian Crisis, and the October Plot were completed prior to the summer of 1957, and were submitted as an integral part of my doctoral dissertation to Yale in September 1957. Mr. Storry's treatment of these incidents did not come to my attention until much later. By far one of the most revealing accounts of the March Plot is to be found in Aoki, *The Pacific War, 1,* 131–41.

2. Harold D. Lasswell and Abraham Kaplan, *Power and Society* (New Haven, 1950), p. 241.

men dared mention it even in their private conversations, and ordinary people did not learn of it until after the war.

Either participating in or backing the conspiracy were influential generals of Ugaki's clique, which was then in power. Cooperating with the army elite were the extremists of the Cherry Society.[3] Lieutenant Colonel Hashimoto, it appears, acted as the liaison between the two groups since he headed the Cherry Society and was a member of the Ugaki faction at the same time. Also working closely with both groups was Ōkawa Shūmei, a civilian propagandist, whose chore it was to make contact with ultranationalists as well as certain leftist organizations. Conspicuous for their absence were navy personnel. The unique feature of the unsuccessful coup was that it had the active support in varying degrees of high-ranking officers in the army.[4]

The March Plot has received the attention of many writers,[5] but they have invariably based their accounts on sources which came to light before 1950, principally "Major Tanaka's Notes,"[6] supplemented by the "Secret Records of Japanese Reform Move-

3. See below, pp. 95–102.

4. These included Sugiyama Hajime, Vice Minister of War; Ninomiya Harushige, Assistant Chief of Staff; Koiso Kuniaki, Chief of the Military Affairs Bureau; Nagata Tetsuzan, Chief of the Military Affairs Division; and Tatekawa Yoshitsugu, a section chief in the General Staff. Koiso was probably the prime mover in the early stages of planning. Nagata, who was an immediate subordinate of Koiso, worked out the details of one plan with the aid of Tōjō Hideki and Suzuki Teiichi. Nagata and Tōjō later became the mainstays of the Tōsei (Control) faction of the army.

5. Mori, *Senpū Nijūnen,* pp. 34–35; Yamamoto Katsunosuke, *Nihon o Horoboshita Mono* (Those Who Brought About the Downfall of Japan) (Tokyo, 1949), pp. 115–25; Shiraki Masayuki, *Nihon Seitōshi (Shōwa-hen)* (History of Japanese Political Parties, Shōwa Period) (Tokyo, 1949), pp. 83–87; Wald, "The Young Officers Movement in Japan," pp. 58–81. See also above, n. 1.

6. This is said to have been distributed among the members of the Cherry Society in mimeograph form some time after the October Plot in order to head off a cleavage that was developing within the society. Hence the document is neither polemic nor inciting, but reflective in tone. Major Tanaka Kiyoshi, as an active participant in the March and October Plots, recorded that the role the Cherry Society played was the core of the national reconstruction movement. *Uyehara Checklist,* p. 125, IMT 271.

ments"[7] and the records of the Tokyo War Crime Trials. However, a number of diaries and memoirs of significant value that have appeared since then[8] help both to bring out certain points which the earlier writers have failed to make and to clarify others —among them the shift in plans, subtle changes in objectives, the interplay of personalities, defections from the conspiracy, and the connection between the March Plot and, importantly, the Mukden Incident.

From about the end of May to early December 1930 Ugaki was absent from his office, having undergone a painful operation for tympanitis, and was convalescing most of the time at a seaside resort in Kōzu. During his absence, General Abe Nobuyuki substituted as Acting Minister of War. In early June, Ugaki apparently expressed a desire to resign, for on June 8 Prince Saionji sent Baron Harada to Ugaki's bedside with a message:

> Although I should come to see you in person to make this request, as you know, I am ill; so I have asked Harada to convey my message to you. Certain individuals are circulating rumors saying that you intend to resign. For the sake of the country, I ask you to exercise prudence. Entrust the cares of the Ministry [of War] to someone else. I trust that you will take ample time to rest and fully recover.[9]

Still determined to resign, on June 14 Ugaki summoned Suzuki Fujiya, Chief Cabinet Secretary, and the Permanent and the Parliamentary Vice Ministers of War, and let his intentions be known. Later that evening the two Vice Ministers returned with

7. The Japanese title is "Nihon Kakushin Undō Hiroku." This document is a 477-page typescript report compiled by the Public Peace Section, Bureau of Public Affairs, Ministry of Home Affairs, dated August 1938 and stamped "Top Secret." There is an original copy in the Library of Congress.

8. To mention a few, *Harada Diary;* Ugaki Kazushige, *Ugaki Nikki* (Ugaki Diary) (Tokyo, 1954, hereafter referred to as *Ugaki Diary*); *Ugaki Memoirs; Shidehara Memoirs; Okada Memoirs; Wakatsuki Memoirs.*

9. *Ugaki Diary*, p. 137. Author's translation.

Egi Yoku, Minister of Railways, who came bearing Premier Hamaguchi's personal plea to Ugaki to stay on. Still later Ugaki changed his mind and decided to continue in office. The following morning he sent for Baron Harada and asked him to inform Prince Saionji of his decision. Harada hastened to Saionji's side in Okitsu and was back at seven the same day with the following:

> Never before have I made the kind of request that I have made to you. It was only that I had deep reasons for doing so. I feel relieved, having received your message. I shall tell you in detail what I have in mind when you or I will visit the other, depending upon who recovers first. Pray, take care and be on your feet soon.[10]

The tone of Saionji's language should be carefully noted. Seldom before, perhaps never, had he expressed such cordial regard for and implicit faith in any person. A man as adroit as Ugaki must have instantly sensed that he was marked as a candidate for a future premiership by Saionji, the designator of prime ministers. It therefore does not seem reasonable that Ugaki would have sought by unlawful and highly risky means to acquire power when it was virtually assured him by legitimate means. The language of the message in Japanese is almost unbecoming a man of Saionji's eminence. The seemingly solicitous language is replete with political significance. It can only be taken as reflecting a domestic situation so shaky that in the face of the rising tide of military power Saionji was desperate enough to enlist the support of an influential army man whose integrity and ability he could trust.

The precise period of Ugaki's stay in Kōzu is not known. However, since Abe's temporary assignment lasted from June 16 to December 10, it is presumed that Ugaki spent most of the intervening months at the seaside resort away from the sultry heat

10. Ibid., p. 138. Author's translation.

of Tokyo. Referring to this period when Ugaki was absent, Shidehara wrote:

> It is probably true that while Ugaki was away, army officers—whether young or advanced in age I do not know—gathered to conspire at the Minister of War's official residence. One day I received a letter from Ugaki in Kōzu. In it he expressed deep concern for the disquieting situation. He implored me to exert my utmost and pledged his moral support. By the time Ugaki returned to Tokyo, the plan for the coup was already in an advanced stage.[11]

The implication of "Major Tanaka's Notes" is that these army officers continued to meet throughout the months of January and February under Ugaki's nose. Nothing is said about Ugaki's having frowned upon the meetings, still less disapproved them. In fact, this source alleges that on the night of January 13 Ugaki himself participated in a meeting at which national reconstruction was discussed. But Major Tanaka does not specify whether the meeting was held to plan the coup or merely to deplore the low level of conduct to which Diet members had sunk.[12]

About this time something happened that was to plague Ugaki's political career—perhaps even trouble his conscience—and to make it difficult for him to disavow completely any part in the March Plot.

According to "Major Tanaka's Notes," Lieutenant Colonels Hashimoto Kingorō, Sakata Yoshirō, and Nemoto Hiroshi and Major Tanaka himself met on the afternoon of February 7 at Colonel Shigetō's home in Shinagawa, Tokyo. There they reached a decision with respect to the first phase of the plan for national reconstruction—the means by which the existing government was to be brought to an end. The scheme was as follows:

11. *Shidehara Memoirs,* p. 186. Author's translation.
12. See above, pp. 80–83.

1. The coup was to be staged about February 20, the day on which the labor bill would be submitted to the Diet. Simultaneously, Ōkawa's confidants were to bomb the Premier's residence and the party headquarters of the Seiyūkai and the Minseitō. Mock bombs were to be used (for loud noise rather than destruction).

2. Ōkawa was to arrange for 10,000 demonstrators to converge on the Diet Building.

3. Under the guise of protecting the Diet Building, the troops were to isolate it by surrounding the premises. Members of the Cherry Society were to stand guard at strategic points on the roads leading to the Diet Building.

4. At the height of the confusion, either Major General Koiso Kuniaki or Tatekawa Yoshitsugu was to enter the Diet and from the dais demand the resignation of the cabinet en masse.

5. By prior arrangement, Ugaki was to receive the imperial mandate to form a new cabinet.

6. A further meeting was to be held on February 8 at Major General Tatekawa's home to continue discussion on means of liquidating the existing government and seizing power. The completed plan was then to be submitted to General Ugaki.

According to this schedule, Ugaki would be told of the plot after February 8. Hence it can be presumed that he had no part in the conspiracy up to this point. Yet Major Tanaka's earlier statement, noted above, shows that Ugaki was present at a meeting on the night of January 13.

Mori, on his own initiative, planned a mass meeting of the Seiyūkai in Shiba Park while Ōkawa was holding a mass meeting of the Proletarian party at Hibiya Park on the day assigned for the March Plot. After sundown the mob was to be treated to free saké, after which it was to pour into the Diet Building and effect a junction with Ōkawa's force.[13]

13. Iwabuchi Tatsuo, *Gunbatsu no Keifu* (The Lineage of Military Cliques) (Tokyo, 1948), p. 35 (hereafter referred to as Iwabuchi, *Military Cliques*).

This was, indeed, a strange alignment, since Mori's confidential adviser was Kita Ikki, a known rival of Ōkawa.[14] Moreover, Mori identified himself closely with General Araki, who presumably would not have anything to do with the Ugaki faction. Nevertheless, Mori was well informed about the plans and activities of the Ōkawa faction. Otherwise he would not have issued a secret order to the members of the Seiyūkai, at the height of its assault on the Minseitō, to cease attacking Ugaki. Mori's conduct may perhaps be explained by noting that, as an opportunist, he could not bear to see Ōkawa walk off with the laurels. The surest way to be assured a seat at the council table when the new government was formed was to take part in the *putsch*.

In addition to these plans for phase one, Colonel Nagata Tetsuzan is known to have been working on phase two, the constructive portion of the program. It was worked out with the thoroughness typical of him, from the text of the memorial that Ugaki was to present to the throne to a detailed program for the political administration of Japan.

All evidence points to Ōkawa as the man selected to meet Ugaki, explain the plans, and enlist his support. The following testimony by Colonel Hashimoto at the War Crimes Trials corroborates this point:

> Once Ōkawa came to me and proposed a plan to make General Ugaki the Prime Minister to carry out the program of national reconstruction. I told him that I was thoroughly in accord with him, but I suggested that he first approach General Ugaki to see what he thought of it.

14. One of the reasons for the cleavage between Kita and Ōkawa is said to have been disagreement over the role of the army. Kita maintained that the army's program for national reconstruction was nothing but military fascism and not a genuine revolution. Ōkawa, who was more of an opportunist, maintained that it was no concern of his what the army's program was labeled, because he was merely utilizing the movement in the army for the attainment of his own goal.

> The same evening Ōkawa came back and said that General Ugaki did not seem disinclined about the venture. Then Ōkawa asked me if I could get some bombs for him. He needed the kind which made a loud noise just for the effect. I got the type he wanted.[15]

This testimony by Hashimoto is in keeping with the story which Ugaki told Baron Harada on November 8, 1931:

> Koiso, Chief of the Military Affairs Bureau, came and implored me to meet Ōkawa . . . but since I recalled having met him some five or six years previously, I declined. However, among other things, Koiso and Ōkawa came from the same prefecture and, for other reasons, he persisted on my meeting Ōkawa again. I had to give in.
>
> According to my diary, I met Ōkawa on the night of February 11. His story was, "Today's parliamentary government is not worthy of having the administration of Japan entrusted to its care. . . . We intend to get popular movements under way to attack the evils of the present government. It may even be necessary to resort to direct action. In the event troops are mobilized, I ask of you to work to support such actions and not suppress them."
>
> I said, "That is an outrage. If you so much as harm innocent subjects, disrupt the peace of Tokyo, or jeopardize the security of the imperial family, it would be the duty of the military to counter such dangers. I cannot accede to any such request."
>
> Then Ōkawa said, "Party cabinets are hopeless. Why not form an interim cabinet to institute a dictator government with you as premier?" I replied, "Such an act would be out of accord with anyone who is at

15. IMTFE, *Proceedings,* p. 28,810.

> present a Minister of War. When the cabinet resigns, my position is that I have to resign with it. It is unthinkable that I become a premier and organize my own cabinet."
>
> Finally, Ōkawa said, "We need some bombs to get the popular movement under way. Will you please make some available for me?" I retorted, "I am not in any position to do such a thing." Thus I turned down every request which Ōkawa made.[16]

It must be noted that all along Ugaki's tone is mild, even in refusal. Nowhere did he employ strong categorical language, such as *zettai ni dekinai* (absolutely impossible) or label Ōkawa's proposal an outright act of insurrection. Still less, Ugaki neither admonished nor made an effort to dissuade Ōkawa from committing a grave crime.

Moreover, turning now to Ugaki's own diary, we note a passage recording the conversation which Ōkawa could have misconstrued as meaning that Ugaki was not wholly unsympathetic with Ōkawa's cause. Ugaki states: "I am also keenly aware of the fact that party politics has degenerated. And for the sake of the nation, I feel that something ought to be done about it. Being a soldier, I am always ready to die on the battlefield. Therefore, I shall lay down my life at any time if I can be of service to my country."[17]

It would not be surprising if Ōkawa had reported back to Hashimoto Kingorō that General Ugaki was not unsympathetic toward the venture. Ōkawa now busied himself lining up civilian groups. He made his overtures toward rightist organizations through his confidants, Shimizu Gyōnosuke and Kano Satoshi. Shimizu is said to have obtained from Marquis Tokugawa Yoshichika 200,000 yen. Shimizu promised Tokugawa the post of Minister of the Imperial Household, but the Marquis declined

16. *Harada Diary, 2,* 122–23. Author's translation.
17. *Ugaki Diary,* p. 153. Author's translation.

and designated Prince Konoe instead.[18] As for the leftist groups, he approached the Proletarian party (Musantō) through Matsunobe Shigeji and sent a feeler toward Akamatsu Katsumaro to see where the Social Democratic party (Shakai Minshutō) stood. Overtures were also made toward the extreme leftist Labor Farmer party (Rōdō Nōmintō through Asō Hisashi and Tadokoro Teruaki. It is quite possible that a rapprochement between the leaders of the Labor Farmer party and the extremists of the Cherry Society was being achieved about this time.[19] Meanwhile, Hashimoto obtained mock bombs variously reported as ranging in number from 8 to 300, and turned them over to Shimizu.

By way of rehearsal for the coup, Ōkawa staged two demonstrations: one on March 3 and another about a week later. Although the latter was somewhat more effective than the first, on neither occasion did the participants total more than three or four thousand. His colleagues were taken aback by the poor showing, and Ōkawa himself, realizing that he could not muster enough civilian support to stage a coup, turned to General Koiso Kuniaki, Chief of the Military Affairs Bureau, requesting that the army mobilize some troops. Ugaki does not recall for sure whether it was General Sugiyama Hajime, Vice Minister of War, or Koiso who told him, "They [Ōkawa and his civilian colleagues]

18. *Harada Diary, 2,* 27, 333. See Aoki, *The Pacific War, 1,* 138–39, for an interesting character sketch of Shimizu Gyōnosuke and the part he played in the plot.

19. One writer states that the relationship between the two groups became friendly and even cordial. In January 1931, at a district convention of the Labor Farmer party in Hiroshima, a party leader is said to have observed, "The present military are exceedingly well disposed toward us. From the general grades down to the company grades, the officers are, if not actual supporters, sympathetic toward our party. The young officers at the Army Headquarters have organized a secret society to overthrow the present parties" (author's translation). This attitude of mutual sympathy presaged the open conversion of Sano Gaku and Nabeyama Sadachika, Communist leaders, to ultranationalism in June 1933. Kinoshita Hanji, *Nihon Fashizumu-shi* (History of Japanese Fascism), *1* (Tokyo, 1949), 109 (hereafter referred to as Kinoshita, *Japanese Fascism*).

The fact that in the spring of 1931 Hashimoto and his fellow officers donned civilian clothes and witnessed incognito three of the proletariat

are earnestly asking for active support from the army,"[20] but he flatly turned down the proposal.

Meanwhile, on March 7 Ugaki had received a formal message from Ōkawa written in grandiose language and the classic style. In it Ōkawa warned Ugaki not to become a tool of corrupt political parties and urged him to rise to save the country from its plight. This is the document Ugaki cited later to prove that he had not been party to the conspiracy.

Now alarmed by the serious turn of events, Ugaki summoned Sugiyama, Vice Minister of War, and Koiso, Chief of the Military Affairs Bureau, and issued a stern order to put an immediate stop to the coup d'état.[21] Just to make certain, however, Koiso on about March 10 again sounded out Ugaki and was again upbraided: "Don't be a fool! Do you think you can use His Majesty's troops for such a purpose?" Koiso then began to talk of halting the coup.[22]

The March Plot collapsed when Koiso changed his mind. Unreconciled to the sudden turn of events, Ōkawa visited Tōyama Mitsuru, the time-honored ultranationalist, at his bedside, only to be told that nothing could be done. Ōkawa's next decision was to stage the coup singlehandedly. General Tatekawa volunteered to cast his lot with him. On the 18th, surprising as it may seem, Ugaki sent Kōmoto Daisaku to Ōkawa to tell him to put a stop to the plot.[23] On the same night Marquis Tokugawa Yoshichika pleaded with Ōkawa to give up his plan; otherwise he, too,

---

parties stage a demonstration march on the Diet Building was indicative of their interest in the political movements of the masses, whose activities reached their height that year. Aoki, *The Pacific War, 1,* 126; Akamatsu Katsumaro, *Nihon Shakai Undō-shi* (History of Social Movements in Japan) (Tokyo, 1952), pp. 280–81. It is well to bear in mind that Ōkawa's schemes tended to be impressive in scale only. He was quite inept in matters of finance and in working out details. Therefore, his ability to establish proper working relationships with the various extremist groups was also open to question. Yatsugi, *Shōwa Jinbutsu Hiroku,* pp. 173–74.

20. *Ugaki Diary,* p. 157. Author's translation.
21. *Ugaki Memoirs,* p. 244.
22. *Ugaki Diary,* p. 154. Author's translation.
23. Aoki, *The Pacific War, 1,* 139.

would feel obliged to join him. Ōkawa was reluctant to draw Tokugawa into a venture which, now that the army had withdrawn its support, was destined to fail. The same night Ōkawa decided to abandon the plot.

Several significant developments within the army also contributed to Koiso's vacillation and the eventual collapse of the plot. Perhaps the most sobering in effect was the angry denunciation from the anti-Ugaki faction.[24] About March 10, Colonel Nagata, probably on orders of his superior officer, assembled the field-grade officers and confided to them the secret plan in order to enlist their support. Colonel Yamaoka Shigeatsu, a section chief in the Department of Military Education, rose in indignation and said, "This is an outrage, to conspire like this! I'll start right now with you and arrest you."[25] A few days later Nagata suffered another setback when Isoya, Chief of Staff of the First Division, went to Lieutenant General Mazaki Jinzaburō, his commanding officer, to report on the plans for the coup, only to be sharply rebuked. "The army will fall apart if we do such a thing," said Mazaki. "I will not mobilize the troops no matter who issues the order. Hurry back to the Ministry of War and tell Nagata so."[26] Another source quotes Mazaki as saying, "I will on my own responsibility punish anyone—minister or vice minister—who issues such an order."[27]

Mazaki's strong stand only intensified the cleavage between the Ugaki and the anti-Ugaki factions and resulted in a series of sordid retaliations. Mazaki, who was slated for promotion to Commanding General of the Kwantung Army, was ordered at the last minute to head the Formosan Army, a position of lesser importance. In his stead, Honjō Shigeru, a comparatively pliable

24. This group, which later came to be known as the Kōdō-ha (Imperial Way faction), was headed by Lieutenant Generals Araki Sadao and Mazaki Jinzaburō, Major Generals Yanagawa Heisaku and Hata Shinji, and Colonels Kobata Toshishirō, Yamashita Tomoyuki, and Yamaoka Shigeatsu.

25. Iwabuchi, *Military Cliques,* p. 39. Author's translation.

26. *Ugaki Memoirs,* p. 236. Author's translation.

27. Iwabuchi, *Military Cliques,* p. 39. Author's translation.

general, was assigned to lead the Kwantung Army. It has been suggested that Mazaki was sent off to Formosa because Ninomiya Harushige, Koiso, and Tatekawa, later supporters of the Kwantung Army's actions in Manchuria, could not risk having Mazaki wreck their plans again.[28]

The collapse of the plot was also due to opposition from within the Ugaki faction. The defectors included Colonels Okamura Yasuji, Yamashita, and Nagata Tetsuzan, and Lieutenant Colonel Suzuki Teiichi—all of whom contended that the settlement of Manchurian problems came first. In fact, they had arbitrarily set 1934 as the deadline for working out positive solutions. It was not that these men did not see the eventual necessity of internal reconstruction, but that they opposed the plot on the ground that it was still premature.

This group also realized that by resorting to gradualism the control of the government could be won by more legitimate means, and once power was seized, the internal changes that the direct actionists were stressing could be instituted at will. This line of thinking was identified with the Tōsei-ha (Control faction), which by 1937 managed to assume a position of dominance among the warring cliques.

The Cherry Society

As a part of the analysis of domestic factors leading to the Manchurian invasion, there remains the task of assessing the role of the extremists of the Cherry Society in the March Plot and in the Mukden Incident.

28. Mazaki suffered more deprivation at the hands of the Ugaki clique. In 1934, after Hayashi Senjūrō succeeded Araki and became the Minister of War, Nagata took revenge by removing Mazaki from the post of Inspector General of Military Education. However, Nagata was made to pay with his life for his arbitrary action. In August 1935 Lieutenant Colonel Aizawa Saburō, an admirer of Mazaki, slashed Nagata in his office in broad daylight. Aizawa, in turn, was executed after an outbreak by the young officers of the Kōdō-ha on February 26, 1936. The ghost of the quashed March Plot finally returned to haunt Ugaki himself. In January 1937 he received the imperial mandate to form a cabinet. Though the Big

An informal group of captains, majors, and lieutenant colonels began to meet at the Army Officers' Club at Kudan in Tokyo toward the end of September 1930. A sense of urgency aroused by the forced ratification by the government of the London Naval Treaty was initially responsible for prompting these men to meet.[1] The group was without a formal designation at first, but by the end of November it had come to be known as the Cherry Society (Sakura-kai), cherry blossoms having for many centuries been associated with the Japanese warrior. The principal sponsors were Lieutenant Colonels Hashimoto Kingorō, Higuchi Sueichirō, and Sakata Yoshirō. At first they commanded the attention of only a handful of members, but eventually the group was to count about a hundred members, though attendance at any one meeting did not exceed forty to fifty. Officers from the General Staff comprised about 60 per cent of the total, with the remainder coming from the Ministry of War and the Office of the Inspector General of Military Education.

The group, by no means unified, included extremists as well as moderates, although both were greatly outnumbered by neutralists. The extremists were preoccupied with the destruction of the existing forms of government to the point of minimizing the significance of the constructive phase. They maintained that a new and improved order would emerge spontaneously upon the elimination of the now decrepit old order. It is not difficult to appreciate the emotional appeal which their passionate arguments must have exercised upon the minds of the comparatively naïve and uninformed elements of society.

The arguments of the moderates or the gradualists commanded only a meager following because their program was time-consuming and unspectacular. Moreover, the men of this group did not

---

Three of the army recommended three candidates for the post of Minister of War, all three declined the appointment. Without anyone to fill the post, Ugaki's efforts to form a cabinet failed. He thus paid a price for having pushed the program of arms reduction in the 1920s and having refused to cooperate at the time of the March Plot.

1. See Aoki, *The Pacific War, 1,* 122–24.

present their thesis with the passion and zeal of their competitors, the extremists. The moderates maintained that, before any action could be contemplated, the objectives of the national reconstruction had to be carefully outlined, and the rationale of the movement stated in understandable terms. In stark contrast to the extremists, the moderates prescribed the removal of only the cancerous growth in society, leaving the healthy tissues intact, thus keeping the destructive process to a bare minimum.[2] Finally, the neutralists, who comprised the bulk of the group, preferred not to commit themselves in one way or another.

The principal pastime of this loosely knit group was to eat together in the evening and engage in lively discussion of current affairs. Especially spirited were the conversations involving national reform and Manchuria and Mongolia. It would not have been at all surprising if at times the extremists carried the day with their fiery talk. It was in part to offset the undue influence they exercised and to prevent the Cherry Society from turning into a terroristic organization that Major Tanaka Kiyoshi and Captains Watanabe Fujio, Iwaaze Hideo, and Yamaoka hastened the completion of concrete plans for national reconstruction.

Hashimoto headed the Russian Specialist faction, the radical element within the group. He had recently returned from service as a military attaché in Istanbul, and while stationed there he had watched with interest the progress of Turkey under the strong leadership of Kemal Atatürk. He had also observed at close hand Russia's Five-Year Plan and the resurgence of Italy and Germany under Mussolini and Hitler. On his month-long voyage home Hashimoto pondered the problem of how to reform Japan, shaping his dreams into a comprehensive plan. Once back in the General Staff office he worked out the means of implementing it. This was some time after January 1930.[3]

2. For cleavages of a similar nature cf. above, p. 95, and below, pp. 196–97.

3. See IMTFE, *Judgment* (Tokyo, 1948), pp. 532–33. These pages contain a translation of a brief passage from Hashimoto's book, *The Road to the Reconstruction of the World.*

Hashimoto stealthily made up an attendance book and endeavored to muster like-minded officers under his banner. Things did not always go smoothly, however, especially after Lieutenant Colonels Mutō Akira and Kawabe Torashirō joined the society. These men bitterly criticized him and his views. According to a reasonably reliable source, Hashimoto's faction numbered barely 10 per cent of the entire group. Thus, even by generous allowance, the nucleus of the extremists could not have totaled more than ten. Hashimoto once engaged Ōkawa as an after-dinner speaker, but his lecture produced little sympathetic response among the members of the group.[4]

However, it was not without reason that Hashimoto's group was given prominence to the point where it overshadowed the existence of the much larger but amorphous nonmilitant group. "Major Tanaka's Notes" refers to the Hashimoto clique as a "secret society," prepared to resort to direct action to effect national reconstruction.[5] According to Hashimoto's own testimony at the War Crimes Trials:

> In October 1930, I inaugurated a study and discussion group with a view to instituting a national reform. Its members consisted of officers of the rank of lieutenant colonel and lower. The so-called Cherry Society was not a secret society. Neither did it have its own bylaws, nor was a membership fee charged. The society had no connection with the Kwantung Army or its

4. Matsumura, *Miyakezaka,* pp. 46–47.

5. Shiraki, *Nihon Seitōshi,* p. 80. The committee comprising Lieutenant Colonels Sakata Yoshirō, Nemoto Hiroshi, Hashimoto Kingorō, Major Tanaka Kiyoshi, and Captains Chō Isamu and Tanaka Wataru were delegated with the task of drawing up the plans for national reconstruction. Aoki, *The Pacific War, 1,* 124–25. It is noteworthy that of the six mentioned above, four—Sakata, Nemoto, Hashimoto, and Tanaka—were participants in the preliminary discussion of the March Plot which was held at the residence of Colonel Shigetō on the night of February 7, 1931. Ibid., p. 107.

> officers. No discussion was held relative to the Manchurian problems, nor did the society have any connection with the Mukden Incident.
>
> In March 1931, I participated in the planning of the March Plot for the purpose of inaugurating national reform. Ōkawa Shūmei planned the plot with a view to placing General Ugaki at the head of a cabinet. The plan fell through because General Ugaki himself disapproved. The March Plot was not linked with the Mukden Incident.[6]

Hashimoto's testimony is corroborated by that of Major General Tanaka Ryūkichi, who turned prosecution witness at the trials. He stated, "The Meeting in October did not touch at all on the question of Manchuria because Japan was plagued with extremely acute domestic problems at the time."[7]

Tanaka Ryūkichi, however, contradicted himself when he was asked to testify about Captain Chō Isamu, who played a leading part in the October Plot with Hashimoto: "Captain Chō told me in Shanghai that the purpose of the Cherry Society was twofold: first, to carry out internal revolution or reconstruction; second, to solve the Manchurian problems."[8]

The conclusion to be drawn is that, inasmuch as Hashimoto himself denied the existence of the Cherry Society as a corporate body, it is immaterial whether the society as a group had any dealings with the Kwantung Army; the real question is whether any members of the Cherry Society as individuals conspired with the staff of the Kwantung Army or were sympathetic with its designs. While the testimony of Wachi Takaji at the trials proves rather convincingly that Hashimoto for one was not in communication with the members of the Kwantung Army,[9] it cannot

6. IMTFE, *Proceedings*, p. 28,793.
7. Ibid., p. 1961.
8. Ibid., p. 1963.
9. For a fuller discussion see below, p. 201.

thereby be concluded that Hashimoto was indifferent to its objectives. His testimony at the trials to the contrary notwithstanding, it is clear from an earlier report prepared for the General Staff in 1930—to be discussed shortly—that Hashimoto was just as ready as Chō to tie national reconstruction and the Manchurian problem together. And it is highly probable that there were quite a few others among the extremists, both in the Cherry Society and in the high offices of the army, who tended to associate the two issues rather closely.

However, as the crisis at home and on the continent deepened with every passing day, this duality in their objectives had to be resolved. It was obvious that both issues could not be settled simultaneously and that priorities had to be thrashed out. This was, indeed, a momentous issue, and it was inevitable that in the ensuing controversy a split in the camp should occur. In the case of the March Plot this was precisely what happened, materially contributing to the fiasco that followed.

The nature of the schism needs closer scrutiny. There is evidence that Hashimoto was convinced early of the need to give priority to internal reconstruction over foreign adventure. This was not quite the case with Ōkawa. As an official in the employ of the South Manchuria Railway Company, he was just as much a continental expansionist as he was an internal reconstructionist. Becoming impatient with the desultory progress of the Japanese government in Manchuria, he launched a campaign of his own as early as April 1929 to take the Manchurian question directly to the Japanese people. His success attracted the attention and cooperation of the General Staff. It is not at all surprising, therefore, that he soon had a following among certain field-grade officers who were strongly imbued with the notion that immediate action ought to be taken in Manchuria.[10]

But it was gradually concluded that a prerequisite to successful Japanese action in Manchuria was the establishment of a military-controlled government at home. It must have been

10. IMTFE, *Judgment,* p. 87.

this line of reasoning that slowly but surely began to pervade the thinking of the members of the Chinese Intelligence Section under Colonel Shigetō Chiaki and the Russian Intelligence Section under Lieutenant Colonel Hashimoto Kingorō of the General Staff. So fervent were these men in their conviction that their conclusion found its way into the *1930 Report on the State of the Nation,* an annual publication by the intelligence section of the General Staff which heretofore had devoted itself exclusively to the question of strategy vis-à-vis potential enemy nations. That portion of the report which broke precedent read: "If a positive solution of the Manchurian problems is to be sought, it is inevitable that national reconstruction must precede it. Our thinking has been dominated by this one thought."[11] This was tantamount to declaring that the General Staff was now making Japan's internal administration its business.

We can only deduce that the issue at stake was that of priority. Defection of a group of influential army officers has been already mentioned. At the head of the group was Nagata, followed by Okamura, Yamashita, and Suzuki. It was their contention that the proper time had not yet arrived to institute internal reconstruction and that positive settlement of the Manchurian and Mongolian questions must come first.

There is probably no clear-cut explanation why men such as Shigetō and Ōkawa should have given priority to internal reconstruction. Suffice it to note that the cause apparently had the full backing of highly placed army officers. Moreover, there is always the element of pride. Once the factions had taken sides, each would have had to stick to its argument. It is significant that the highly formal letter which Ōkawa addressed to Ugaki on March 6 contained no reference whatsoever to Japan's continental problems, despite the fact that Manchuria was Ōkawa's preoccupation.

Perhaps the most persuasive reason why the Manchurian problem may have undergone temporary eclipse in the minds of the

11. Kinoshita, *Japanese Fascism, 1,* 107. Author's translation.

right-wing revolutionists was the dazzling prospect of their becoming the masters of Japan overnight. Not only did these leaders appear to have become oblivious to the Manchurian problem, they were even suspected by the young officers of the Kita faction of having betrayed the ideals of national reconstruction. In premature anticipation of the success of the coup, Ōkawa, Hashimoto, and Shigetō gave themselves up to debauchery for days on end at a Japanese-style restaurant, the Kinryū-tei, in Tokyo. It is not at all surprising that the more serious-minded officers, principally of company grade, broke off and formed a splinter group—the Little Cherry Society—under the leadership of Lieutenant Colonel Mitsui Sakichi and Lieutenant Sugaha Saburō. In short, the handful of zealous army officers who tried to direct the activities of the Cherry Society for their own ends never quite succeeded.

Sources of Military Provocation

In the Disarmament Conference, scheduled to meet early in 1932 in Geneva, the military saw nothing but disaster, particularly after the Hamaguchi government had scored a resounding victory over the Naval General Staff in the ratification of the London Naval Treaty. Understandably, the army die-hards took the navy defeat as a signal for a showdown with the government. Since the early twenties the army had been subjected to a series of drastic manpower reductions, with telling effect on the morale of its career officers; rightly or wrongly it felt it could retreat no more.

In the initial curtailment of army personnel in 1922 some 60,000 officers and men had been demobilized. Under the second arms reduction program of 1923 two independent garrison units and five military preparatory schools were dissolved. Neither of these two programs, however, approached in devastation the blow which the third retrenchment program administered to army morale. During the second Katō government in 1925 under War Minister Ugaki, four divisions—the 13th at Takata, the 15th at

Toyohashi, the 17th at Okayama, and the 18th at Kurume—were demobilized, resulting in the discharge of some 34,000 men and officers and the decommissioning of 6,000 mounts.

The officers who were forced to accept involuntary retirement were particularly resentful of the government's drastic retrenchment program. This was not only the end of their military careers—one of the very few channels through which men of ordinary background in Japan could rise to eminence—but, unlike their brethren in Western countries, Japanese officers by training and outlook were neither suitable nor desirable for civilian employment. About the only vocations open to them were positions in high schools as instructors in military drill, a poor substitute for the relatively higher glamor and prestige of military office.

And the prospects of those fortunate officers who remained in regular service were dim and getting dimmer. It was virtually pre-ordained that their careers would terminate after a colonelcy. If an officer rose to generalship, it was by sheer good fortune. Thus it came about that even in Japan, where by tradition military careers were held in high esteem, the observation could be made that "aboard a streetcar people would no longer offer their seats to an officer, and parents, as eager as they were to marry their daughters off, became hesitant about giving them to young officers.[1]

The world-wide demand for disarmament in the post-Versailles decade of international good will was given sharp local emphasis in Japan with the financial crisis in 1927, and armed forces reduction became not merely a slogan but a pressing necessity. Through 1930 and 1931 under the retrenchment policy of Inoue Junnosuke, Minister of Finance, the Hamaguchi and Wakatsuki governments were able to effect a considerable reduction in civil and military expenditures. As a part of Inoue's economy drive, not long after the Hamaguchi government succeeded Tanaka's, an army reorganization committee was formed under the chairmanship of General Ugaki, then Minister of War. After two

1. *Shidehara Memoirs,* p. 167. Author's translation.

and a half years of protracted study, on May 1, 1931, the Big Three of the army—War Minister Minami, Chief of the General Staff Kanaya, and Inspector General of Military Education Mutō —met to arrive at a decision. The three were fully cognizant of the far-reaching impact of their decision, once it was made and announced. They therefore required several more meetings before they reached unanimity of opinion. Their verdict was that further reductions in armament expenditures were unfeasible and that any budgetary surplus that might be realized by readjustment should be allocated to strengthening other branches of the armed forces by replacing obsolete equipment. The decision proved very unpopular in the face of the suffering that was becoming more widespread and acute as the economic crisis continued to mount.

Harada reported in his diary that in mid-July of 1931 the army had a plan to preclude any possibility of further arms reduction.[2] Kanaya, Chief of the General Staff, and Minami, Minister of War, each was to have a private audience with the Emperor, at which time they were to report that a further reduction of armaments was impossible. Thereafter, the army could parry any efforts by the cabinet to push through the retrenchment program by asserting that "once something has been reported to the Emperor, it can no longer be rescinded."[3]

When Prince Saionji was alerted by Harada to the army's scheme, he took steps to caution the Emperor through Suzuki, the Grand Chamberlain, not to commit himself in any way should either Kanaya or Minami approach him with matters pertaining to disarmament. It is presumed that the army failed to follow through with its scheme, since Harada does not report on the outcome of the purported audience.

The antagonism between the government and the army was further heightened by an incident that occurred at the Conference of Division Commanders on August 4, 1931. Minami, character-

2. *Harada Diary, 2,* 7.
3. Ibid.

izing the government as run by uninformed and irresponsible people, deplored the fact that they were capitalizing on the current economic and financial crisis to arouse strong sentiments for disarmament on the home front. Moreover, he accused critics of the army of spreading the false rumor that, impervious to the domestic crisis, the armed forces were asking far too large a sum of money for their budget. The truth of the matter, he said, was that the army authorities had drawn up the army reorganization plan on the basis of minimum needs, and that this meant a real sacrifice to the military.

Minami then touched upon the disquieting developments in Manchuria and Mongolia and by inference blamed Shidehara's weak-kneed diplomacy for the predicament Japan found herself in. He exhorted the members of the armed forces to redouble their efforts to cope with the mounting crisis.[4]

While the language of his blustering denunciation was enough to incense the younger members of the Minseitō in the Lower House of the Diet, his statement nevertheless represented the consensus of the elites of the army. Breaking precedent, leading members of the army in addition to division commanders had attended the conference. These included Generals Suzuki Takao, Inoue Ikutarō, and Shirakawa Yoshinori, all of whom were members of the Supreme War Council; General Hayashi Senjūrō, Commander of the Tokyo Garrison; General Kanaya Hanzō, Chief of the General Staff; and General Mutō Nobuyoshi, Inspector General of Military Education. These generals reportedly prevailed upon Minami to express at the next cabinet meeting the army's profound dissatisfaction with Shidehara's policy.[5]

As matters turned out, at the cabinet meeting on August 6 it was Shidehara who took the initiative and reprimanded Minami for his indiscretion in releasing his address to the public. The

4. *Tōkyō Nichinichi Shinbun* (August 5, 1931), cited in *Harada Diary, 2,* 17.

5. *Tōkyō Asahi* (August 5, 1931), pp. 1–2, cited in Takeuchi, *War and Diplomacy in the Japanese Empire,* p. 345.

Foreign Minister was distressed that Minami's ill-advised utterances might arouse undue concern in the United States, Great Britain, and China at a highly tense moment in Japanese-Chinese relationships.[6]

In this situation, Minister of Finance Inoue made the fatal error of failing to assess correctly the sharp political repercussions of his ill-timed deflationary policy. During the decade of the twenties the trend toward concentration of capital in the hands of the zaibatsu continued to a point where the polarization of society into the haves and have-nots became obvious even to the average Japanese on the street. A handful of gigantic family holding companies[7] controlled a chain of subsidiaries in virtually every field of heavy industry, mining, finance, insurance, and banking, with a resultant influence in government through both the bureaucracy and political parties. Since in the same period the political influence of the militarists was on the wane and political authority seemed to be gravitating toward the Diet and the zaibatsu, the two naturally incurred the enmity of the military.

As the only means available to reduce substantially the budgetary deficit, throughout the summer of 1931 Inoue pressed for a lowering of military and naval expenditures despite bitter opposition. And by early September Inoue and Minami had reached substantial agreement on this thorny question. However, when Minami bore the agreement back to the Ministry of War, he was rebuffed by Koiso, Chief of the Military Affairs Bureau, and Onodera Chōjirō, the Accountant General.[8] Consequently, the agreement reached after much labor was nullified, and the negotiations were right back where they had been in early summer. This rather obscure incident may be taken as just another instance in which the military decided to defy the government and fight back.

6. Ibid. (August 7, 1931), p. 1.
7. The larger ones included Mitsui, Mitsubishi, Sumitomo, and Yasuda.
8. *Harada Diary, 2,* 42–43, 45.

Agrarian Impoverishment and the Young Officers

No evidence has been uncovered thus far to indicate that Japan's agrarian problems had any immediate bearing on the March Plot, the Mukden Incident, or the October Plot. It is more appropriate to say that these plots were planned by a relatively restricted group of army officers to further the immediate interest of their own clique rather than to bring comprehensive benefits to a large segment of the underemployed Japanese agrarian population.[1]

In the twenties the number of agricultural households remained virtually stationary at about five and a half million, and there were no pronounced changes in the size or distribution of the farms. The trend was toward an increase in farming families cultivating medium-sized plots from one and a quarter to five acres, with a decrease in the very large and the very small. There was comparatively little change in the system of land tenure, though the number of tenant farmers tended to decline while the number of those who owned part of the land and rented the rest grew. Rice continued to be the chief food crop, and well over half the cultivated area was devoted to it.

In the middle twenties the price of rice maintained a fairly high level, in part because of the absence of bumper crops and recurrence of several poor harvests. But from 1927 to 1930 there was a succession of large crops, with the one in 1930 being exceptionally heavy.

1. In contrast, the abortive coups which came later—on May 15, 1932, and February 26, 1936—were closely tied in with Japan's agrarian problems. The bitter but futile struggle which young officers of company grade, with the backing of civilian satellite organizations—see Yanaga, *Japan since Perry,* pp. 502–05, on Ketsumeidan (Blood Brotherhood League) and Aikoku Kinrōtō (Patriotic Workers' Society)—carried out against the Tōsei-ha in order to pave the way for internal reconstruction can be understood only when cast against the backdrop of the extreme impoverishment of Japan's agrarian population. This is true even though the young officers themselves admittedly had no comprehensive program of their own.

Since 1927 the government had tried under a valorization scheme to support the price of rice by purchasing surplus rice whenever its market price fell below a fixed figure.[2] However, the price continued to fall steadily, and within a period of four months in 1930–31 the price of one *koku*[3] of rice collapsed from twenty-seven to eighteen yen.

Moreover, there was a long-term deterrent to any rise in the price of domestically produced rice. Under the encouragement of the government, which effected improvements in irrigation and the use of fertilizer, the output of rice in Korea increased by 30 per cent in the twenty-year period following annexation in 1910. Similar development had taken place in Formosa, though on a smaller scale.

Between 1927 and 1929, imports from these two areas averaged about 13 per cent of Japan's domestic production. This amount enabled her to meet the increase in demand created by the ever-growing population. However, from the point of view of the Japanese farmers, an increase in population brought no benefits, since the inflow of rice from these two colonies and the ever-present possibility of an influx of inferior and cheaper rice from Southeast Asia tended to keep the price of domestically produced rice depressed.

Although certain agrarian groups, such as the Imperial Agricultural Society (Teikoku Nōkai), agitated in favor of restricting imports, such a step would have been politically hazardous. A well-known scholar of Japan's economy has observed that "to have listened to such a demand would, however, have produced trouble among the urban population, besides endangering both industrial development and strategic advantages."[4] To put it bluntly, the backward, inarticulate mass of the farming populace benefited neither from the rise in national income due to

2. G. C. Allen, *A Short Economic History of Modern Japan, 1867–1937* (London, Allen and Unwin, 1946), p. 109.

3. Equivalent to 5.12 American bushels.

4. Allen, *A Short Economic History of Modern Japan,* p. 110.

the industrialization of Japan nor from the enlarged demand for rice due to the growth in population.

However, the sudden collapse of the rice market was not the only blow the Japanese farmers sustained in 1930. Raw silk, their principal source of cash income and their second most important agriculture product, suffered an even more disastrous drop in price when the American demand slackened.

Between 1914 an 1921 sericulture saw a threefold increase in production, until two fifths of all farming households were engaged in that occupation as a secondary source of income. This remarkable increase in the production of raw silk in turn meant an additional demand for female workers who came mainly from farming households. Wages which a farmer's daughters earned, together with the sale of cocoons, comprised a very important part of the farmer's cash income, since much of his rice production was either consumed by his family or, in the case of tenant farmers, passed to the landlords as rent.

Commenting on the highly sensitive role raw silk played in the agrarian economy, Professor Allen writes:

> At a time when very little additional land was available for cereal cultivation, this outlet was most valuable to the peasants. Such improvements in their standard of living as occurred in this period—and they can hardly be considered substantial—are attributable largely to fresh opportunities to engage in industrial occupations and, in particular, to participate in this rapidly growing silk trade. Any disturbance to the growth of that trade was bound to have disastrous consequences for them.[5]

In 1923 the average export price of raw silk per 100 *kin*[6] was 2,150 yen. After 1925 the export price tended to fall, because

5. Ibid.
6. One *kin* is equivalent to 1.323 pounds.

of the rise in the exchange value of the yen. In April 1929 the export price was 1,420 yen, which still compared favorably with the 800–900 yen of pre-World War I prices. However, after the collapse of the American market, the price slumped to 540 yen by October 1930, and it continued to fall for the next two years, hitting a low of 390 yen in June 1932. This spelled double disaster for the farmers, since their cash income had already been drastically reduced when the price of rice had collapsed.

Over the course of three years there was almost a 50 per cent reduction in the income from rice, silk, and oats. Rice and silk were said to have comprised roughly 70 per cent of the cash income of Japanese farmers. In terms of ratio, the rate of decline in the annual income of Japanese farm households from rice, silk, and oats was 62 for 1930 and 52 for 1931, assuming 100 as an index figure for 1929.[7]

Ironically, in contrast to the overabundance of rice in other parts of Japan, the five prefectures in the northeast corner of Honshū and Hokkaidō were ravaged by an unusually early frost in 1931, which caused extensive damage to the crops. Many farm households, on the verge of starvation, were compelled to sell their daughters to procurers.

Despite the misery and poverty which hung like a heavy pall over the countryside of Japan, the relief measures instituted by the Minseitō government were wholly inadequate and slow in being administered. Of some 140 million yen earmarked for the relief of farmers, only a little over 4 million had actually been spent by February 1931.[8] The acute condition of the agrarian population was reflected in the frequency of tenancy disputes (as indicated in Table 1), which continued to mount through 1931.

7. Kiyozawa Retsu, "Goichigo Jiken no Shakaiteki Konkyo" (Social Origin of the May 15, 1932 Incident), *Kaizō* (November 1933), p. 265 (hereafter referred to as Kiyozawa, *May 15, 1932 Incident*).

8. Muramatsu Yūji, "Taiheiyō Sensō Boppatsu to Nihon Keizai" (The Outbreak of the Pacific War and the Japanese Economy), *Taiheiyō Sensō Genin Ron* (Causes of the Pacific War), ed. Ueda Katsuo (Tokyo, 1953), p. 566.

The acute distress suffered by the peasantry was not by any means a new development on the Japanese social scene; for centuries the peasant had been exploited by feudal regimes.[9] Tokugawa agrarian policy may be characterized by the saying, "Impose taxes upon farmers to such an extent that they can neither live nor die,"[10] or, "Peasants and rape seeds—the more they are squeezed, the more is gained."[11] The farmer's lot would

TABLE 1. *Number of Tenancy Disputes, 1926–1932*

Year	*Disputes*	*Participating Tenants*
1926	2,751	151,061
1927	2,052	91,336
1928	1,866	75,136
1929	2,434	81,998
1930	2,478	58,565
1931	3,419	81,135
1932	3,414	61,499

Source: Tōyama, Imai, and Fujiwara, *Shōwa-shi* (History of the Shōwa Era) (Tokyo, 1955), p. 45.

9. On the eve of the Meiji Restoration, the *samurai* (warrior class) numbered about two million or roughly 6–7 per cent of Japan's population. The maintenance of this large idle class in an agricultural economy had placed a heavy burden on the nonprivileged peasant class, which constituted about 75 per cent of the population. The annual land tax paid in rice by the peasant constituted the major source of revenue for the *shōgun* and *daimyō* (feudal lords). Though it varied from province to province, the revenue amounted to 40–50 per cent of the total yield of paddy fields. Allen, *A Short Economic History of Modern Japan,* p. 11. For precise delineation of the term Meiji Restoration, see Albert M. Craig, *Chōshū in the Meiji Restoration* (Cambridge, 1961), pp. 360–61.

10. E. Herbert Norman, *Japan's Emergence as a Modern State* (New York, Institute of Pacific Relations, 1940), p. 21.

11. It goes without saying that exploitation and oppression of the peasants gave rise to innumerable agrarian uprisings during the Tokugawa

have been more tolerable had it shown some signs of improvement, as had other sectors of the nation's economy as the result of the Meiji Restoration.

Japan's modern agriculture owed its distorted development to two factors. The first was the shaping it received in the political settlements of the early Meiji era, and the second was the enormous growth in Japan's population in modern times.

The former theme has received a classic treatment in E. Herbert Norman's book *Japan's Emergence as a Modern State.*[12] The author maintains that the two factors which accelerated Japan's transition from a feudal to a modern state were, first, that Tokugawa feudalism was in its last hours and the regime collapsed without prolonged and wasteful civil war; and second, that external pressures exerted by the Western nations left no choice for Japan but to concentrate her national resources in building her defense structure by banking heavily on the only sizable resource Japan had, namely revenues from land taxation. Under this program it was inevitable that the peasants were made to shoulder the extremely high cost required to modernize in a short span of time.[13]

The policy goal pursued by Japan is succinctly stated by Norman:

> The policy of the Meiji Government was to initiate strategic industries, to endow lavishly the defense forces, to subsidize generously a narrow and comparatively weak merchant-banking class in order to en-

period. For details see Hugh Borton, "Peasant Uprisings in Japan of Tokugawa Period," *Transactions of the Asiatic Society of Japan,* 2d ser. *16* (1938).

12. See in particular chap. 5, "The Agrarian Settlement and Its Social Consequences," pp. 136–66.

13. In 1899 the land tax on rural sites was raised from 2.5 per cent to 3.3 per cent. In 1905 it was raised again, later reaching 11.5 per cent on the most highly taxed sites. Allen, *A Short Economic History of Modern Japan,* p. 44. The theme that the main impetus for the post-Restoration modernization program came from external pressure is admirably summarized in Craig, p. 373.

> courage its entry into the field of industry. *The reverse side of this policy was marked by a disproportionately heavy tax burden on the agricultural classes,* by the stinting of enterprises less vital than those connected with defense, and by a general impatience at any sign of unrest or democratic protest which might precipitate a domestic crisis and so hinder or retard the task of reconstruction. Nevertheless, it was this policy which succeeded in the very speedy creation of industries, a merchant marine, an overseas market, and an efficient navy.[14]

In the words of Bertrand Russell, "Modern Japan is almost exactly what it was intended to be by the men who made the revolution of 1867."[15]

In the early decades of the twentieth century, moreover, the farmers steadily lost ground to other sectors in the national economy. As shown in Table 2, of enormous political significance was the fact that, whereas the per capita share in the national income by the primary industries[16] followed a steady path of decline from about 1922 through 1940, the income of the secondary and tertiary industries rose steadily upward from about 1915 until 1930, resulting in a rather conspicuous gap in the standard of living between the agrarian population and the urban population engaged in other sectors of the economy. As Table 3, on labor wage indices, indicates, even after the depression had set in, urban wages did not show a decline anything like that of the farmers' income.

Still another indication of the imbalance of the agrarian and

14. *Japan's Emergence as a Modern State,* p. 208. Italics added.

15. Quoted in G. C. Allen, *Japan: The Hungry Guest* (New York, Dutton, 1938), p. 116.

16. Primary industries include agriculture, forestry, fisheries, and mining. Of course, the latter three together equal only a small fraction of the overwhelmingly large agricultural industry. Secondary industries comprise manufacturing and construction. Tertiary industries comprise the service industries: transportation and communication, wholesale and retail, finance, public services, professions, rentals, etc.

TABLE 2. *Ratio of Per Capita Income of Those Engaged in Primary Industries to Per Capita Income of Those Engaged in the Remaining Sectors (Secondary + Tertiary) of the National Economy on the Basis of Quinquennial Average*

Periods	
1903–07	36%
1908–12	39%
1913–17	42%
1918–22	40%
1923–27	32%
1928–32	27%
1933–37	29%
1938–42	27%

Source: Yamada Yūzō, *Nihon Kokumin Shotoku Suikei Shiryō* (Statistical Estimates of Japan's National Income) (Tokyo, 1951), pp . 128, 130 (hereafter referred to as Yamada, *National Income*).

TABLE 3. *Indices of Labor Wages in Japan, 1924–1930 (1921–1923 = 100)*

Year (June)	*Index*
1924	104
1925	103
1926	103
1927	101
1928	102
1929	102
1930	95

Source: Kiyozawa, *May 15, 1932, Incident,* p. 267.

urban economies in September 1931 was the discrepancy in Tokyo between the average wholesale index and the average index price on agricultural products. Using 1920 as the base year with an index of 100, the index for produce had shrunk to 37.5 in comparison with the average wholesale index of 54.4 and the index of 42.1 for farming equipment and supplies—both appreciably higher indices than for produce but still substantially reduced from those of 1920.[17]

Although space will not permit us to explore all the intricate causes underlying the profound discrepancy in per capita income between the farming population, which comprised approximately half of Japan's working population in the 1928–32 period,[18] and those engaged in secondary and tertiary industries—a discrepancy which gave rise to the phenomenon known as the "dual economy"—the population problem certainly was a contributing factor of great importance.

Between 1914 and 1930 the population of Japan proper increased by 25 per cent, or from 51 million to 64 million in absolute figures. In the mid-twenties, even before financial crisis had overtaken the country, the national economy had experienced considerable difficulty in annually absorbing the approximately 450,000 new workers seeking employment. This large semi-stagnant reservoir of surplus population was at best semi-employed, a condition marked by irregularity of work and insecurity of employment, and, when employed, subject to long hours of work at meager wages. The semi-employed surplus lived on the fringes of the urban economy and like driftwood tended to shift back and forth between the cities and the villages in response to the ebb and flow of the nation's economic activities. In the latter half of the twenties the movement of this surplus population was more heavily in the direction of the rural areas than toward the cities, with the result that the standard of living in the already congested villages was depressed to a

17. Kiyozawa, *May 15, 1932 Incident,* p. 266.
18. Yamada Yūzō, *National Income,* p. 130.

point where, in some localities such as northeast Honshū, it became intolerable.[19]

Among the writers of tracts espousing the agrarian cause, Gondō Seikyō and Tachibana Kōsaburō attracted considerable attention. Both men attributed the existing social ills of Japan to the deplorable state of the once healthy villages. On the other hand, they saw in the unbridled growth of huge urban centers the eventual undoing of Japan, likening them to cancerous growths which would sap the nation's strength.[20]

They associated with this urban-rural imbalance the growing influence of big business in politics, the top-heavy bureaucratic administration, and the military, suspecting these three elements of collusion for further selfish ends. They feared that this state of affairs was responsible for the unhealthy class differentiations and the steady deterioration in the lot of the average man on the street. They expressed a nostalgic longing for values of primitive communalism, wherein they envisioned more local autonomy,

19. From July 1929 to June 1930 the number of workers discharged from factories and mines employing more than 50 amounted to 660,000. Of these unemployed workers, 300,000 returned immediately to their native villages. Thus, allowing for a lag for those who drifted back to the villages after some lapse of time, it must be presumed that the majority of the unemployed eventually found their way back to the country. Cited in Tōyama, Imai, and Fujiwara, *Shōwa-shi* (History of the Shōwa Era) (Tokyo, 1955), pp. 39–40.

20. Maruyama Masao, in discussing the impact of the "agriculture-first" principle on the development of fascism in Japan, observes that this principle tended to exercise a restraining influence upon the proclivity inherent in fascistic movement to regiment thinking and to foster a highly centralized economy. Gondō in *Jichi Minpan* (Principles of Autonomous People) and *Nōson Jikyū Ron* (Essay on the Salvation of Farm Villages) indicated that he was a thoroughgoing agrarian, even to the extent of showing an antinationalistic tendency. Tachibana did not categorically disapprove large-scale manufacturing industries. Maruyama Masao, *Gendai Seiji no Shisō to Kōdō* (Thought and Actions Underlying Contemporary Politics), *1* (Tokyo, 1958), 39–40, 44 (hereafter referred to as Maruyama, *Contemporary Politics*). For a description of the various schools of thought among the agrarian-centered nationalists, see Scalapino, *Democracy and the Party Movement in Prewar Japan,* pp. 356–57.

less interference from the central authority, and more familial ties. At the apex of the amorphous national state they posited an emperor whose function was to reign in the Confucian manner, living an exemplary life and thus serving as a model to be emulated rather than ruling by rigid codes of law.

Although Gondō had had little or no direct dealings with the Army extremists, his two works influenced the thinking of the young officers who were responsible for the assassination of Premier Inukai in May 1932.

Many young officers themselves came from poor country districts. Since the wretched conditions at home affected the morale of the draftees for whose training they were responsible, it is not at all surprising that the officers took a paternalistic interest in the family welfare of peasant soldiers.[21] As they brooded over the plight of the farmers, many began to entertain a distrust of the parliamentary government, which was ineffective in alleviating agrarian problems, and the zaibatsu, which they suspected of exercising a corrupting influence on the government. Thus many young officers turned to champion radical programs to better the economic status of the underprivileged peasantry against the big business interests of the cities.[22]

Actually, the young officers did not rise in open rebellion until the May 15, 1932, Incident. However, that their deep discontent

21. That the depressed living conditions in the farming communities affected even General Honjō, Commander in Chief of the Kwantung Army, is borne out by the testimony of Katakura Tadashi: "Lieutenant General Honjō saw Ambassador Yoshizawa in the presence of Miyake, Ishihara, and myself. Among the three points Honjō mentioned, the third was his hope that, in view of the fact that the soldiers who had served devotedly in the incident had come from the fishing villages and farms in Japan, the living conditions of the farming communities would be improved" (IMTFE, *Proceedings,* p. 19,004).

22. For a cogent description of the social and economic conditions in the thirties which provoked the young officers into taking matters into their own hands and the climate of opinion which enabled the military and the ultranationalists to dominate Japan, see "The Nationalistic and Militaristic Reaction" in Edwin O. Reischauer, *Japan, Past and Present* (New York, 1954), pp. 157–85.

with the existing form of government in 1931 acted as powerful force in nurturing the March and October Plots and the Mukden Incident cannot be denied.

4.
MOUNTING CRISIS IN JAPANESE-CHINESE RELATIONS

With the final settlement on April 28, 1929, of the Tsinan Incident, followed by the recognition of the Nationalist regime on June 28, it appeared that relations between China and Japan had at last returned to normal. To cap this, there followed the halcyon days of the spring of 1930 when, with the Minseitō back in power, Shidehara restored China's tariff autonomy. Nevertheless, even while the tide was changing visibly in China's favor, her officials made no secret of the fact that Japan would be called upon to relinquish additional special concessions in China. The stage was thus set for the deterioration of Japanese-Chinese relations which led inevitably to the Manchurian crisis.[1]

Minister Saburi's "Suicide"

At this critical juncture two unfortunate incidents followed hard on each other. Taken separately, neither could have been serious; together they deepened suspicion between the two nations.

First came the inexplicable death of Saburi Sadao, Japan's Minister to the Nanking government. Although Saburi was originally slated for promotion to the post of Ambassador to Moscow, after some persuasion he had accepted the lesser post at Nanking.

1. The brief interlude of relaxation of tension in Sino-Japanese relations is described in Horiuchi Kanjō, *Chūgoku no Arashi no Naka de* (In the Storms in China) (Tokyo, 1950), pp. 65–81.

The Foreign Office's explanation was that Saburi was the logical choice because, having attended the Peking Tariff Conference in 1928, he was well versed in the problems of Sino-Japanese trade.

It was early in October 1929 that Minister Saburi arrived in Shanghai to undertake the onerous task of revising the unequal treaties. His arrival in Nanking was hailed with much fanfare, since he was regarded as a personal friend of Chiang Kai-shek. Saburi engaged in a series of conversation with Chang, C. T. Wang, and other key officials of the Nanking government. In late November he returned by way of North China to consult Shidehara in Tokyo; the report was that he had brought highly important proposals for discussion. While officials at Nanking awaited his return, his stay in Tokyo lengthened to a week. Meanwhile, the delicate Japanese-Chinese relations showed signs of deteriorating, and Shigemitsu, the Japanese Consul General at Shanghai, becoming more and more anxious by the day, wired Tokyo time and again to no avail. Then, on November 29, there suddenly appeared bulletins posted at street corners in Shanghai reporting Minister Saburi's "suicide."

Shidehara claimed that Saburi had cleared all business with him and was set to return to Nanking when he suddenly died. Although his death is a mystery to this day, there were circumstances which could have given him a feeling of complete frustration. Saburi's return to Tokyo, for instance, coincided with a period of extraordinary confusion at the Foreign Office, whose key men, feverishly engaged in preparing instructions and documents for the delegation attending the London Naval Conference, were unable to devote the time and attention to the China problem which the situation demanded.

To the end, Shidehara doubted that Saburi actually committed suicide. The pistol which he purportedly used was identified as not his, and his own was found packed in his suitcase. Also, although Saburi's body was found with the pistol in his right hand, the bullet had entered his head from the left temple and came out from the right.[1] This unnatural death electrified public opinion in China. Some suspected that his proposals, being too favorable to China, had been rejected by the Foreign Office.

Saburi's death was followed by an incident even more destructive to Japanese-Chinese accord: the Japanese government decided on Obata Torikichi, the former Ambassador to Turkey as successor to Saburi. No one could blame officials of the Nanking government for suspecting that Obata was chosen because of his firm attitude toward China. The Chinese had not forgotten that back in 1915 Obata had participated in the negotiations for the Twenty-One Demands as a counselor to Minister Hioki Yasu. As might be expected, the Nanking government flatly refused *agrément* for Obata. Shigemitsu spent the last two days of December in Nanking in an unsuccessful effort to persuade Chiang and C. T. Wang to retract their refusal.

Japan, now in the awkward position of being unable to appoint a full-fledged minister, appointed Shigemitsu as Acting Minister. Chinese feelings toward Japan progressed from bad to worse. Meanwhile, Japanese ultranationalists and the extremists of the military were busily fanning the sentiments of the people in an effort to produce a get-tough policy toward China.

China's Positive Diplomacy

Throughout the early months of 1931 Shigemitsu, in the capacity of Acting Minister, continued negotiations with the Nanking government with a view to revising the treaties.[1] The onerous issues of Manchuria were discreetly set aside in order that an accord might first be reached on issues pertaining to China proper. It was Shigemitsu's hope that the touchy subject of Manchuria could be brought up in an improved atmosphere after the initial goal had been attained.

1. *Shidehara Memoirs,* pp. 92–95.
1. Shigemitsu, *Shōwa no Dōran, 1,* 42–43.

However, in the spring, C. T. Wang, Nanking's able Minister of Foreign Affairs, seeing that the tide was running in China's favor, publicly announced the five stages by which China intended to recover her full rights.

1. Restoration of customs autonomy
2. Abolishment of extraterritoriality
3. Restoration of foreign settlements
4. Restoration of leased territories
5. Restoration of railroads, rights to navigate inland waterways, and rights to engage in coastal trade.

Wang's schedule called for recovery of these rights in a comparatively short span of time. Moreover, it was made known that should the schedule tend to lag as the result of deliberate delays on the part of foreign powers, Wang would abrogate such treaties unilaterally.

Shigemitsu was quick to perceive the almost insurmountable difficulties that the execution of such policies would pose in Sino-Japanese negotiations, especially in respect to Manchuria, and was determined to visit Tokyo to say this. Before leaving Shanghai, he called on Wang, who not only reiterated his fivefold program but added that it also applied to Manchuria, indicating that he thought the Kwantung Leased Territory and the operation of the South Manchuria Railway must be restored to China. Since the statement came directly from the Foreign Minister, Shigemitsu was deeply distressed: this meant complete nullification of all the groundwork he had done up to that time.

Shigemitsu could not help being puzzled by Wang's change of attitude, because it was not consonant with the understanding reached by Minister Saburi and Wang that the touchy question of Manchuria would be set aside until another issue—the unequal treaties with respect to China proper—had been amicably settled.

The already difficult situation was further aggravated by the irresponsible action of a Japanese news agency. Despite Shigemitsu's insistence that the home government not publish any portion of his conversation with Minister Wang, the Rengō news agency indiscreetly released the story, causing most unfortunate repercussions in both Japan and China. The Japanese military were so incensed by the news that it made the continuation of Shidehara's conciliatory policy impossible.

Early in April 1931 Shigemitsu headed for Tokyo. His proposals to the home government were (1) to make broad concessions in China proper at once to relax Japanese-Chinese tensions; (2) to keep the powers informed of the current Japanese-Chinese dispute by making a full report to the League of Nations; (3) to formulate an over-all China policy at once. There was no doubt in Shigemitsu's mind that the time to act was now if Japan were to avert a major crisis with China.

One can well appreciate Shigemitsu's disappointment when he reached Tokyo. It turned out that the Wakatsuki cabinet, which had just been installed, was a weak government committed to continuing the policies of the Hamaguchi cabinet, its predecessor. It simply did not have enough vigor and imagination to strike forth boldly in a new direction. His proposal to restore promptly to China foreign settlements of small value—such as Soochow and Hangchow—was rejected. He was told that the Privy Council would not tolerate such a proposal. A cabinet member even called Shigemitsu's attention to the fact that his general pro-Chinese attitude would put Shidehara in an untenable position. It appears that by then many influential members of the Privy Council and the Seiyūkai had succumbed to the ultranationalistic appeals of Itō Miyoji and Mori Kaku. Morever, though the Hamaguchi government managed to have the London Naval Treaty ratified, its momentary success gave rise to such a violent reaction from rightist elements that the net effect was to enable the proponents of the doctrine of the "independence of the supreme command" to become more firmly entrenched than before.

Since neither government was in a mood to make any concession, it was apparent to Shigemitsu that it was merely a question of time before the negotiations would reach an impasse. All that remained for Japan to do was sound the alarm and forewarn the world that, despite the fact that Japan had exercised every precautionary measure, a clash was certain to come.

On April 29 Shigemitsu said his farewells to Shidehara and Tani. As he recalled, it was, indeed, a departure full of foreboding. The parting catch phrase was "to reach a stalemate, if one must, on a sound ground." In other words, Japan ought to deport herself at all times in such a manner that when and if the Japanese-Chinese breach occurred, her conduct would be above reproach in the eyes of the world.

Railroad Negotiations[1]

It will be recalled that, during Marshal Chang's short-lived rule from Peking, Yamamoto Jōtarō, president of the South Manchuria Railway Company, extracted from the Marshal concessions to build five railways in Manchuria.[2] After Chang's sudden death, Saitō, a director of the company, took up residence in Mukden preparatory to resuming the railroad negotiations with Chang Hsueh-liang, the Marshal's son. However, Hayashi, the Consul General assigned to Saitō to assist him in the negotiations, deliberately postponed the discussions despite the anxiety of Tanaka and Mori until the difficult question of the Tsinan Incident was settled. Lest premature resumption of the touchy question arouse the feelings of the Chinese people, Hayashi tactfully laid aside the railway issues and shifted the subject of his negotiations to that of the rights of Japanese residents to lease land and engage in business enterprises.

1. For a quarter of a century after 1905, international politics in Manchuria for the most part had revolved around the issue of railroad building. A comprehensive treatment of this intricate subject is to be found in the *Lytton Report*, pp. 42–49. The treatment in the present book is confined to the highlights of events in the period after 1925.

2. See above p. 16.

On January 14, 1929, stating that he was acting under direct orders from Premier Tanaka, Hayashi again broached to the younger Chang the immediate approval of the extension of the Kitun Line to Huining. Chang and the Northeast Political Council had once before refused to approve the Japanese request on the ground that the elder Chang had made his consent under duress at a critical moment when he was pressed by the Nationalist armies.

Again, Hayashi made no headway. The younger Chang perfunctorily referred the matter to Nanking. From Chiang Kai-shek came the reply that inasmuch as China was now a unified nation, all matters pertaining to foreign relations were to be referred directly to the central government. If Japan should again bring up the matter of railroad concessions in Manchuria and Mongolia, Chang was not to listen.[3]

Moreover, there were controversies over the issue of through traffic. The Chinese were operating nearly one thousand kilometers of their own railways by 1921 and, according to the *Lytton Report,* for two years prior to the Mukden Incident they attempted to operate the various lines as a unified system, by routing all freight exclusively over their lines to Yingkow, the port

3. To fully appreciate Japan's vexation when the railroad negotiations reached an impasse, one must go back another four years to 1925. In the words of the late H. F. MacNair: "In the years just after the Washington Conference, the Chinese sought by obstructionism and numerous devices to make life as uncomfortable as possible for the Japanese in Manchuria. Contrary to the Peking declaration which accompanied the Sino-Japanese Treaty of 1905, the Chinese in 1925 began to construct rail lines paralleling the tracks of the South Manchuria Railway." MacNair and Lach, *Modern Far Eastern International Relations* (New York, Van Nostrand, 1950), p. 351. The completion in October 1927 of the Tatung Line from Tahushan to Tungliao was to the Japanese simply a revival of the earlier Chinhai Line. The latter's construction was abandoned when Russia and Japan jointly protested that it paralleled the South Manchuria Railway. Also in the planning stages were the Chinhai Line and railroads connecting the various coal mines to compete against Fushun, a huge open-pit coal mine owned and developed by the South Manchuria Railway Company.

of exit. The through-traffic controversy, in turn, gave rise to a bitter war of rates between the Chinese lines and the South Manchuria Railway Company. The Chinese railroads had an advantage over the Japanese because of the decline in the value of Chinese silver currency at the time. The Japanese were also apprehensive over the plan to dredge the Port of Hulutao, for upon completion of it, Hulutao and Yingkow would have flanked Dairen from both sides to divert a sizable portion of its marine cargoes.

Contrary to Kōmoto's grandiose dream, the demise of Marshal Chang did not bring the solution of Japan's problems in Manchuria and Mongolia any closer. His son, Chang Hsueh-liang, though still a youth, turned out to be a tactful and cautious negotiator. He took extra care not to show the Japanese that he knew who was responsible for his father's death, lest they cease to negotiate with him. He was firmly resolved, however, that they would not receive any concessions whatever.

It was not long before Tanaka and Mori became restive over the slow progress of the negotiations. Early in 1929 Tokyo sent a secret directive to Japanese authorities in Mukden to draw up a plan entailing the use of police power, if necessary, to bring the issues of railroad concessions and the rights of Japanese residents to a quick settlement.

In Mukden, Morishima Morito of the Consulate General met with Saitō, a director of the South Manchuria Railway Company. and Hata, the chief of the local Army Special Service Agency. Together they worked out a detailed plan providing a step-by-step sequence through which control over the railroads and the exercise of rights of residents were to be put into effect. In case they should have to take unilateral measures, the plan provided for the disposition of the police officials and also for concerted action with the Kwantung Army if armed conflict with the Chinese troops should ensue.

Although the plan was ready to be put into operation the instant word came from Tokyo, that order never came: the Tanaka government had suddenly been confronted with an explosive political issue at home—whether the Japanese signers of the recently concluded Kellogg-Briand Pact had committed lese majesty in accepting the treaty "in the name of the people" and not of the Emperor.

Chang Hsueh-liang, in an effort to gain control over the Chinese Eastern Railway, engaged the Soviets in a series of military encounters from July to December 1929. Although Chang was unsuccessful in his attempts, the incident served as a reminder to the Kwantung Army of Chang's determination to oust foreign interests from Manchuria. Perhaps even more significant, however, to the Kwantung Army was the fact that the support the Chinese expected from the Western nations failed to materialize. Might the Kwantung Army have taken this as a cue that were it to start an action in Manchuria it, too, would have a relatively free hand to do as it pleased?

Other Irritants

In Manchuria the governing policy of the Chinese officials was to limit the exceptional privileges of the Japanese residents as much as possible in order to strengthen their own authority. The Sino-Japanese Treaty of 1915 stated: "Japanese subjects shall be free to reside and travel in South Manchuria and to engage in business and manufacture of any kind whatsoever." In the interior of South Manchuria, however, these rights were restricted by a provision that required the Japanese to carry travel permits and observe local laws, though the Chinese officials were not to enforce this regulation until they had come to an understanding with the Japanese Consul.

Apparently what happened was that the Chinese authorities, without submitting their regulations to the Japanese Consul, exerted pressure upon the Japanese residents, sometimes by severe police measures, to evict them from many cities and towns in South Manchuria and eastern Inner Mongolia. Chinese landlords were discouraged from renting houses to Japanese. The Japanese also complained that Chinese authorities refused to issue travel permits and harassed them by illegal taxes.

Chinese authorities answered by pointing out that the Japanese were attempting to reside and conduct business in all parts of Manchuria in disregard of the treaty provision which limited their residence to South Manchuria. The basic factor contributing to Japanese-Chinese differences was the unwillingness on the part of the Chinese authorities to observe the provisions of the Treaty of 1915, on the ground that it lacked "fundamental validity."[1]

Another irritant was the constant controversy over the right to lease land. The Treaty of 1915 provided that "Japanese subjects in South Manchuria may, by negotiation, lease land necessary for erecting suitable buildings for trade and manufacture or for prosecuting agricultural enterprises." The phrase "lease by negotiation" was defined by an exchange of notes between the two governments to mean "a long-term lease of not more than thirty years and also the possibility of its unconditional renewal." For some unexplained reason the word "possibility" was missing from the Japanese version, with the result that their text read simply "leases for a long term up to thirty years and unconditionally renewable."[2] It was inevitable that disputes should arise. The Japanese insisted that their land leases were renewable at their sole option, and this in effect was tantamount to the right of perpetual use. And such an interpretation was unacceptable to the Chinese, especially in view of the upsurge of the rights recovery movement.

Obstacles of various sorts were erected to prevent the Japanese from leasing land. Most widespread in effect were provincial and local orders flatly decreeing that leasing of land to Japa-

1. *Lytton Report,* p. 53.

2. Ibid., p. 54. In the land-lease dispute involving a farm near Mukden, the Consulate General removed the Chinese narrow-gauge tracks which cut across the land, lest the issue give the Kwantung Army a pretext to start an incident. See Morishima, *Conspiracy,* pp. 39–41.

nese was punishable under the criminal laws. In some instances special fees and taxes which were payable in advance were levied upon leased land. In others, local officials were prohibited from approving transfers of leases under threat of punishment.

Another source of trouble was the status and treatment accorded the many Korean farmers who immigrated to Chientao, an area adjacent to Korea.[3]

After the Mukden Incident Japanese publicists busied themselves in describing hundreds of provocative incidents in China proper and Manchuria: "Among the fair-minded students there never was any doubt that the Chinese during and after the Nationalist revolution of 1925–28 had needlessly irritated the Japanese on a good many occasions, and if each irritation in itself has been only a pinprick, it was still the case where a thousand pinpricks equaled a slash of the sabre."[4]

From the Chinese point of view, however, Japanese complaints of provocation were nothing but rationalizations, and the incidents themselves nothing but expressions of irrepressible indignation over Japan's assumption that certain rights and privileges had been legally established when in fact the Chinese had never intended that the treaties were to be so construed.

Japan's Consulate General at Mukden realized that it was but a question of time when all the issues outstanding since the time of the Russo-Japanese War would have to be settled. On numerous occasions it had urged the home government to begin negotiations with the Chinese government as soon as possible. Thus, to prepare for the forthcoming conference with the Chinese, early in 1931 the Consulate General had obtained the services of a specialist in documents from the home office in Tokyo. Under his supervision and with the cooperation of the Public Relations Division of the South Manchuria Railway Company, the task of sorting and classifying a mass of documents which had ac-

3. See below, pp. 143–44.

4. R. H. Ferrell, "The Mukden Incident: September 18–19, 1931," *Journal of Modern History, 27* (1955), 67.

cumulated at the Consulate General ever since its opening some forty years before was begun.

Documents especially needing clarification were those pertaining to certain rights and privileges which the government in Tokyo assumed were firmly established when in reality they rested on weak treaty rights. Notable examples were the assumed rights over land attached to the South Manchuria Railway Company in Fushun, Antung, and Yingkow; the assumed power to police the Mukden-Antung Railroad; and the assumed judicial power over Chinese criminal offenders in the Kwantung Leased Territory.[5]

The "railroad town" sections of such important Manchurian cities as Mukden, Changchun, and Antung actually included large, heavily populated areas of these cities.

The "railway guards" were regular Japanese soldiers. Their acts offended the Chinese officials as well as the public, because they often carried their police functions into adjoining districts or engaged in maneuvers without permission of Chinese authorities. The legal basis for Japan's right to maintain these guards was controversial. It went back to the original Russo-Chinese Agreement of 1896, which granted to the Chinese Eastern Railway "the absolute and exclusive right of administration of its lands." From the outset, China denied Russia's claim that this gave her the right to guard the railway line with Russian troops.

In the Portsmouth Treaty of 1905, Russia and Japan agreed on the right to maintain the railway guards "not to exceed fifteen men per kilometer." However, in the Treaty of Peking signed by China and Japan later in the same year, the Chinese government would not accede to this particular provision in the Portsmouth Treaty. China and Japan did make reference to the touchy subject in Article II of the supplementary agreement of December 22, 1905, which was appended to the Sino-Japanese Treaty of Peking:

5. Morishima, *Conspiracy,* p. 45.

> In view of the earnest desire expressed by the Imperial Chinese Government to have the Japanese and Russian troops and railway guards in Manchuria withdrawn as soon as possible, and in order to meet this desire, the Imperial Japanese Government, in the event of Russia's agreeing to the withdrawal of her railway guards, or in case other proper measures are agreed to between China and Russia, consents to take similar steps accordingly. When tranquillity shall have been re-established in Manchuria and China shall have become herself capable of affording full protection to the lives and property of foreigners, Japan will withdraw her railway guards simultaneously with Russia.[6]

Subsequently, by the terms of the Sino-Soviet Agreement of 1924, Russia withdrew her guards. Japan, however, would not withdraw hers contending that tranquillity had not been established in Manchuria and that China was not capable of affording full protection to foreigners.

The two loopholes in Article II were that it did not define precisely the point at which "tranquillity shall have been re-established in Manchuria and China shall have become herself capable of affording full protection to the lives and property of foreigners" and that it failed to specify the part empowered to determine when and if these conditions had been fulfilled.

Finally, it is noteworthy that China, by acceding to the phrase "in Manchuria and China," strengthened Japan's contention that Manchuria did indeed constitute a unique territory separate from China proper. However, before even a semblance of order could be achieved out of the hodgepodge of documents, Japanese-Chinese relations had deteriorated to a critical point.

6. Quoted in the *Lytton Report,* p. 52.

5. THE ACTORS

Accomplices in Tokyo

After the collapse of the March Plot, both the army extremists[1] and the civilian ultranationalists[2] for the time being abandoned the idea of internal reconstruction and turned their attention to Manchuria. In the summer of 1931 Major Chō Isamu contacted and enlisted the support of a select group of about a hundred army officers from the twenty-eighth to the forty-second[3] graduating classes of the Military Academy. Jointly the officers published a pamphlet entitled "A Manifesto Concerning Manchurian Problems" and distributed it throughout Japan among their fellow classmates. In addition, some of the officers of this group who were stationed in Tokyo supplemented the pamphlet by circulating their own private appeals throughout Japan. There is no available information regarding either the names or the exact number of individuals who comprised the nucleus of Major Chō's group. Like Hashimoto's group in the Cherry Society, it was probably not very large.

At the civilian level the counterpart of Major Chō's role was performed by Ōkawa Shūmei. At the request of Hashimoto and

1. This group included Colonel Shigetō Chiaki, Lieutenant Colonels Nemoto Hiroshi and Hashimoto Kingorō, and Major Chō Isamu. Backing them were Major Generals Koiso Kuniaki, Ninomiya Harushige, and Tatekawa Yoshitsugu and Colonel Nagata Tetsuzan.

2. Ōkawa Shūmei and Mori Kaku were among the most prominent in this group.

3. These classes covered a period from 1916 to 1930.

Chō, Ōkawa toured Japan and made speeches in some twenty major cities from the latter part of June to early September. His speeches interwove two themes: that Manchuria must be brought under the control of Japan, and that at home the time was ripe for a complete rejection of party politics and a thorough reconstruction of the government. On the whole, Ōkawa's campaign was effective, reflecting in part the phenomenon that in time of economic distress the words of a demagogue tend to command a larger following than in normal times.

It is not improbable that, as the immediate superior of Hashimoto and Shigetō, Major General Tatekawa of the General Staff not only gave his moral support but may even have gone so far as covertly to direct the activities of these two field-grade officers. According to the testimony of Tanaka Ryūkichi at the Tokyo War Crimes Trials, General Tatekawa stated in early 1929 that if Manchuria were not placed under the control of Japan, Japan simply could not develop into a national-defense state and therefore a world power. Tatekawa then sent Major Tanaka to Manchuria to study its resources. Tanaka returned to report that Manchuria was not endowed with enough basic resources to become a self-sustaining state. The area was found to be particularly wanting in petroleum.

Tanaka went on to testify that despite his findings, at a meeting of the Chiefs of Staff in August 1929 Tatekawa saw to it that a plan for developing Manchuria into a self-sufficient area was distributed among those who attended the conference. This material was prepared with a definitive objective: to inculcate the notion that Manchuria was the lifeline of Japan.[4]

In the spring of 1931 Lieutenant Colonel Ishihara arranged with Colonel Nagata, then chief of the General Affairs Section in the Ministry of War, to have two large howitzers of 24-cm. caliber quietly transferred from Port Arthur to Mukden.[5] A huge

4. Testimony of Tanaka Ryūkichi, IMTFE, *Proceedings,* pp. 2002–03.

5. One writer thinks that General Tatekawa may have had some knowledge of the transfer of these howitzers, but feigned ignorance. Matsumura, *Miyakezaka,* p. 39.

shed was built within the garrison compound to conceal the guns, one of which was carefully trained on the North Barracks; the other was aimed at the hangars housing the Chinese fighter planes. The reason for this was that the Chinese were armed with several score of the latest fighter planes purchased from France. The Kwantung Army had none. Therefore, in the event of armed conflict, the planes had to be prevented from taking to the air. On the night of the Mukden Incident shells were dropped around the hangars in such a pattern that, although neither the hangars nor the planes inside were harmed, the Chinese were prevented from taking off.[6]

Thus it is definite that the field-grade officers of the Kwantung Army were in touch with the field-grade officers of the Ministry of War and the General Staff.[7] The howitzer mountings were permanently anchored in concrete, and while we have no word from either Nagata or Ishihara that the basic purpose of the guns was to support an offensive, it is certain that they were moved to Mukden with a reasonable expectation of early use.

Itagaki Seishirō

There is very little doubt that Colonel Itagaki was the prime mover behind the Mukden Incident; after it was over, Morishima, the section chief of the Asia Bureau of the Foreign Office, visited

6. Takamiya Taihei, "Waribashi kara Umareta Manshū Jihen" (The Manchurian Incident, Which Started from a Fall of a Chopstick [i.e. flipping of a coin]), *Shōwa Memo,* Supplement to *Bungei Shunju* (July 1954), pp. 28–29.

7. Representing the clique which was plotting the Mukden Incident, Hanaya visited Tokyo several times in the summer of 1931 to sound out the reaction of certain members of army headquarters toward the secret undertaking. In his article some 25 years later, Hanaya has shown the varying degrees to which he divulged the plan, depending on his estimate of their reliability: Hashimoto and Nemoto 95 per cent, Tatekawa and Shigetō 90 per cent, Nagata 85 per cent, and Koiso and Ninomiya 50 per cent. Hanaya Tadashi, "Manshū Jihen wa Kōshite Keikaku Sareta" (This is how the Manchurian Incident Was Planned), *Himerareta Shōwashi,* p. 43 (hereafter referred to as Hanaya, *Himerareta Shōwashi*).

Mukden and reported back to Tokyo that Honjō, Commander in Chief of the Kwantung Army, was virtually confined to quarters. Itagaki, Ishihara, and Hanaya were at the controls of military activities in Manchuria. Since Major General Miyake Mitsuharu, Chief of Staff of the Kwantung Army, could no longer assert his authority, the three were left to do as they pleased. Whenever Itagaki and Hanaya indulged in wine after the incident, they boasted:

> The Manchurian Incident was planned well in advance. Field pieces were arranged in positions around Mukden as early as July 25. Since we succeeded in Manchuria, our next move is to engineer a coup d'état after we return to Japan and crush the party government and set up a government based on national socialism with the Emperor at the center. Capitalists, such as Mitsui and Mitsubishi, will be liquidated and there will be equitable distribution of wealth. You can rest assured that we will do this.[1]

Itagaki, unlike Ishihara, was neither a theoretician nor a brilliant strategist. However, he possessed soldierly qualities. He had stamina and fortitude. He was open to suggestions from his subordinates and thus was able to win their loyalty. For his knack of pushing projects through he was nicknamed "the Locomotive."

The gist of Itagaki's lengthy testimony at the Tokyo War Crimes Trials was as follows: As the Chinese officers and men became imbued with vigorous anti-Japanese sentiment, they became openly frank and boastful of the superiority of their army because, they said, their men had had more combat experience in the frequent internal wars in which they had participated. Itagaki further observed that Chinese troops were shifted about so as to encircle Japanese garrisons along the South Manchuria Rail-

1. *Harada Diary, 2,* 77. Author's translation.

way.[2] Japanese troops totaling several ten thousands in number were sparsely distributed over a distance of almost 1,000 kilometers and pitted against some 200,000 Chinese troops.[3] In the eyes of staff officers the situation was fraught with great danger.

Moreover, the Kwantung Army did not have a single aircraft to match the several scores of late-model fighter planes the Chinese Army had just purchased from France. At this critical juncture in the relations between two nations, war could have been averted only if Japan had been willing to relinquish entirely the rights and interests she had acquired in Manchuria. But such a retreat would not have been feasible strategically, and national sentiment in Japan would not have tolerated it.

Although the Kwantung Army needed additional troops and equipment, army headquarters in Tokyo would not accede to its requests. In view of the imminent collision with Chinese troops, therefore, the Kwantung Army had to devise emergency countermeasures, and about a year prior to the Mukden Incident had mapped out a plan whereby it hoped to cope with contingencies with only the troops and equipment on hand.

In the event of hostilities, the Kwantung Army's strategy was to concentrate its main force in the vicinity of Mukden and deliver a heavy blow to the nucleus of Chinese forces concentrated in the area. The transfer of the two heavy howitzers from Port Arthur to Mukden was an integral part of this emergency measure. This, in brief, was Itagaki's statement, made to mitigate the charges brought against him for the part he played in the Mukden Incident.

In private, however, Itagaki was being considerably more positive in his views.[4] In May 1930 he told a friend that there were many unsolved problems between China and Japan of such

2. IMTFE, *Proceedings,* pp. 30,256–85.

3. According to the testimony of General Honjō Shigeru, the Commander of the Kwantung Army at the time of the Mukden Incident, the army consisted of the Railway Guard Battalions and the Second Infantry Division from Sendai, totaling 10,500 men. IMTFE, *Exhibit* 2403.

4. IMTFE, *Judgment,* p. 535.

a serious nature that they could no longer be handled by diplomacy; hence there was no choice left but to use force. He advocated that Marshal Chang Hsueh-liang be driven out of Manchuria in order that a new state might be established in accordance with the principle of *Kōdō,* or benevolent imperial rule. Despite the fact that Itagaki was through and through a man of action, it is possible that his associates influenced him into believing that once *Kōdō* had gained a foothold in Manchuria, it could be transplanted to Japan, where the spiritual regeneration of the Shōwa era could be fostered.

Ishihara Kanji

In June preceding the Mukden Incident the office of the General Staff summoned to Tokyo the Chief of Staff of the Kwantung Army, Major General Miyake Mitsuharu, to impress upon him the peaceful course the central government intended to pursue in Manchuria. He was also briefed on the necessity of exercising surveillance in order to localize any incident should a conflict occur between the Kwantung Army and Chang Hsueh-liang. As we have seen, officers in the high command of the Kwantung Army, like Lieutenant Colonel Ishihara Kanji and his fellow activists thought differently.[1] Ishihara vigorously deprecated the conciliatory policy of the Tokyo government as weak kneed, all but stating openly that he had a mind to act in defiance of the army authorities in Tokyo when the time arrived.

Ishihara's association with the Kwantung Army began in October 1928 after the untimely death of Chang Tso-lin. Upon graduating from the War College at the top of his class, the way was open for him to embark on the gay and colorful career of a military attaché in some European capital. Instead, by his own insistence, he chose to join the Kwantung Army as Chief of Mili-

1. The gist of Ishihara's role in the Mukden Incident described in this and the three following paragraphs are a summary of statements from Itō, *Gunbatsu Kōbōshi, 2,* 191–92.

tary Operations in order to study at first hand the strategic problems of Manchuria and China vis-à-vis Russia.

Brilliant and aloof, he made no effort to conceal his belief in his superiority as a strategist. At headquarters in Port Arthur he proceeded to work out the first phase of his plan—the occupation of Manchuria. In the beginning he thrashed out the strategic problems with Major Hanaya Tadashi. The twosome was later joined by Colonel Itagaki Seishirō when he arrived as the Senior Staff Officer in May 1929. Although Itagaki initially objected to Ishihara's plans, he succumbed to the latter's zeal and by 1930 had consented to assume leadership in the conspiracy. The trio was later joined by one more accomplice, Captain Imada Shintarō. These men together laid the plans for blasting rail lines, assaulting the North Barracks under cover of darkness, occupying Mukden and other key cities, disrupting peace and order and terrorizing the public, maintaining liaison with the Japanese army in Korea, and winning the support of headquarters in Tokyo. Their plans were completed by January 1931, and in a sense the Mukden Incident was a product manufactured by these four army officers.

Some months after the Incident, Lieutenant Colonel Ishihara, reminiscing, said: "Indeed, that evening in Changchun was the actual inception of the Manchurian crisis." He was referring to July 3, 1929, when the staff of the Kwantung Army spent the first night of their field trip at a hotel in Changchun. There Ishihara gave a discourse concerning modern warfare. He suggested that a study be undertaken to delineate the means by which Manchuria would be administered after its occupation by Japanese troops. The research project was assigned to a Captain Sakuma, who was to complete it within a year from the date. It is not known whether Sakuma accomplished his task.

Another likely source for such a master plan was the Research Section of the South Manchuria Railway Company, which from the time of its founding was considered the brains of the Kwantung Army. It was established by President Gotō Shinpei almost simultaneously with the founding of the company after the Russo-Japanese War. Ōkawa Shūmei had been associated with the Research Section since 1919, becoming its director in 1929. Inevitably Ōkawa's idealistic schemes became a part of the plans of that organization. These schemes were referred to by grandiose slogans like "concord among the five nationalities" (Manchus, Chinese, Mongolians, Koreans, Japanese—sometimes with White Russians as the sixth nationality) and "a Utopia based on the kingly way." Such schemes included a generous leavening of a peculiar revolutionary spirit based on an indiscriminate mixture of rightist and leftist doctrines. The Research Section maintained elaborate establishments in Dairen and Tokyo and engaged in broad research projects pertaining to the political and economic problems of Manchuria and Inner Mongolia. On the basis of those findings it drafted long-term plans and policies for the development and exploitation of these areas. As the eyes of Japan's imperialism on the continent, it functioned like its counterparts in the colonial offices of the many European powers in the late nineteenth century.

Another master plan, whose existence has been vaguely suggested, was drawn up by the staff of the Kwantung Army. It was, in fact, a broad program of political and economic reform encompassing Manchuria and Japan proper under the aegis of a Nazi-type, one-party system. The complete contents of this so-called bible of the reform was known only to a select few among the extremist officers of the Kwantung Army. In order to further its purpose of taking over the government, it employed the Communist technique of cells whose members, by undercover activities, were to subvert the various ministries and departments of the government. Through such means the over-all pattern of total national reconstruction was eventually to emerge. It is not known whether a copy of this plan is still extant.

It is possible that the plan described above was either closely related to, or identical with, another plan in the custody of the Kwantung Army and labeled top secret. Copies of this plan, each bearing a stamped serial number, were distributed to a select few. Morishima Morito, the Japanese Consul in Mukden, succeeded in obtaining a copy by stealth through the efforts of a medical doctor, Morita Fukumatsu, a long-time resident of Mukden. It revealed among other things the Kwantung Army's plans for the occupation of the whole of Manchuria from Shanhaikwan to Manchouli; for its administration, finances, and banking; for the disposition of customs and gabelle; and for the operation of a postal service. The text of this plan is not available.

The only plan with details readily available is the one found in a book by Yamamoto Katsunosuke.[2] This plan was said to have been presented by a staff officer of the Kwantung Army at a gathering in Manchouli some time in 1929 under the title "Plan for the Annexation of Manchuria and Mongolia by the Kwantung Army." It is suggested that this unnamed staff officer may have been Lieutenant Colonel Ishihara.

Briefly, Part One deals with "the restoration of peace and order." It provides for dissolving the Chinese military and civil administrative establishments, disbanding the Chinese Army, disarming troops, confiscating public and private properties, and apprehending escaped soldiers and bandits. Expenses for the operations were to be met by taxation and by income realized from disposing of confiscated properties.

Part Two pertains to administrative policy. The territory was to be entrusted to a military government simple in structure but highly effective. Government interference was to be kept to a minimum except for the maintenance of peace and order. Nominally, the economic development of the area was to be based on laissez faire among the three nationalities: Chinese, Korean, and Japanese. Actually, however, the traditional colonial pattern of a large native population subjected to exploitation by a ruling foreign minority would have been followed. The Chinese were designated for labor and the retail trade, the Koreans were to

2. *Nihon o Horoboshita Mono,* pp. 127–38. See also Asahi, *Taiheiyō, 1,* 366–69.

develop rice fields, and the Japanese were to engage in large-scale enterprises.

The plan counsels against sudden and drastic changes in administrative procedures. The capital was to be located in either Harbin or Changchun. Under the office of governor general there were to be six departments: general affairs, military, civil administration, provincial administration, army division chiefs, and provost marshal. Manchuria and Inner Mongolia were to be divided into ten provinces. Law courts were to be established at the seat of each provincial government. Approximately four divisions were to be assigned to guard the borders against Russian invasion.

That Ishihara's primary interest was in Manchuria is borne out by the fact that he sternly reprimanded Major Chō for his active participation in the October Plot, with which Ōkawa also was associated.[3] Ishihara's preoccupation with the continent stemmed from both the overriding strategic importance he attached to Manchuria and Mongolia vis-à-vis Russia and the economic potentiality of a region that Japan would have to draw upon if she were to attain the dream of every strategist—a state with a self-contained national defense.

Notwithstanding Ishihara's views, the so-called Miyazaki Report on the natural resources of Manchuria, prepared by the Research Section of the South Manchuria Railway Company, maintained that the resources of Manchuria alone were inadequate to make Japan self-sufficient enough to cope with the world-wide trend toward autarky. The report stressed the absolute necessity of developing the resources of North China. There is little doubt that the leaders of the Japanese army who were concerned with converting Japan into a national-defense state took this advice to heart. Hence the military operations of the Kwantung Army in North China and Inner Mongolia following the Manchurian crisis and lasting through 1936 in defiance of the Saitō and Okada governments were events linking the Man-

3. See below, pp. 201–02.

churian crisis with the China Incident, and ultimately with the Greater East Asia War.

After World War II, Ishihara was asked by Sung Te-ho, a correspondent from Chungking, why it was that Japan in the thirties was so highly apprehensive of a Soviet thrust from Siberia. Ishihara replied that, despite the imminent threat from the north, the defensive strength of the existing regime in Manchuria was appallingly inadequate to cope with the Soviets. However, since China and Japan were continually at odds with each other, it was impossible to come to terms over Manchuria, a region of vital importance to Japan by virtue of its history and geographical location. It was thus decided to cut Manchuria off from China proper in order that Japan might exercise freer rein over this area. Ishihara also pointed out that his idea for an independent Manchuria was put into effect with the understanding and backing of Chinese residents in Manchuria. It is presumed that he was referring to individuals such as Yu Chung-han, who spearheaded the independence movement, and later became a key official of Manchukuo. That Ishihara and his fellow alarmists had somewhat exaggerated the Soviet threat in 1931 was later revealed when, in 1936, the Russians relinquished to Japan their interest in the Chinese Eastern Railway.[4]

While Ishihara may not have shared Ōkawa's enthusiasm for internal reconstruction of Japan, in matters pertaining to the philosophy guiding the administration of Manchuria he seems to have accepted some ideas of Ōkawa while rejecting others.

With the naïveté often typical of soldiers, Ishihara apparently believed in absolute equality of political rights among the different nationalities residing in Manchuria. If the plan submitted by a staff officer at Manchouli were Ishihara's own idea, however, he does not seem to have extended his notions of equality to cover economic rights. Among other things he advocated the immediate

4. See M. Vinacke, *A History of the Far East in Modern Times* (New York, 1950), p. 525; also David J. Dallin, *Soviet Russia and the Far East* (New Haven, 1953), pp. 17–21.

restoration to Manchuria of the South Manchuria Railway Company (the advance guard of Japanese imperialism), Port Arthur, and Dairen. Moreover, Japanese rights and privileges of every description in Manchuria were to be restored unconditionally to Manchuria. Only by taking such drastic steps did he believe that Japan and Manchuria could put up a united front against Russia's encroachment. But the turn of events in Manchuria following the Mukden Incident went contrary to Ishihara's wishful thinking.

The Wanpaoshan Incident

Two events in the summer of 1931 preceded the Mukden Incident. In early July about a hundred Korean farmers were attacked by four hundred irate Chinese farmers at Wanpaoshan, a village eighteen miles north of Changchun. The trouble began when a group of Koreans, after having leased a large tract of land near Wanpaoshan, proceeded to irrigate it by digging a ditch several miles long across land occupied by the Chinese farmers.

The Chinese farmers protested en masse to the authorities at Wanpaoshan. Thereupon Chinese police were sent to the site and the Koreans were told to leave the area at once. At this point the Japanese Consul at Changchun stepped in, dispatching the consular police to back the Koreans. Negotiations ensued but without results. Exasperated, the Chinese farmers took matters into their own hands, drove the Koreans away, and began to fill in the ditch, at which point the Japanese consular police countered by opening fire on the Chinese farmers and scattering them. Then the Koreans returned and completed the ditch under the watchful eyes of the Japanese police.

Although there were no casualties, the repercussions were immediate. A series of anti-Chinese riots broke out in Korea, starting at Inchon on July 1 and spreading to Seoul, Pusan, and Pyongyang. All told, 393 Chinese were massacred and their property destroyed. The Chinese retaliated with anti-Japanese activities in Tsingtao, Shanghai, Tientsin, and other cities with large Japanese resident populations. For example, at Inchang on the upper Yangtze, members of the Anti-Japanese Association attacked a Japanese hospital.

The Chinese government protested against the stationing of Japanese consular police in China and also charged that the Koreans were living outside the Chientao District, the only area in which they were permitted to reside by virtue of the Chientao Agreement of September 4, 1909.[1]

At the root of the trouble lay the now all-too-familiar question of Japan's right to engage in commerce and lease land in Manchuria, and here her demands flew directly in the face of China's fervent rights recovery movement. Moreover, as long as the Nanking government and Chang Hsueh-liang refused to recognize the exceptional relationship between Japan and Manchuria, any basic solution of the Wanpaoshan Incident was impossible.

The Death of Nakamura Shintarō

Negotiations to settle the Wanpaoshan Incident had barely begun when the tale of the death of a Japanese intelligence officer at the hands of Chinese troops in the region bordering Inner Mongolia trickled into the office of the Japanese Consul General at Tsitsihar. As the culmination of a long series of altercations between the two nations, no other incident gave the military and ultranationalists in Japan a more persuasive argument in favor of using force to settle once and for all the outstanding issues pertaining to Manchuria.

Captain Nakamura Shintarō was a Japanese army officer on active duty. In early June he left Harbin on a military mission and traveled westward, accompanied by a Japanese assistant and

1. See the *Lytton Report*, pp. 62–63, for a comprehensive treatment of this incident.

Russian and Mongolian interpreters. They detrained at Ilikotu, a station on the western section of the Chinese Eastern Railway, on June 9 and headed south toward Taonan along the Hinganling mountain range. About June 27, after the party had reached an eating place in Solun near the terminus of the Taoan-Solun Line, the men were arrested by Chinese soldiers under Kuan Yu-hing, Commander of the Third Regiment of the Reclamation Army. Several days later Nakamura and his party were taken to a hill in back of the barracks and shot; their bodies were cremated.

In Harbin the party obtained traveling permits. At the time, Captain Nakamura declared himself to be an agricultural expert and did not state his true identity. After the arrest in Solun, the Chinese soldiers discovered on the men a Japanese military map, surveying instruments, six revolvers, and narcotic drugs for nonmedical purposes; it was therefore only natural that they suspected Nakamura and his party of being military spies or officers on a special military mission.

The Japanese insisted that the execution of Captain Nakamura and his aides was unwarranted, despite the questionable nature of their mission. Even more objectionable was the arrogant attitude of the Chinese and the affront to the Japanese army and nation. The Chinese authorities in Manchuria were accused of forestalling official inquiries, evading responsibility, and being insincere in their efforts to track down those responsible for ordering the execution.

The initial investigation was instituted by Governor Tsang Shih-yi of Liaoning Province, but Consul General Hayashi called on General Yung Chen, the Chinese Chief of Staff, and informed him that the findings were unacceptable to the Japanese. Meanwhile, Major Mori had conducted an independent investigation on behalf of the Japanese General Staff.

Marshal Chang Hsueh-liang, having been informed of the seriousness of the situation by General Yung Chen, instructed the latter and Governor Tsang Shih-yi to conduct a second inquiry without delay. Marshal Chang also sent to Tokyo his adviser, Major Shibayama, who arrived there on September 12 to explain the Marshal's sincere desire to settle the case amicably.

In addition, Marshal Chang sent Tang Ei-ho, a high official, to Tokyo to hold conversations with Foreign Minister Shidehara, War Minister Minami, and other high officials. The object of the special missions was to ascertain whether any common ground could be found for solving outstanding Sino-Japanese differences in Manchuria. Although it was now futile, Marshal Chang made additional concessions by announcing on September 16 that the Nakamura case, to comply with Japanese demand, would be handled by Governor Tsang Shih-yi and the Manchurian authorities instead of by the Nanking government. Inasmuch as Marshal Chang had previously refused to deal directly with the Tokyo government in the case of the railroad negotiations,[1] this was a major concession.

At this highly critical juncture, there was clearly something seriously amiss in the liaison between the Marshal and the Nanking government. On September 14 the Nanking government announced that it would appeal the case of Captain Nakamura to the League of Nations. On the 15th it countered Japan's demand to settle all outstanding issues between the two countries by declaring that the Wanpaoshan and all subsequent incidents were the responsibility of Japan.[2] Needless to say, these ill-timed statements only nullified Marshal Chang Hsueh-liang's desperate efforts to localize Sino-Japanese disputes and avert all-out war.

Meanwhile, on September 16 the second Chinese Commission of Investigation returned to Mukden from Solun with Commander Kuan Yu-hing under arrest. On September 18, the day of the Mukden Incident, General Yung Chen informed the Japanese Consul that Commander Kuan would be immediately tried before a court-martial for the death of Captain Nakamura. After the Kwantung Army occupied Mukden, it found Commander Kuan still detained in the military prison there.

1. See above, p. 125.
2. *Shigemitsu Memoirs,* p. 104.

The dilatory attitude of the Chinese officials in the early stages of the incident and the series of delays following it had tried the patience of the Japanese people. In Tokyo the Association of Full Generals counseled the Minister of War to assume a firmer attitude toward China. The Imperial Veterans' Association took to inciting the public by demanding immediate settlement of the Nakamura Incident. And, to add fuel to the already explosive situation, there were other incidents. In Tsingtao an unruly Chinese mob demonstrated in denunciation of the activities of the local Japanese patriotic societies, and negotiations relevant to the incident of the Japanese maneuvers across the Tumen River on the Manchurian-Korean border had yet to be undertaken. In the course of September, "settlement of all pending issues, if necessary by force" became a popular slogan in Japan.

Mori Kaku again made his appearance on the troubled scene. He traveled about Korea and Manchuria from the middle of July to the middle of August, at one point visiting the site of mob violence in the Wanpaoshan Incident. He was accompanied by several fellow members of the Seiyūkai and a news reporter.[3] Ostensibly the purpose of his trip was a tour of inspection, but his real intention, suggests Yamaura, his biographer, was to effect a complete about-face in Shidehara's China policy. Before Mori left Tokyo he said, "There is really no need for me to visit the site of the Wanpaoshan Incident. The Investigating Commission will take care of that. I have a different idea [implying that he had far more important business in mind]."[4]

Prior to his departure Mori had made careful arrangements with the army authorities in Manchuria; upon his arrival he was therefore greeted and accorded special courtesy by military police at every stop. At Antung, Mukden, Kirin, Changchun, Harbin, Dairen, and Chientao he met with the local Japanese residents in round-table conferences to sound out their reactions to the current crisis. Yamaura reported that the Japanese residents of

3. Yamazaki Takeshi, Tōjō Sadashi, and a journalist, Yamaura Kanichi.

4. Yamaura, *Mori Kaku,* p. 695. Author's translation. Bracketed phrase supplied.

Chientao and Kirin especially were experiencing difficulties with the local Chinese authorities. Those who had arrived quite recently were leaving the area and only those with deep roots were staying on.

In Mukden, Mori held private talks with Honjō. Commanding General of the Kwantung Army; Miyake Mitsuharu, Chief of Staff; Itagaki Seishirō, a high-ranking officer of the Staff; Doihara, head of the Army Special Service Agency[5] in Mukden; and Miura, head of the Mukden Military Police. Mori also met Colonel Kōmoto Daisaku, who had perpetrated the murder of Chang Tso-lin. Kōmoto acted as a liaison agent for Mori in his contacts with Itagaki and Ishihara. It was through Mori's good office that Kōmoto in 1932 became a director of the South Manchuria Railway Company.

In Dairen at a banquet held in Mori's honor by Uchida Yasuya, president of the company, Mori bluntly criticized the railroad's action in discharging a large number of company employees when it ought to have been taking on more personnel, the way a general increases his forces before a battle. Yamaura states that, among the directors, only Sogō Shinji[6] was cooperating with the Kwantung Army. President Uchida and the others[7] stood for the status quo and a nonaggravation policy.

Since the party to which Mori belonged was not in power at the time, he met the high officers of the Kwantung Army in a private capacity. However, once the Seiyūkai returned to power

5. An organization devoted largely to the gathering of political intelligence.

6. As a continental expansionist Sogō had seen eye to eye with Mori as early as 1917. He facilitated matters for the military by acting as a liaison official between the South Manchuria Railway Company and the Kwantung Army. He was politely shunned by the other directors of the company on account of his close association with the army.

7. Eguchi Sadanaga, vice president, was affiliated with the Mitsubishi interests and the Minseitō. Kimura Eiichi was formerly an official of the Foreign Office. Godō Takuo was then still politically uncommitted, though later he joined the ranks of the national reconstructionists.

the following December, Mori exerted his utmost efforts to push the Manchurian crisis to its conclusion. For the part he played in bringing Manchuria under Japanese control, he was posthumously awarded the Second Order of Merit.

Colonel Doihara Kenji of the Kwantung Army was another individual busily fishing in troubled waters. Just before the Mukden Incident he traveled to Shanghai, Nanking, and other parts of China on an undisclosed mission. He arrived in Tokyo on September 10 and immediately went into conference with Minister of War Minami, Vice Minister of War Sugiyama, Chief of the General Staff Kanaya, Vice Chief of the General Staff Ninomiya, Chief of Military Affairs Bureau Nagata, and Major Shibayama, adviser to Chang Hsueh-liang. His mission was to apprise key personnel at army headquarters that the Kwantung Army was in no mood to stand idly by in the face of further provocations and to make certain that, in the event of armed conflict with the enemy, headquarters would support such an action. Doihara told members of the staff that the Chinese authorities had no intention of reaching an amicable settlement with the Japanese representatives over the Nakamura Incident. Nevertheless, both Minami and Kanaya counseled Doihara to exercise prudence.

To fellow activists in Tokyo, in utmost stealth, Doihara communicated "the plans to start action from our side" and asked for their vigorous support. Colonel Hashimoto Kingorō countered with a fervent plea for the postponement of military action in Manchuria until October, when the newly established military government in Tokyo would have instituted a program of national reconstruction. With the effete Wakatsuki government swept aside, contended Hashimoto, the Kwantung Army would be free to act as it willed in Manchuria. By so arguing, Hashimoto revived the familiar controversy over the priority between the military coup d'état at home and the settlement of Manchurian problems. It is interesting to note that on this issue Hashimoto himself could not make up his mind. It would appear that, for a while following the abortive March Plot, he conceded priority to the solution of Manchurian problems.[8] However, some time between August and September he seems to have reverted to his original position of going through with internal reconstruction first.

On the 11th, the following day, Doihara called on Foreign Minister Shidehara and Tani, Chief of the Asia Bureau. Shidehara expressed his hope to Doihara that the army would exercise prudence and not engage in precipitous actions.

By the 15th or thereabouts Doihara was on his way back to Manchuria, prepared to press for immediate settlement of all questions then outstanding between China and Japan. Doihara made a stopover in Seoul to see Lieutenant Colonel Kanda and, on the night of the Incident, was en route to Mukden. As outlined above, only the general drift of the conversations which Doihara held with the army leaders on the 10th are known today; however, since Shibayama two days later reported on Chang Hsueh-liang's conciliatory attitude, it is conceivable that the attitude of some of the army leaders had further stiffened to the point where they may have decided to capitalize on the Nakamura Incident, demand everything, and fight in case their demands were rejected. This belief is corroborated by the statement Doihara made to news reporters en route to Mukden. He said that if the Chinese authorities should show reluctance to comply with the demands put before them, there might be trouble. The measures to be taken by the Kwantung Army under certain circumstances were already determined, but Doihara was doubtful that the Foreign Office would be willing to support such actions.[9]

8. See below, particularly pp. 194–96.

9. Tokyo Asahi, September 16, 1931, cited in Takeuchi, *War and Diplomacy in the Japanese Empire,* pp. 348–49.

6.
THE MUKDEN INCIDENT, II

We are now ready once more to focus attention on the fateful day of the Mukden Incident—September 18, 1931. In the afternoon, a formal conference was held between General Yung and Hayashi, the Japanese Consul General, to settle the Nakamura Incident. The Chinese admitted the guilt of their soldiers and expressed their earnest intention to reach a settlement forthwith; it appeared likely that a satisfactory accord could be reached by means of diplomatic negotiation.

The conference adjourned for a recess at eight o'clock. Since the incident involved a Japanese army officer, the Consul General felt that he should confer with an appropriate officer of the Kwantung Army before further statements were made to the Chinese representative. Accordingly, he designated Morishima of the consular staff, who had just come from a meeting of the staff, to locate the officer and take him to the meeting, which was to reconvene later the same evening.[1]

Meanwhile, other high officials of the Japanese Consulate General had been locked in a secret conference discussing the nature of the various demands to be made to the Chinese representatives. These included an official apology, indemnities, punishment of the responsible party, and assurances for the future. On the last topic there was a heated discussion, but in the end they agreed to accept Morishima's proposal: that Japan would open a consulate in Taonan, since China had already given her tacit approval many years previously but had never come to the point

1. IMTFE, *Judgment*, pp. 548–49. IMTFE, *Proceedings*, pp. 3017–18.

of permitting Japan actually to carry out the undertaking.[2] By coincidence, this meeting also ended about eight o'clock the same evening. These were the circumstances which sent Morishima off on the evening of the 18th to look for an appropriate officer of the Kwantung Army.[3]

He first tried to reach Colonel Doihara and then Major Hanaya, but neither could be located. He tried desperately to track down any officer attached to the Army Special Service Agency, but not one could be found. Only later did it become evident that these officers had already assumed their assigned stations in anticipation of the bombing of the railroad at Liutiaohu.

Colonel Itagaki and his fellow conspirators apparently did not make up their minds about the timing of the Incident until they learned from Tokyo that General Tatekawa was being sent to put a stop to their plot.[4]

Portents of military action in Manchuria were evident from about September 12. Shidehara later recalled it was about this

2. Fujimura Toshifusa, a ranking official of the staff who had participated in on-the-spot negotiations at Tsinan in 1927 and 1928, strongly advocated a guarantee occupation of the old section of Mukden enclosed by protective walls. Morishima objected to Fujimura's proposal, stating that to ask the Kwantung Army to mobilize their troops and occupy Mukden was to play right into the army's hands, since that was precisely the kind of pretext it was waiting for to start military action. Morishima, *Conspiracy,* pp. 50–52.

3. Ibid.

4. There have been several theories regarding the premeditated date of the Liutiaohu Incident. The Tokyo War Crimes Tribunal stated: "Upon a consideration of all the fact relating to the incident of 18th of September, the Tribunal unhesitatingly rejects this explanation [an argument by the defense that the Mukden Incident was not premeditated] and holds that Kawakami [a Japanese army officer in charge of a garrison army in Fushun] had orders to take certain action in an emergency, which would occur on the night of the 18th of September" (IMTFE, *Judgment,* p. 547). Morishima, a consular official in Mukden at the time of the Liutiaohu Incident, who probably had more firsthand knowledge of the Incident than any person except those directly implicated in the plot, states in his book, published several years after the War Crimes Trials, that the Incident was originally planned for September 28, but when Tokyo became aware of the plot the date had to be advanced (p. 57). This date is corroborated by Hanaya, *Himerareta Shōwashi,* p. 44.

time that certain delegates from Manchuria came to see him and reported that some young army officers had been making requests for military supplies to be stockpiled at prescribed places by a certain time.[5] On September 17 Chief of Police Terada of Fushun came into Mukden to report to Morishima that he had been forewarned by the officer in charge of the garrison in Fushun to make plans to evacuate and protect Japanese residents and maintain peace and order in town.[6]

Kimura Eiichi,[7] a director of the South Manchuria Railway

5. *Shidehara Memoirs,* p. 170; also his testimony, IMTFE, *Proceedings,* p. 33,589.

6. Shortly before the Incident, Captain Kawakami, in command of the garrison at Fushun (the Second Company of the Second Battalion of the Independent Infantry Garrison), received orders from the headquarters of the Kwantung Army to entrain at Fushun with his company upon the occurrence of a certain emergency. This order, the contents of which were not established at the Tokyo Trials, was probably sent out without Honjō's knowledge [a presumption made by the Tokyo War Crimes Tribunal (IMTFE, *Judgment,* p. 545)] by one of his subordinates—either Itagaki himself or one of his fellow conspirators. Thereupon Kawakami assembled the Japanese police, ex-servicemen, and prominent residents of Fushun on or about September 16 and explained that the findings of the second investigation of the Nakamura Incident would be announced on the 18th and that, depending on the position taken by the Chinese authorities, the crisis in Sino-Japanese relations might come to a head. He therefore asked these men what measures they were prepared to take in the event that his company had to leave Fushun unguarded on September 18 (IMTFE, *Judgment,* p. 546; also testimony by Katakura Tadashi, IMTFE, *Proceedings,* p. 18,933).

Next, Captain Kawakami assembled the officials of the South Manchuria Railway Company in Fushun and announced that in view of the fact that an acute situation might arise after the 17th, an arrangement should be made to have a night train standing by at Fushun in the event his troops had to entrain under emergency orders (IMTFE, *Judgment,* p. 546). It appears that Captain Kawakami made so much out of what was intended to be an alert order that he stirred up a great deal of commotion among the Japanese officials and residents of Fushun. The South Manchuria Railway Company became alarmed and sent one of its directors to Fushun to confirm Kawakami's statements. This director is said to have returned to Mukden on the 17th stating that it did not seem that anything of consequence was in the offing.

7. At that time Morishima and Kimura were working closely together in an attempt to settle the Nakamura Incident (IMTFE, *Judgment,* p. 546). For Kimura's background see above, p. 148, n. 7.

Company, who also anticipated trouble, together with Morishima called on Consul General Hayashi to persuade him to act immediately to prevent the army from starting an incident. However, Hayashi, having had a reassuring talk with Lieutenant General Honjō of the Kwantung Army only three days before, could not bring himself to take the situation as seriously as did Morishima and Kimura. Hayashi interpreted the portents as mere signs of a large-scale maneuver to take place soon, and therefore confined his efforts to sending a private wire calling General Honjō's attention to the disquieting news he was receiving in Mukden. It became evident only after the incident that this telegram, which might have altered the course of events, was intercepted by the members of Honjō's staff at Port Arthur and did not catch up with Honjō until he arrived in Mukden on September 19.

In Tokyo on September 11, meanwhile, War Minister Minami was summoned to the Imperial Palace and sternly cautioned by the Emperor to restore discipline in the army. The Emperor made a particular point of singling out the Kwantung Army.[8]

On September 12 Foreign Minister Shidehara received a cable from Hayashi, the Consul General of Mukden, stating that the company commander of a garrison unit in Fushun had warned that a big incident would break out within a week.[9] Thereupon Shidehara immediately called the attention of Minami to the disquieting situation in Manchuria. The Foreign Minister warned that, if matters were allowed to ride, not only would the young officers blight their own careers but they would put the nation's security in jeopardy.[10]

It was perhaps a few days later that Minami spoke to Kanaya, Chief of the General Staff, of the warning he had been given by the Foreign Minister. Kanaya became apprehensive, for the news

8. *Harada Diary, 2,* 52–53. Kurihara, *Tennō,* p. 58.

9. Testimony by Tanaka Ryūkichi, IMTFE, *Proceedings,* p. 2006.

10. Testimony by Shidehara, ibid., p. 33,589; *Shidehara Memoirs,* pp. 170–71.

followed too closely on the heels of the caution which Minami had received from the Emperor only a short while before.

An emergency meeting was immediately held at the official residence of the Minister of War.[11] It was attended by Minami, Kanaya, Sugiyama, Koiso, Ninomiya, Tatekawa, Nagata, and Imamura. Minami spoke up by saying, "We've already had one incident involving the death of Chang Tso-lin, but you don't think there is any chance that the Kwantung Army would take action without consulting Army Headquarters, do you?"

After various opinions had been expressed by the generals, Tatekawa, scraping his pipe, asserted confidently that there was no need for worry on that score, because the present Kwantung Army was not that stupid. Minami retorted, "Well, it seems as if you have some inside information on the doings of the Kwantung Army." Flustered, Tatekawa said, "No, that I don't know. No, no."[12] Kanaya became suspicious: "Then we had better advise Honjō[13] of the Emperor's admonition of the 11th by telegram." Koiso quickly interposed, "We shall be taking chances by telegram. It might possibly be misinterpreted. Though we will be troubling Tatekawa, let's have him deliver in person the letters by the Minister of War and the Chief of the General Staff." Although Minami and Kanaya had misgivings about the letters not reaching Honjō in time to head off an incident, each wrote a message and handed it to Tatekawa.

Tatekawa returned to his office and summoned Shigetō, Chief of the Chinese Section; Nemoto, Chief of the Chinese Subsection; and Hashimoto of the Russian Section. He issued secret orders, following which two sets of telegrams were dispatched. An official

11. The entire account of this meeting has been selectively taken from Takamiya, *Shōwa Memo,* pp. 28–29.

12. According to Hanaya, Tatekawa replied, "I cannot say that there are not rumors that such plans are afoot" (Hanaya, *Himerareta Shōwashi,* pp. 45–46). This and quotations immediately following are author's translations.

13. Lieutenant General Honjō Shigeru, Commander in Chief of the Kwantung Army.

telegram advising the departure of Tatekawa for Manchuria went out from the General Affairs Section of the General Staff office to General Honjō, of the Kwantung Army. Simultaneously, Hashimoto sent a secret telegram to Itagaki: "Tatekawa is expected to arrive in Mukden tomorrow, hospitable treatment will be appreciated. His mission is to prevent the incident."[14] Meanwhile Tatekawa, having planned his itinerary to arrive in Mukden on September 18,[15] left his office in Tokyo with a nonchalant air on September 15.[16]

When Itagaki and the young officers of the Army Special Service Agency in Mukden saw the cable, they were shocked. If the letters from Minami and Kanaya embodying the Emperor's admonition were to reach simple and honest Honjō, it would spell the end of the plot. On the night of the 16th, Itagaki, Hanaya, Imada, Ishihara, Kawashima, Ono, Kojima, and one or two more officers gathered at the office of the Army Special Service Agency for a crucial meeting. Ishihara had originally planned to start the Incident on the night of September 28, immediately after the harvest of the tall sorghum which, owing to its extreme height, would have otherwise materially hampered the military

14. Yamaguchi Shigeji, *Ishihara Kanji—Higeki no Shōgun* (Ishihara Kanji, The Tragic General) (Tokyo, 1952), p. 112. The Japanese text read, ASU TATEKAWA HŌTENCHAKU NO YOTEI KANTAI TANOMU TOMEOTOKO. It is puzzling that the cable sent from Tokyo, presumably on the 15th, should have read, "Arrive in Mukden tomorrow," because even by the fastest means of transportation it is estimated that the trip would have required about sixty hours from Tokyo to Mukden. Hanaya states that Tatekawa left Tokyo on the night of the 15th (Hanaya, *Himerareta Shōwashi,* p. 46). Author's translation. Hanaya received a separate cable from Hashimoto the gist of which was BARETA TATEKAWA YUKU MAE NI YARE, meaning "(plot) exposed execute (plan) before Tatekawa's arrival." Asahi, *Taiheiyō, 1,* 434. Author's translation.

15. So far, no evidence has been uncovered showing that Tatekawa deliberately chose this date because of a tacit understanding between him and the young officers of the Kwantung Army that the Liutiaohu Incident would be staged on this date.

16. This date is deduced from the fact that Itagaki showed Hashimoto's telegram to Ishihara on September 16 (Yamaguchi, p. 112).

operations.[17] The question now was whether to stage the Incident after discussing the matter with Tatekawa upon his arrival or to go through with it before consulting him. Hanaya argued that it would be more prudent to wait until they had consulted Tatekawa, because of the danger of being branded as traitors if Tatekawa were to bring orders directly from the Emperor calling a halt to the operation. Imada on the other hand insisted that they go ahead with their plans, since the secret had already leaked out and Tatekawa might well put a damper on the venture. In the end the decision was left to chance, and Hanaya carried the day by winning the toss. But on the following day Imada approached Hanaya and again insisted that they carry out their plans before Tatekawa's arrival. Hanaya finally consented to go through with the plans on the night of the 18th; he also assumed full responsibility for the task of persuading Tatekawa.[18]

Meanwhile, on September 17, Lieutenant General Honjō, who had been appointed commander of the Kwantung Army in the August reshuffling of army personnel,[19] had just completed his initial tour of inspection of his troops and installations and was addressing the Second Division at Liaoyang when he received a

17. See above, n. 15.

18. Hanaya, *Himerareta Shōwashi* p. 46. The following is a variant version describing the same episode based on Takamiya, "Waribashi kara Umareta Manshū Jihen," *Shōwa Memo,* pp. 22–31: The younger officers argued that postponement now would mean abandoning the plan forever. Itagaki then proposed leaving the decision to chance. He would stand up a chopstick, and if it fell to the right, they would postpone the operation and discuss it with Tatekawa; but if it fell to the left, they would go ahead without the benefit of Tatekawa's advice. When Itagaki stood the chopstick up, it fell to the right. A moment of silence followed. Then Captain Imada jumped up and refused to accept the vagary of chance. Hanaya, too, sided with Imada. At this point Itagaki reversed himself and joined the two. A round of toasts followed, after which it was decided that Ishihara would draw up the mobilization order to be handed to the battalion commander as soon as the Incident began. The excuse would be given that immediate mobilization was essential and time would not permit waiting for the orders from General Honjō. See also Asahi, *Taiheiyō, 1,* 434–35.

19. See above, pp. 94–95.

telegram from his Chief of Staff Miyake at Port Arthur. The message stated that General Tatekawa was en route to Mukden on a visit and suggested that one of the staff officers, either Itagaki or Ishihara, be detailed to meet Tatekawa and escort him on his tour of inspection.[20] General Honjō chose Colonel Itagaki.

Before Itagaki left Liaoyang, Ishihara said to him, "In view of the decision reached at Mukden last night, we cannot very well back out now. We will have to go through with it." Itagaki replied, "That is the way I feel about it. I am glad that we both see it the same way. I'll take care of matters in Mukden, so will you look after the arrangements in Port Arthur?"[21]

That day, September 18, Ishihara and other members of the staff accompanied General Honjō back to Port Arthur. Itagaki alone proceeded in the opposite direction to Penhsihu on the Anfeng Line and awaited the arrival of General Tatekawa, who was aboard an express train from Antung bound for Mukden.[22]

When Itagaki greeted Tatekawa, the latter complained that he had not been able to rest on the way and was therefore not inclined to discuss business right at the moment. However, he did mention the fact that his superiors were concerned about the reckless conduct of the young officers. Itagaki reassured him that there was no need for worry if this was the object of his visit. He then added that he would see Tatekawa the following day after the General had rested.[23]

Upon arriving at Mukden at about 1 P.M. of the 18th, they were met by Doihara's assistant, Major Hanaya of the Army Special Service Agency, who escorted them to an inn, Kikubun. Tatekawa later told a friend that he allowed himself to be spirited

20. IMTFE, *Judgment,* p. 549.

21. Yamaguchi, *Ishihara Kanji,* p. 112. Author's translation.

22. It was during this stage in his itinerary that General Tatekawa was recognized by a fellow passenger and tried to conceal his identity (Morishima, *Conspiracy,* p. 49).

23. IMTFE, *Proceedings,* p. 30,261.

away to an inn because he did not intend to block the young officers from hatching their plot.[24]

By 9 o'clock Tatekawa lapsed into sleep, having drunk freely of sake. At about 10 o'clock, he was awakened by a bombardment and the crackling of rifle fire. He donned his uniform and staggered out toward the vestibule of the inn, where he was surrounded by waiting soldiers. As the men escorted him back to his room, he was told: "We were ordered to guard you and stop you from walking outdoors, since it is dangerous." Tatekawa was forcibly confined to his quarters even after daybreak of the 19th. It was only after Mukden had been placed fully under the control of Japanese forces that he was led to a room located above the Special Service Agency, where he was joined by General Honjō from Port Arthur. The two exchanged greetings exclaiming, "Are we in for real trouble!"[25]

The Night of September 18

After dining with Tatekawa, Itagaki excused himself and returned to the office of the Army Special Service Agency, apparently expecting a telephone call. This was at about 9 o'clock. At about 10 Itagaki was on the verge of returning to his billet when a telephone message from the garrison troops, probably Lieutenant Kawamoto's patrol, reported the blasting of the railroad line

24. IMTFE, *Judgment,* p. 550.

25. Itō, *Gunbatsu Kōbōshi, 2,* 195. Author's translation. At variance with Itō's story is a firsthand account to the effect that Tatekawa confided to another person in 1932 that he personally went to witness the assault on the city of Mukden on the night of the Incident. Key Kiyokazu Kobayashi, "The Kwantung Army and the Manchurian Incident" (unpublished essay, Columbia University, 1956), p. 59, n. 34. This is a penetrating study principally of the events and actions which occurred on the night of the Mukden Incident and the following day. Mr. Kobayashi, in drawing his own conclusion, has questioned the validity of the assumption made by the Prosecution of the Tokyo Trials that the Mukden Incident represented the "initial phase of a gigantic Japanese conspiracy to conquer the world" (ibid., p. ii).

at Liutiaohu. It required several more calls before Itagaki could make out what had happened—that just after 10 P.M. the rail line of the South Manchuria Railway on the southwest side of the North Barracks had been blasted and that patrolling scouts under Lieutenant Kawamoto of the Third Company[1] had been fired on by enemy troops lying in ambush.[2]

However, there are indications that mobilization in and around Mukden and Fushun were executed on orders from Lieutenant Colonel Shimamoto even before Colonel Itagaki issued his own order. According to Shimamoto, on the night of September 18 he returned from a party slightly intoxicated and went to bed, receiving the initial report by telephone at 10:25 P.M. When he picked up the receiver, he heard the voice of Lieutenant Nagamine Yasuo, the officer on duty at headquarters of the Second Railway General Battalion, saying, "This is an emergency call." Shimamoto asked, "Is this a maneuver?" Nagamine replied, "No, it's real." Shimamoto asked again, "What do you mean by real?" The answer came, "Right now the Hushihtai unit is engaged in battle with Chinese troops."[3] Sobered, Shimamoto at once ordered his battalion to muster,[4] but there were only the First and Fourth Companies on hand at Mukden, since the Third was already engaging the enemy at Hushihtai and the Second was stationed in Fushun, about twenty-five miles to the east.

After notifying Shimamoto, Lieutenant Nagamine, hardly sus-

1. The Third Company of the Second Railway Guard Battalion was sometimes referred to as the Hushihtai Unit; it was under the command of Captain Kawashima Tadashi.

2. Testimony by Itagaki, IMTFE, *Proceedings,* p. 30,262. A slightly different version states that "just a little before 10 P.M. Itagaki received a telephone call from an undisclosed party. Thereupon he took leave of Tatekawa. From the inn he presumably proceeded to the office of the Army Special Service Agency, where he waited for news that the action had started. He then issued the mobilization order drawn up by Ishihara, ordering: 'Officers in charge, execute mobilization. Take your posts, and start action immediately' " (Yamaguchi, *Ishihara Kanji,* pp. 114–15). Author's translation.

3. Mori, *Senpū Nijūnen,* p. 52. Author's translation.

4. Ibid.

pecting that he was calling the brain center of the intrigue, phoned the Army Special Service Agency in Mukden and asked that it relay the emergency message on to Kwantung Army headquarters at Port Arthur. The staff of the Army Special Service Agency delayed transmission of the message to Honjō, the Commanding General, until the Incident was well under way. In addition, Nagamine alerted the headquarters of the Railway Guard Battalion at Kungchuling, the 29th Infantry Regiment at Mukden, the Mukden Military Police Unit, and the Mukden Railway Station, which was requested to have a specified amount of rolling stock ready.[5]

A few minutes before 11 Shimamoto received a direct report from the Third Company that it was engaging Chinese troops in the vicinity of the northwestern approaches to the North Barracks after having pursued them to this point. Thereupon Shimamoto informed Colonel Hirata Yukihiro, Commanding Officer of the 29th Regiment, of his intention to lead the First, Third, and Fourth Companies in a direct assault upon the North Barracks itself, saying that the Second Company from Fushun was proceeding to Liutiaohu as rapidly as possible.

Colonel Hirata approved Shimamoto's decision, and he himself decided to attack the walled city within Mukden.[6] This was later verified by Hirata in testimony at the Tokyo Trials, in which he stated: "The operational plan of the Kwantung Army had been that in case of an emergency the army should concentrate its main forces around Mukden to attack the walled city if the occasion demanded such an action."[7]

Before these two officers could lead their men into action, however, they were summoned to the office of the Mukden Special Service Agency located immediately outside the gate of the 29th Regiment's quarters. There, much to their surprise, they found Colonel Itagaki. Shimamoto received an "army order"

5. Aoki, *The Pacific War, 1,* 149.
6. *Lytton Report,* p. 69.
7. IMTFE, *Proceedings,* p. 19,286.

from Itagaki which, as it turned out, merely affirmed the decision Shimamoto and Hirata had reached earlier with regard to the attack on the North Barracks. In addition, however, Itagaki's order authorized Shimamoto to assume command over the Fifth Railway Guard Battalion from Tiehling, which Itagaki had ordered to hasten to Mukden.[8] Also ordered to come to Mukden from a distance of about a hundred miles was the Third Railway Guard Battalion at Tashihchiao to the southwest. This battalion, however, never made Mukden because, as will be seen shortly, it was ordered by General Honjō to proceed elsewhere.[9] After the momentary interruption by Itagaki, Shimamoto continued on his way to the Mukden Station, where he boarded the train with his First and Fourth Companies at 11:40 P.M. and arrived at Liutiaohu, the scene of the skirmish, shortly after midnight.

Although one source alleges that Itagaki ordered Hirata to attack the walled city within Mukden,[10] Hirata's own account is somewhat different. When he arrived at the office of the Army Special Service Agency, he found that Hanaya, who was supposedly in charge during Doihara's visit to Tokyo, was absent and in his stead Itagaki was busily directing the operation. Hirata said he did not know why Itagaki was there in Mukden, nor was he aware of the fact that Tatekawa was also in Mukden that night.

Hirata testified that Itagaki gave him no direct orders simply because he did not have the right to do so.[11] Hirata had very little to do with Itagaki that night, although when the latter said he thought the attack should stop short of the west wall of the city, despite the fact that Hirata wanted to capture it, Hirata had to persuade Itagaki to acquiesce.[12]

8. Aoki, *The Pacific War, 1,* 150.
9. See below, p. 168.
10. Aoki, *The Pacific War, 1,* 153.
11. IMTFE, *Proceedings,* p. 19,306.
12. Ibid., p. 19,132. Hanaya corroborates the assumption that Shimamoto was kept in the dark (Hanaya, *Himerareta Shōwashi,* p. 44). Also, Morishima Morito of the consular staff at Mukden wrote in his book, "For

Other units also apparently were caught unawares. Ishihara Kanji stated in his deposition [13] that the Second Company from Fushun, despite the pre-incident flurry for which its commanding officer, Captain Kawakami Seiichi, was responsible, arrived in Mukden on the early morning of the 19th in no shape for combat. The only reasonable assumption is that Captain Kawakami was never told of the pending incident, although he was warned that an emergency might occur.

In another part of Manchuria, in a red-brick barrack in Changchun, a handful of Japanese soldiers of the Hasebe Brigade was overhauling a pack artillery piece on the evening of September 18. When night fell, they were still tinkering with the breech mechanism but were unable to put it back into working order. They finally gave up and left the mechanism in a disassembled state on the shop floor for the night.

During the night came the sudden call for mobilization. The infantry unit split into two. One half proceeded to Nanling to attack the Chinese artillery unit there, while the other half attacked an infantry unit at Kuanchangtzu. The dismantled artillery piece could not be put to use, and as a result the casualties sustained by the Hasebe Brigade were said to have been heavier than expected.[14] If this story is true, Hasebe cannot be charged with complicity in the conspiracy any more than Hirata, Shimamoto, or Kawakami. Taken together, these instances corraborate reservations made in the *Lytton Report* that the findings do "not exclude the hypothesis that the officers on the spot may have thought they were acting in self-defense." Similarly, the observation that on the night of September 18 the Japanese by their own

---

the sake of their reputations, I make a special note of the fact that the mobilization order [from Itagaki] came as a complete surprise to Shimamoto and Hirata [that night] . . . the actual plotting of the Incident was the work of two or three men and was confined to Itagaki and his confidants" (Morishima, *Conspiracy,* p. 58). Author's translation.

13. IMTFE, *Exhibit,* No. 2584, cited in Kobayashi, "The Kwantung Army and the Manchurian Incident," p. 38.

14. Matsumura, *Miyakezaka,* p. 38.

admission executed "with swiftness and precision"[15] a plan that had been laid out in advance needs to be qualified. The wording of the *Report* on its face suggests that the whole of the Kwantung Army was aware of Itagaki's plot, when in reality even the garrison officers in Mukden were taken by surprise, as were those in more remote regions such as Changchun.

With respect to the question of the high degree of preparation shown, it would seem that the testimony by Katakura Tadashi was reasonably true and correct. At the War Crimes Trials he stated that since the Kwantung Army was a small force in comparison with the Chinese in Manchuria,[16] the standing policy of the army was that, in the event of an emergency, it would execute a carefully worked out operational plan depending for success upon its thoroughly trained troops.[17]

It is now time to assess the role played by Colonel Itagaki on the night of September 18. At 10:40 P.M. there was a sudden telephone call for Morishima, who was asked to hasten to the Army Special Service Agency because Chinese troops had bombed the tracks of the South Manchuria Railway at Liutiaohu and Japanese troops were already engaging them. Morishima hurriedly summoned his staff to report to the Consulate General, instructing it to come prepared to work all night, and then rushed to the office of the Army Special Service Agency. There, much to his surprise, in a brightly lit room he found Colonel Itagaki and the office personnel in a flurry of activity. Itagaki told Morishima that the Army had been mobilized because an important Japanese right relating to the South Manchuria Railway had been violated, and asked him for the cooperation of the Consulate General. Morishima asked who had issued the mobilization order. Itagaki replied, "Since it was an emergency situation and the command-

15. See above, p. 6.

16. The ratio was roughly one to thirteen. Toyoshima Fusatarō, "Chōsengun Ekkyō Shingeki su" (Japan's Korea Army Crosses the Border and Advances), *Himerareta Shōwashi,* p. 55 (hereafter referred to as Toyoshima, *Himerareta Shōwashi*).

17. IMTFE, *Proceedings,* p. 18,939.

ing officer was in Port Arthur, I issued the order in his behalf." Morishima repeatedly emphasized the necessity of seeking a peaceful solution by means of diplomatic negotiations. Itagaki became provoked and retorted harshly, "Does the Consulate General wish to interfere with the prerogative of the Imperial Command after it has been invoked?" Hanaya, who by then was back in the office and standing by, drew his service sword and menacingly brandished it, roaring, "No meddler in the Supreme Command will be tolerated." Realizing the futility of arguing with army officers in such a high state of excitement, Morishima returned to the Consulate General and reported the entire affair to the Consul General.[18]

Who placed the bomb on the rail bed? For some inexplicable reason, this point does not seem to have been clarified by the War Crimes Tribunal at Tokyo. According to Morishima and Hanaya it was Captain Imada Shintarō[19] of the Army Special Service Agency who directed the blasting of the rail. On the night of September 18 he accompanied a railroad maintenance worker on a hand car to a spot north of Liutiaohu and ordered the blasting. The bomb employed in the explosion was selected with a view to keeping the damage to a minimum. When the maintenance worker protested that his duty was the maintenance of the railroad and not its destruction, Imada drew his sword and forced him to set the bomb against the rail.[20] After the explosion, sentries were posted at the site; when railroad crewmen tried to approach it the next day, they were rudely driven away.

Presumably the actual damage to the rail was of such a minor nature that neither Captain Imada nor his confederates cared to have the facts disclosed. Therefore, representatives from the Kwantung Army, the Mukden Consulate General, and Manchukuo met before the Lytton Commission arrived, in order to avoid making contradictory statements to the Commission. The

18. Morishima, *Conspiracy*, pp. 52–53.
19. He later became Major General and died after World War II.
20. Morishima, p. 58. Hanaya, *Himerareta Shōwashi*, pp. 44, 46–47.

Lytton Commission, however, refrained from assessing the responsibility for the explosion, stating that its mission lay in settling the issues which had arisen subsequent to it.[21]

Meanwhile, what was Honjō, Commanding General of the Kwantung Army, doing at this critical juncture? As noted previously, he had delivered an address at the headquarters of the Second Division at Liaoyang on the afternoon of September 18 and had returned to Port Arthur with his staff at about 9 o'clock that night.

At 11:30 P.M. Katakura Tadashi received a telephone call from Captain Konishi, officer of the day. Katakura rushed to headquarters. After he read the telegram from Mukden, he ran to the residence of General Miyake, the Chief of Staff. It was therefore around 11:40 P.M. when General Honjō learned from his Chief of Staff of the hostilities between the Chinese and Japanese troops at Liutiaohu. At the time General Honjō received the news, he was in his quarters taking a bath,[22] which would indicate that this benign General was not aware of the drastic actions which Itagaki and his associates had planned for that night.

It must be noted, moreover, that there was a lag of approximately one hour between the time Lieutenant Nagamine at the headquarters of the Second Railway Guard Battalion in Mukden relayed the initial report from the Third Company of its encounter with enemy troops to the Mukden Army Special Service Agency (10:30) and the time Katakura was informed of the incident in Port Arthur (11:30).[23] The delay, because of its length, was presumably deliberate, and it should be noted that it occurred at the Special Service Agency, where Itagaki was frantically issuing mobilization orders with the specific intention

21. *Lytton Report,* p. 68.

22. Ferrell, "The Mukden Incident," *Journal of Modern History, 27* (1955), 72.

23. See above, pp. 160–61.

of aggravating the situation in order that the clash at Hushihtai might be turned into a major incident.

Honjō called a staff meeting. Ishihara cautiously handed to the General the mobilization order which the former had drawn up after he had parted company with Itagaki at Liaoyang the previous day. There followed a few anxious moments, for Ishihara well knew by then that Itagaki had on his own issued the mobilization order, and if General Honjō were to refuse to authorize it Itagaki presumably had but one way out—hara-kiri. Honjō meditated for a few moments with his eyes closed; then having made up his mind to authorize the action already taken by his subordinates in Mukden, he stated resolutely, "Let the matter be carried out on my own responsibility."[24]

Katakura Tadashi has testified that Ishihara was nevertheless annoyed by Honjō's subsequent indecisive handling of the developing operations; for twice during the same evening he modified his original plans, thereby losing precious moments when instant mobilization was tactically essential.[25] Initially, Honjō ordered the military operations to be carried out according to a predetermined plan defensive in nature and localized in scope: Japanese forces in Manchuria were to concentrate in and around Mukden and wait for the enemy to make its move.

However, after receiving the second report from Mukden stating that one company of Japanese troops at Hushihtai was engaging three to four hundred enemy troops armed with machine guns and that the enemy was receiving reinforcements, Honjō took steps to reinforce his local forces in order that they might separately engage the enemy troops in the locality in which they were stationed.[26] Presumably it was at this point that Honjō issued the blanket order which brought all Japanese forces in Manchuria into action. The Commander in Chief of the Japa-

24. Testimony by Takeda Hisashi, IMTFE, *Proceedings,* p. 19,326.
25. Ibid., p. 18,939.
26. Ibid., p. 18,894.

nese Garrison Army in Korea was asked to send reinforcements in accordance with prearranged plans, so that the Kwantung Army could take the offensive. The Second Overseas Fleet was requested to leave Port Arthur and steam toward Yingkow.[27]

Honjō then made a further modification in his strategy, calling for partial abandonment of the initial phase of trying to draw the brunt of the enemy attack toward Mukden. His revised plan—and here one can almost detect the guiding hand of Colonel Ishihara—called for the Hasebe Brigade in Changchun to receive a counterorder to stay put, since the situation in the north around Changchun and Kirin was obscure. Also noteworthy is the fact that in a single stroke General Honjō's final order altered the orders initially issued by Colonel Itagaki to the Third Railway Guard Battalion at Tashihchiao. Whereas, according to Itagaki's instruction, the unit was to go to Mukden to support the action of the Second Railway Guard Battalion, Honjō's final instruction ordered it to attack the enemy troops at Yingkow, a port city approximately twelve miles west of the town where it was stationed.[28]

General Honjō left Port Arthur for Mukden between 3 and 3:30 A.M. of September 19. He took with him Ishihara and the main body of staff officers, but left behind most of the heads of the various departments—i.e. ordinance, medical, intendance, legal, etc., to clear up affairs in Port Arthur.[29]

When Honjō arrived in Mukden, Hayashi must have reproved him for permitting the military action of the Kwantung Army to get out of hand despite the warning he had cabled to the General.[30]

It was then that Honjō became suspicious, for he had not

27. See the *Lytton Report,* p. 69; IMTFE, *Judgment,* p. 558; Hanaya, *Himerareta Shōwashi,* p. 47.

28. For details of General Honjō's orders given between 1:30 and 2:30 A.M. on September 19, 1931, see Kobayashi, "The Kwantung Army and the Manchurian Incident," p. 33 and appendix 1.

29. Testimony by Katakura Tadashi, IMTFE, *Proceedings,* p. 18,896.

30. See above, p. 154.

read such a telegram. He immediately sent Lieutenant Colonel Shimamoto to Port Arthur to investigate the circumstances of the delay in Hayashi's telegram. On September 20 Itagaki and Katakura paid a visit to Hayashi and explained the matter fully,[31] although there is no evidence that the Consul General expressed satisfaction with their explanation. So incensed did Katakura become over this incident that on the following day, the 21st, he returned to the Consulate General to give vent to his anger and to reprove Hayashi for interfering with military operations.[32]

On the night of September 19 the staff officers of the Kwantung Army held a conference in Mukden. Because of the succession of telegrams from Tokyo calling for nonaggravation and nonextension of the military situation, Honjō's second and third orders—taking the offensive by calling for reinforcements from the Korean Army, and then extending the theater of conflict to Changchun and Kirin—had to be abandoned. It is highly probable that Ishihara objected strenuously to Honjō's effort to comply with the directives from Tokyo. To secure the northern plains of Manchuria against a possible thrust later from the Soviet army was almost an obsession with Ishihara. Under these circumstances it is not difficult to see that General Honjō experienced great difficulty in turning down Ishihara and other young officers itching for further action.[33]

Katakura was sent out to bring Tatekawa to the meeting. Much to Ishihara's disappointment, Tatekawa sided with General Honjō. He strongly stressed the opinion that no matter what the Chinese did Japan should not advance her forces into northern Manchuria.[34]

31. Testimony by Katakura, ibid., pp. 18,934–35.

32. Morishima, *Conspiracy*, p. 56.

33. IMTFE, *Proceedings*, p. 18,901.

34. Ibid., p. 18,905; also see below, pp. 178–79. As the Chief of the Division of Strategy, Tatekawa had composed a plan of his own, "An Outline of the Solution of Manchurian Problems," and circulated the draft copies among his section chiefs. His plan called for a full year to reach fulfillment.

Crossing the Yalu

It would have been little short of recklessness had the officers of the Kwantung Army planned the Mukden Incident without taking into account reinforcements which they hoped to receive from Korea. Sometime between 1:20 and 2 A.M. on September 19 Lieutenant General Hayashi Senjūrō, Commander of the Korean Army, received an urgent call from General Honjō of the Kwantung Army requesting an immediate dispatch of reinforcements to Mukden.[1]

At 6:24 A.M. a detachment of the Japanese air force stationed at Pyongyang suddenly took off for Mukden.[2] On whose order these planes were moved—a highly relevant point—has not been clarified by the various writers who have dealt with the question of the unauthorized crossing of the Yalu.[3] There are seemingly only two alternative explanations. Either General Hayashi issued an order authorizing the departure, or the members of the flying corps decided to take off on their own. The weight of circumstantial evidence seems to tip the scale slightly in favor of the latter. It is generally known that the Korean Army was intercepting communications between Mukden and army headquarters in Tokyo about this time. Even more significant is the fact that Lieutenant Colonel Kanda Masatane, a staff officer of the Korean Army, was in personal contact with Lieutenant Colonel Ishihara Kanji of the Kwantung Army.[4] Thus it is quite conceivable that either a junior staff officer of the Korean Army or the

1. Aoki, *The Pacific War, 1,* 150.

2. Japan proper and Korea were on the same standard time. At present, Seoul time is half an hour behind Tokyo time. Manchuria, however, was one hour behind Japan and Korea.

3. Mori, *Senpū Nijūnen,* p. 56; Matsumura, *Miyakezaka,* p. 41; Morishima, *Conspiracy,* p. 64; Itō, *Gunbatsu Kōbōshi, 2,* 167–69; Takeuchi, *War and Diplomacy in the Japanese Empire,* p. 353; Hanaya, *Himerareta Shōwashi,* pp. 47–48; Toyoshima, *Himerareta Shōwashi,* pp. 52–58; Asahi, *Taiheiyō, 2,* 6–18. Readers are cautioned that the accounts found in these publications are spotty and not infrequently at variance with one another.

4. Itō, *Gunbatsu Kōbōshi, 2,* 168, 192, Matsumura, *Miyakezaka,* p. 41.

squadron leader of the flying corps was incited by the activists of the Kwantung Army into issuing an unauthorized order.

By early dawn General Hayashi almost certainly had ordered the various contingents of the Twentieth Division in Seoul and Pyongyang to proceed by rail to the Korean-Manchurian border to await further instructions. Already concentrated at the border town of Shingishū were approximately 4,000 men of the Thirty-Ninth Mixed Brigade, which had reportedly been engaging in maneuvers since the 16th. It is noteworthy that the Thirty-Ninth Brigade did not cross the Yalu on the morning of the 19th, since it could have done so in an hour had General Hayashi so ordered. That he did not intend to is implied in the text of the telegram he addressed to the Minister of War and the Chief of the General Staff the same morning: "In response to an urgent request from the Kwantung Army, I have decided on my own and am about to send my troops across the border. Request is made to secure promptly His Majesty's sanction."[5] The intent of this telegram seems to be that while General Hayashi had on his own initiative taken preliminary steps to mobilize his troops, he would await imperial sanction before executing the crucial act of crossing the border.[6]

Tokyo was dismayed when it learned of the precipitate action of the Korean Army, for its hands were full trying to restrain the Kwantung Army. The Minister of War wired General Hayashi:

5. Itō, *2*, 168. Author's translation.

6. Somewhat more difficult to explain is the curious statement by one writer that at 8 A.M. of the 19th a telegraphic instruction went out to General Hayashi from the office of the General Staff to mobilize one brigade at once to support the actions of the independent garrisons in Manchuria (Mori, *Senpū Nijūnen,* p. 56). What gives this statement an air of unreality is that General Hayashi did not act upon the instructions, although they came, supposedly, while he was anxiously waiting for a response from Tokyo. The same writer goes on to say that at 1 P.M. another wire had to be dispatched to countermand the earlier instructions, since the emergency session of the cabinet had decided in the meantime "not to enlarge the incident." All this is in direct contradiction to the statement by another writer, who asserts that Army headquarters in Tokyo was shocked when it learned of the mobilization of the Korean

"Arbitrary crossing of the border is absolutely inadmissible. Stand by until imperial sanction is secured."[7] At the same time emergency orders were dashed off to General Muro of the Twentieth Division, to General Yoshimura who was aboard the train with the Brigade, and to the gendarmery at Shingishū and the independent garrison at Antō, to "stop mobilizing" and to "report the present location of the Brigade."[8] Yoshimura's Brigade was made to detrain near Shingishū. It was only then that Tokyo heaved a deep sigh of relief.

Army headquarters at Tokyo, after a conference, decided to go ahead and take steps to secure imperial sanction. Some of the younger members of the staff persisted in the conviction that the Korean Army should be permitted to cross the Yalu, and the matter of securing imperial sanction should be deferred until the mission had been accomplished. However, Colonel Nagata Tetsuzan, Chief of the Military Affairs Section, resisted and with the backing of General Kanaya, Chief of the General Staff, headquarters was able to adhere to its initial decision.

In the meantime, determined not to allow the Korean Army to join the conflict in Manchuria, the government had taken steps through the Minister of the Imperial Household to forestall General Kanaya should he apply for an audience to secure His Majesty's sanction to cross the Yalu. Thus, when General Kanaya requested an audience on the 20th, he was told that the Emperor was indisposed, and the Minister of War had no choice but to advise General Hayashi by wire to hold his troops at the border.

In the higher circles of the government strong criticism was

Army (Matsumura, *Miyakezaka,* p. 41). Conceivably, General Kanaya could have been in the dark as to the doings of his immediate subordinates, Ninomiya, Tatekawa, and Hashimoto—all fellow conspirators in the March Plot. Nevertheless, even if the Japanese army at this time had been riddled with rank insubordination, this statement, in which Kanaya is seen as a tool of his subordinates, does not explain why General Hayashi did not carry out the order and send his troops across the Yalu shortly after 8 A.M. on the 19th.

7. Itō, *2,* 168. Author's translation.

8. Mori, p. 41.

being directed against Premier Wakatsuki for assuming a defeatist attitude. On the evening of the 19th the Premier summoned Baron Harada, Prince Saionji's private secretary, and complained:

> For one thing, I have received reports from neither the Foreign Office nor the Ministry of War. When I rebuked the Minister of War by asking him, "Isn't it an outrage to send troops from Korea without an order from the government?" he replied, "There was a precedent for mobilizing without imperial sanction at the time of the Tanaka cabinet." So you can see, I am unable to restore order under the present circumstances. What do you suppose I ought to do? . . . It is not that I am asking you to consult Prince Saionji, but I am really in a fix.[9]

When Harada reported Wakatsuki's unhappy plight to the Grand Chamberlain and the Minister of the Imperial Household, neither of the gentlemen took kindly to Wakatsuki's negative attitude.

On September 20 Harada called on Shidehara. The Minister of Foreign Affairs expressed his misgivings regarding Wakatsuki's attitude. Moreover, Shidehara seemed displeased with the lukewarm attitude shown by cabinet members with party backgrounds toward efforts to restrain the unbridled actions of the army. On the 21st Harada went to Kyoto to report to Prince Saionji on his current findings on the cabinet's action. There Harada was told to instruct Kido Kōichi, Chief Secretary to the Keeper of Privy Seal, that the Emperor must not under any circumstances sanction the unauthorized mobilization of the Korean Army should either the Chief of the General Staff or the Minister of War report to His Majesty on the incident. Instead, the Emperor should withhold his word and intimate that he would give the matter further thought.

Meanwhile, on the afternoon of September 20, high army offi-

9. *Harada Diary, 2,* 64–65. Author's translation.

cials[10] met at the residence of the Minister of War to discuss what position the army ought to take with respect to the crisis in Manchuria. After the conference Minami set forth the army's views. Of the five points which he made, only those relevant to the relationship between the army and the Foreign Office are cited here.

> 2. Cabinet approval must be obtained before Japanese troops stationed in Korea cross the Korean frontier. In case of necessity, however, if approval from Tokyo cannot be obtained in time, the Commanders in Chief of the Kwantung Army and the Korean Army are given the authority to take appropriate measures.
>
> 4. Solution of problems pertaining to Manchuria should be sought at the local level and not between Nanking and Tokyo.
>
> 5. The army agrees with the government in its policy of nonaggravation, but desires to point out that the nonaggravation of the situation does not necessarily mean the nonenlargement of the theater of operations. This point is made clear to the government.[11]

Among other things, these statements of policy suggest (1) a divergence in points of view within high army circles toward the Foreign Office, (2) a preponderance of those who preferred to allow the Kwantung Army a wide latitude in its actions.

Point number 2 strongly suggests that the army was willing to make concessions to the government. Presumably, General Kanaya was the only person present who spoke up for nonen-

10. Those present at the conference included Minami, Minister of War; Kanaya, Chief of the General Staff; Mutō, Inspector General of Military Education; Sugiyama, Vice Minister of War; Ninomiya, Vice Chief of Staff; Araki, Vice Chief of Military Education; and Koiso, Chief of the Military Affairs Bureau of the Ministry of War.

11. *Tōkyō Asahi,* September 21, 1931, quoted in Takeuchi, *War and Diplomacy in the Japanese Empire,* p. 352.

largement of military operations. The remainder stood for a hands-off policy, insofar as headquarters' direction of the Kwantung and Korean Armies was concerned. It is quite possible that some men, like Koiso and Araki, even came out strongly for giving free rein to the Kwantung Army, so that Manchuria could be brought under Japan's control with a minimum of delay. Minami, the War Minister, was in a ticklish situation. Not only did he condone, he was positively in favor of the actions taken by his subordinates.

The seemingly pious pronouncement concerning cabinet approval in the opening clause, moreover, is completely nullified by the reservation made in the succeeding clause. For one thing a situation of emergency already existed in Manchuria. For another, it is almost impossible not to create tension whenever troops are stationed on foreign soil where they are not welcome. Because of the ever-present possibility that the radicals of the Kwantung Army might take matters into their own hands, and because hostilities not only between the Japanese and Chinese troops but also among the several Chinese factions were in progress,[12] Japanese commanding officers in Manchuria or Korea did not have to look far for a situation of emergency.

Actually, the second statement was tantamount to allowing the Kwantung Army and the Korean Army to take military action on any provocation. It indicated that the majority of the Japanese officers at the highest level unmistakably favored action in Manchuria. It would also seem that these high army officials had few qualms about crossing the Yalu, an international frontier, without declaring war. Of course in this instance, Japan, as a signatory to the League Covenant and the Kellogg-Briand Pact, officially designated the armed conflict as an "incident" and China refused to recognize that a state of war existed. Nor were they

12. See Map 7 attached to the *Lytton Report* for the military situation in Manchuria about September 30, 1931. General Chang Hai-peng, in the vicinity of Taonan, and General Hsi Hsia, poised just east of Kirin, are designated as generals of doubtful allegiance.

unduly concerned about freely mobilizing His Majesty's troops and moving them onto foreign soil without imperial sanction.[13]

Since by this time there was no duly constituted local Chinese authority with which the Kwantung Army could negotiate, statement 4 could mean but one thing: the army was determined to settle the Manchurian questions by means of force. The army shunned diplomatic settlements of any sort between Nanking and Tokyo, because such settlements would have meant success for the moderate policy represented by Shidehara and Shigemitsu.

Statement 5, like statement 2, is self-contradictory. One cannot but wonder how it would have been possible to enlarge upon military operations without aggravating the situation. It can only be interpreted as an expression of the army's wishful and absurd thinking that the occupation could be extended over the whole of Manchuria without interference from either the Chinese or the Japanese governments.

It was possibly on the 20th that an interesting episode occurred at a cabinet meeting.[14] Minami read a report on the Liutiaohu Incident and subsequent events. Shidehara, in his memoirs, remarks that it went into somewhat more detail than the reports found in the press. Minami's report concluded with an appended notation stating in effect that it was hoped the conflict would not be further enlarged. Shidehara then pressed Minami, saying, "There isn't much that can be done about what has already happened, but 'hope,' mere wishful thinking, will not do. Can you

13. Article XIII of the Meiji Constitution read, "The Emperor declares war, makes peace, and concludes treaties."

14. In his memoirs (p. 172), Shidehara states that he does not recall whether this episode occurred on the 20th or the 21st. It is suggested, however, that this cabinet meeting probably took place during the morning of the 20th. The statements—especially 2 and 5—made by Minami after the high-level meeting of the army men on the afternoon of the same day, strongly suggest that they were made to hedge against the commitment he was pressed to make earlier the same day. To pursue this point a bit farther, on the 21st Minami sought the cabinet's approval to send an additional three to four thousand troops from Korea to Manchuria. It hardly seems possible that he could on the same day pledge nonenlargement of the military operation on the one hand and on the other ask for an increase in fighting forces.

guarantee that the conflict will not be further enlarged?" The Minister of War said, "Wait a moment," and left the room with the written report. After a while he came back with the same report to which the notation "will be guaranteed" had been added.

At long last, the members of the cabinet breathed more easily. It was only then that the Foreign Office, for the first time, felt sufficiently confident to wire the Japanese delegation in Geneva an account of the Mukden Incident. This episode illustrates that it was not within Minami's power to determine the course of the Manchurian crisis but that he was speaking in behalf of a powerful group which manipulated him from behind the scene. We have just noted how Minami's report was rigidly edited and how he dared not change a word without the consent of this amorphous body of army men.[15]

At the extraordinary meeting of the cabinet on the morning of September 21 Minami tried to get the cabinet to agree to send three to four thousand troops to Changchun and Chientao, a district in the southeastern part of Manchuria and partially bordering on Korea, in view of the critical situation which prevailed in these localities. Minami had the audacity to suggest to the cabinet members that they were being consulted as a matter of form. The Minister of War maintained that the army could go ahead and dispatch troops from Korea without consulting them if it so desired, since the decision had been reached by the so-called Big Three of the army.

Shidehara, Inoue, and other members of the cabinet vociferously opposed Minami's proposal and counseled caution by re-

15. Harada, in his diary, gives some inkling of the kind of situation with which Minami had to contend. "When I saw the Minister of Finance on September 4, 1931, Inoue said to me, 'The Minister of War held ideas very similar to mine with respect to military reorganization; so we came to an understanding on all matters before we parted company. However, after he returned to his ministry, he was rebuffed by Onodera Chōjirō, Accountant General, and Koiso Kuniaki, Chief of the Military Affairs Bureau. So Minami had to come back and retract everything we had agreed upon, with the result that we were right back where we had started.' " *Harada Diary, 2,* 45. Author's translation.

minding him of the decision reached on September 19 not to aggravate the situation. The session ended inconclusively at 5 o'clock that day.

Since fighting continued daily on the Manchurian side of the Yalu, it was doubtful whether the Korean Army could be restrained indefinitely. Even while the cabinet was engaged in heated discussions over the very problem, 4,000 troops of the Thirty-Ninth Mixed Brigade, concentrated at Shingishū, crossed over into Manchuria. The troops could no longer wait for authorization from General Kanaya, Chief of the General Staff.[16] How did this eruptive, defiant action by the Korean Army come about on the heels of the Mukden Incident? The answer to this question must be sought in the actions of the Kwantung Army. We may start with the fact that for a time immediately after the opening of hostilities there was indecision in the high councils of the Kwantung Army with respect to the question of strategy.

When Kwantung Army headquarters moved up to Mukden from Port Arthur on the morning of September 19, there was a strong inclination on the part of the army to settle the Manchurian and Mongolian issues once and for all. When General Tatekawa heard of this, he is said to have counseled, "The establishment of a new administrative regime in South Manchuria comes first. If we dawdle, there will be intervention by some third power. We must make haste. Northern Manchuria, I would say, comes later."[17]

Lieutenant Colonel Ishihara, the master strategist of the Kwantung Army, thought differently. He was irresistibly attracted toward Harbin because he was primarily concerned with Rus-

16. According to one source, "It was a known fact that General Hayashi's staff was in touch with Lieutenant Colonel Ishihara of the Kwantung Army. Hayashi was said to have been railroaded by his staff into ordering his troops to cross the border. It was even rumored that Hayashi, unable to make up his mind, was trembling in his office." Matsumura, *Miyakezaka*, pp. 42–43. Author's translation.

17. Ibid., p. 39. Author's translation. See also Asahi, *Taiheiyō, 2,* 29–30, and Supplement, pp. 5–6.

sian intervention. Once strategic command of the northern plains had been secured, the Kwantung Army would be in the advantageous position of possessing interior lines of communication according to the classic strategy employed by Napoleon at Leipzig.

Though Tatekawa listened to Ishihara's plan, he already had his hands full trying to stabilize the situation in and around Mukden. Moreover, he countered by saying that if the Kwantung Army advanced into the northern plains, the Russians would be provoked into intervening. Also to be contended with was the order from army headquarters in Tokyo to withdraw to the railway zone of the South Manchuria Railway—the reverse, so to speak, of the nonaggravation policy.

Meanwhile, an urgent call came in to headquarters in Mukden from the Army Special Service Agency in Kirin. The Japanese army detachment there was trying to draft Hsi Ch'ia[18] to act as a front for the army regime, but he did not dare oblige as long as stragglers from the North Barracks in Mukden occupied Kirin. All of a sudden headquarters' eyes were trained on Kirin. Technically, of course, the army was not permitted to engage in military actions outside the railway zone without imperial sanction. General Honjō, Commanding General of the Kwantung Army, counseled caution and delayed making any decisive move. Extremists among his staff, however, were fearful that Tokyo might decide to impose further stringent restrictions on the actions of the Kwantung Army. They feared that at any moment they would be ordered to relinquish the huge advantages they had gained in a short time.

On September 21, three days after the Mukden Incident, Colonel Itagaki finally prevailed upon General Honjō to order an attack on Kirin. Once the decision had been reached, the attack was launched swiftly and boldly. Ishihara rounded up all available troops, incorporated them into the Second Division under

18. Once Chief of Staff of the Kirin Army, he later headed the puppet regime of Kirin under the tutelage of the Kwantung Army.

General Tamon, and made a dash for Kirin, leaving Mukden completely unguarded. Kirin was occupied without firing a shot. What happened next is a story already known. Hsi Ch'ia reluctantly proclaimed the independence of the province of Kirin under the threat of General Tamon, who held a revolver to his head.[19]

The Korean Army, which was itching for action, immediately seized the opportunity to fill the vacuum and crossed the Yalu into Manchuria. The unauthorized crossing of the border was excused by Korean Army spokesmen on the grounds that Mukden was in peril without Japanese soldiers for protection. After arriving in Mukden, detachments were sent to occupy Liaoyuan and Hsinmin. This phase of the operation was completed on September 22.[20]

News of the precipitate moves of the Kwantung and Korean Armies, reached the General Staff at 5:30 P.M. on September 21 and deeply distressed General Kanaya. The next day he hastened to the Imperial Palace to see whether the Emperor would grant an ex post facto sanction for the unauthorized mobilization of the Korean Army. It is presumed that by this time Kido had apprised the Emperor of Saionji's counsel not to sanction the action of the Korean Army,[21] since the Emperor refused Kanaya's petition, stating that there was no decision by the government to cover the cost of the expedition.[22] Minami, equally concerned,

19. Morishima, *Conspiracy,* p. 75. For a singular eye-witness account of the Kwantung Army's Kirin operation and its subsequent hostile attitude toward the members of Japan's Foreign Office, see Ishii, *Gaikōkan no Isshō,* pp. 181–90.

20. Asahi, *Taiheiyō, 2,* 16–17. One can only be puzzled by Exhibit 3423 of the IMTFE, which cites from *Man-Mitsu-Dai-Nikki* (Manchurian Secret Great Diary) that the Chief of the General Staff, under date of September 22, 1931, sent a top secret order to the commanders of the Kwantung Army and the Korean Army authorizing the dispatch of the Korean Army into Manchuria. First, on the 19th, the Office of the General Staff was compelled to rescind a mobilization order to the Korean Army dispatched earlier the same day; secondly, why would the Office of the General Staff issue an order for an action already completed?

21. See above, p. 172.

22. *Wakatsuki Memoirs,* p. 377.

sent General Sugiyama, his Vice Minister, to see Wakatsuki. Sugiyama pleaded with the Premier to hasten to the Imperial Palace the same night and report to the Emperor that the commander of the Korean Army had arbitrarily dispatched one brigade into Manchuria and that the details would be reported to His Majesty after the matter had received attention at the cabinet meeting the next day.

On the morning of September 23 the Emperor summoned Wakatsuki and said, "The government's policy not to aggravate the situation is, indeed, an appropriate one. You will see to it that this policy is carried out."[23] When Wakatsuki withdrew, he found Kanaya in the waiting room. The General had come in utmost secrecy to plead with Wakatsuki to report to the Emperor that the expedition by the Korean Army had been passed upon by the cabinet. Without the Premier's word, Kanaya said, he could not receive the Emperor's sanction. Wakatsuki remained adamant in the face of Kanaya's plea and returned to his residence.

Harada gives no reason for Wakatsuki's refusal. Legally speaking, this was a problem only between the Emperor and the Chief of the General Staff. As a student of the Meiji Constitution observes, "The supreme military command . . . is exercised by the Emperor not through the ministers of the Departments of War and the Navy but through the Chiefs of the General Staff of the Navy and War, who are responsible only to the Emperor. The General Staffs are organizations independent of the Cabinet and discharge their business under the direct control and supervision of the Emperor."[24]

If what is quoted here had been the established practice, then the actions of both Kanaya and Minami were extraordinary. The aid which they sought from Wakatsuki was more in the nature of a personal favor than anything else. What then was responsible

23. *Harada Diary, 2,* 71. Author's translation.

24. Nakano, *The Ordinance Power of the Japanese Emperor,* pp. 154–55.

for creating this curious situation in which two full generals had to solicit the Premier for his moral support? The only answer seems to lie in the manner in which the Emperor had interposed the authority of the civil government between himself and the army. We therefore come to the crucial question: Was this either by established practice or by constitutional interpretation the proper way of disposing of the issue? It is apparent that the verdict should be negative. The real charge should have been that General Hayashi of the Korean Army had overstepped his authority. And since the line of command in case of military operation came down from the Chief of the General Staff, Kanaya too was responsible for the improper act of Hayashi. But the effect of the Emperor's failure to assert at a crucial juncture the constitutional authority which rightfully was his must be presumed to have had an unfortunate and far-reaching effect on the future conduct and behavior of the military men. Actually, Hayashi had encroached upon the imperial prerogative and the Emperor could have simply stated so. In the last analysis, the responsibility of advising the Emperor on the course of action to take rested with the men who surrounded him: Among others the Grand Chamberlain, the Lord Keeper of Privy Seal, the Minister of the Imperial Household, Saionji, and the Premier himself.

The cabinet met on September 23. The members expressed their indignation at Minami's inability to compel the Kwantung Army to comply with the government's order. Certain members went so far as to disavow the government's responsibility for military ventures which the Kwantung Army might undertake in the future without receiving prior consent. Referring to this particular meeting, Harada in his diary wrote, "At any rate the Minister of Foreign Affairs, the Minister of War, and the Minister of Finance reached an agreement. Minami promised that he would not take independent action thereafter."[25] It was reliably reported that even the Chief of the General Staff had sided with Shidehara's nonaggravation policy.[26]

25. *Harada Diary, 2,* 73–74. Author's translation.
26. Takeuchi, *War and Diplomacy in the Japanese Empire,* p. 354, n. 58.

The cabinet was left with no choice but to appropriate funds for the Korean Army lest it be left without subsistence in the field. Moreover, if the Korean Army were withdrawn from Manchuria, it was not certain whether the Kwantung Army with a force of 11,000 could hold its ground against some 250,000 Chinese soldiers[27] in the event of a counterattack on a wide front. There was also the fear that, without adequate armed protection, the life and property of the Japanese residents might be seriously jeopardized. It was not that Inoue, the Minister of Finance, approved of the additional expenditures for the Korean Army; he was merely submitting formally to a fait accompli. Moreover, Minami pleaded with Wakatsuki to save Kanaya's face. The Prime Minister had no choice but to proceed to the Imperial Palace the same evening to report to the Emperor that he intended to defray the additional expenditures which the Korean Army had incurred by its actions.

After Wakatsuki, both Minami and Kanaya had audiences with the Emperor. Kanaya did not emerge from his unscathed; the Emperor reprimanded him with the terse words, "Hereafter, take heed."[28] Kanaya is said to have come away from the audience completely mortified.

With the opening of hostilities, unstinting cooperation from the directors and officials of the South Manchuria Railway Company became indispensable to the mobility of the Kwantung Army. It has been indicated already that the majority of the directors, except for Sogō, were oriented to Shidehara's foreign policy. Therefore, the Wakatsuki government thought of summoning President Uchida and Vice President Eguchi to Tokyo

27. The Chinese regulars with the Fengtien Army as the nucleus numbered about 250,000. Chang Hsueh-liang at the time had approximately 110,000 troops directly under his command, stationed in and about Peking and Tientsin. The remaining 140,000 were stationed roughly as follows in the four provinces: Fengtien 45,000; Kirin 55,000; Heilungkiang 25,000; and Jehol 15,000. Toyoshima, *Himerareta Shōwashi,* p. 55.

28. *Wakatsuki Memoirs,* p. 378. Author's translation.

for a conference, with a view to using their influence to restrain the unbridled actions of the Kwantung Army.

Uchida and Eguchi had booked passage aboard the same ship from Dairen to Tokyo. Sogō, who sensed what would be in store for the two men in Tokyo, quickly resorted to a divisive tactic. He succeeded in persuading Uchida to change his itinerary and proceed to Tokyo by rail via Mukden and Seoul. Thus Eguchi had to sail alone from Dairen. In Mukden, Uchida met General Honjō for a conversation. The staff of the Kwantung Army joined forces and talked Uchida into taking sides with the army, to follow up the Mukden Incident with vigorous military action until the whole of Manchuria fell under Japan's control.

Buoyant with enthusiasm, Uchida summoned the directors and executives of the Mukden office and pledged the undivided support of the South Manchuria Railway Company to the Kwantung Army. He made a statement to the effect that Japan must fight until her ultimate objectives had been attained. The directors were flabbergasted to hear such a statement from Uchida, for it represented a complete departure from Shidehara's diplomacy. En route to Tokyo, in Seoul, Governor Ugaki and General Hayashi, Commander of the Korean Army, awaited Uchida's arrival, and they too voiced full support. After arriving in Japan, Uchida continued to talk in the same vein, much to the disappointment of his friends.

On October 14 Saionji told Harada, "Uchida dropped in today, so I listened to his story and was greatly disappointed in him. Though on the one hand he talked about exercising prudence in order to enable the League of Nations to maintain its prestige and to reciprocate America's friendly attitude, on the other hand when our conversation dwelt upon Manchuria, I was amazed by his positive views. He must have succumbed to the atmosphere in Manchuria and perhaps has even been browbeaten by the army."[29]

29. *Harada Diary, 2,* 93. Author's translation.

On the following day, October 15, Shidehara described to Harada a conversation he had had with Uchida. "Last night I had a talk with Uchida," he said. "Since he assumed such a positive attitude with respect to Manchuria, I told him. 'If you think you can get by with what you are saying, why don't you take over my office and see for yourself?' He suddenly shifted his stand and said, 'Oh no, we cannot do any such thing. There is the League and America to consider.' "[30]

Thus it is quite clear that Uchida, while recognizing the necessity for Japan to conduct her foreign relations within the framework of the League and other treaty commitments, nevertheless shared the objectives of the Kwantung Army in respect to Manchuria, which were wholly inconsistent with those of the Foreign Office.

Sidelights at Nanking and Tokyo

In a last-minute attempt to ease Japanese-Chinese tensions, Shigemitsu and T. V. Soong, Finance Minister of the Nationalist regime, had agreed to visit Manchuria together. They had booked passage aboard a steamer scheduled to sail from Shanghai on September 20, 1931, when the Mukden Incident suddenly broke out. Undaunted, Shigemitsu continued his efforts. On the morning of the 19th, after receiving news of the Liutiaohu Incident, he called on Soong and expressed regret that their efforts had come too late, but at the same time expressed his determination to settle the Incident as quickly as possible. Soong agreed that an early settlement was desirable, and suggested that the two continue with their original plan to go to Manchuria. Shigemitsu responded that he would try immediately to get the approval of the home office if Mr. Soong would kindly wait.

Chang Chun, a graduate of the Japanese Military Academy

30. Ibid., p. 95. Author's translation.

who chanced to be with them, asked Shigemitsu, "Do you really think the Japanese government can localize the conflict by restraining the army?" Shigemitsu could only reply, "Irrespective of the outcome, the Japanese government has decided to localize the incident. We shall have to do everything we can."[1]

Shigemitsu reported to Shidehara the conversation he had had with Soong. At the end of the message he stressed the absolute necessity of prompt action. As in the Saburi case, there was a delay. Shigemitsu had to send a follow-up telegram emphasizing the urgency of the situation. Meanwhile, the Kwantung Army continued to enlarge its theater of operations. Since localization of the conflict no longer appeared practicable, Shigemitsu concluded that Shidehara was deliberately withholding a reply to Soong's suggestion.

In Tokyo, Shidehara was heartened by the report from Shigemitsu on his conversation with Soong. Elated, he reported the fact to the Minister of War and to the Emperor and followed it by dispatching a congratulatory telegram to Shigemitsu on September 21: "Well done! Make every effort to complete the action." He wanted Shigemitsu immediately to take up the Manchurian issues with Soong along the lines he had suggested. In addition, the Foreign Minister suggested that the conversations extend over all outstanding Sino-Japanese problems.

When Shigemitsu saw Soong, the latter said: "The enlargement of the theater of conflict in Manchuria subsequent to our conversation has been entirely the doing of the Japanese army according to their plans. The matter is out of our hands. China has already appealed directly to the League. There is no point in opening conversations with the Japanese government at this stage."

To counter the unbridled actions of the Kwantung Army in Manchuria the Chinese resorted to every possible means of re-

1. The desperate attempt by Shigemitsu and T. V. Soong to head off Sino-Japanese collision is taken from *Shigemitsu Memoirs,* pp. 105 ff. Author's translation.

sistance short of military action. Shigemitsu expressed his apprehension to the home government in the following terms:

> The Chinese government is fully aware of the gravity of the situation. Though they will adhere to their time-honored practice of not resisting by force, they are bringing into motion every means and method to combat Japan. Not only has the Nationalist government unity of leadership now, but the anti-Japanese machinery which is experienced and disciplined has begun to operate. Economic boycott is bad enough, but now the nationwide student organization, which did not so much as stir in the Korean incident,[2] has taken up the cudgels. Its actions are fraught with extreme consequences. Anti-Japanese sentiment is even more violent than that which flared up during the time of the Twenty-One Demands and is expected to become worse. In the present situation there is no telling when the sparks may leap to regions other than Manchuria. In this connection, it is requested of the government that it especially warn the navy[3] to exercise utmost prudence.[4]

While Shidehara awaited the aforementioned disappointing report from Shigemitsu on the response from T. V. Soong, Shidehara summoned Chiang Tso-pin, the Chinese Minister to Japan, and said:

> I understand that your country has appealed the case of the Liutiaohu Incident to Geneva. This strikes me as

2. An incident in Pyongyang, Korea, on July 5, 1931. Chinese residents in the city were persecuted in retaliation for the Wanpaoshan Incident which had occurred two days earlier in Manchuria.

3. Shigemitsu does not explain why the Japanese navy was singled out. However, in view of the fact that the Shanghai Incident which started on January 28, 1932, was a navy show—a counterpart to the army's Mukden Incident—it is presumed that he had grounds for concern.

4. Shigemitsu, *Shōwa no Dōran, 1,* 53–54. Author's translation.

> an ill-advised move. At the League, nations unfamiliar with the situation in the Far East will argue the issues back and forth until they have turned the place into a debating contest. It will be most humiliating for any nation to admit its fault under such circumstances. Instead, each country is bound to defend its position obstinately. That is certainly not the way to bring two parties to terms. I believe that the best way is to hold direct conversations between China and Japan. It is stated in the League Covenant that every means of diplomacy[5] ought to be explored before an issue is brought to the League's attention. I, for one, cannot see why it is not possible for us to come to terms were our representatives to engage in frank discussion before airing the issue before the forum of nations.[6]

Shidehara states that from 5 o'clock in the afternoon to 8 in the evening he took extra pains to explain and to win Chiang over to his approach to the Sino-Japanese rift. Chiang seemed

5. The Covenant of the League did not enunciate this thesis as clearly as does the United Nations Charter under Article 33, paragraph 1. It must be presumed that Shidehara had inferred the statement from Article 13, paragraph 1 of the Covenant, which read, "The Members of the League agree that whenever any dispute shall arise between them which they recognize to be suitable for submission to arbitration or judicial settlement, and which cannot be satisfactorily settled by diplomacy, they will submit the whole subject-matter to arbitration or judicial settlement," and Article 15, paragraph 1, which read, "If there should arise between Members of the League any dispute likely to lead to a rupture, which is not submitted to arbitration or judicial settlement in accordance with Article 13, the Members of the League agree that they will submit the matter to the Council." The Chinese delegates at Geneva, however, appealed under Article 11, paragraph 1: "any war or threat of war, whether immediately affecting any of the Members of the League or not, is hereby declared a matter of concern to the whole League, and the League shall take any action that may be deemed wise and effectual to safeguard the peace of nations."

6. *Shidehara Memoirs*, p. 174. Author's translation.

to agree with Shidehara's point of view, and apparently went back and sent a long telegram to his home government. After that, however, Chiang declined to see Shidehara for a long time, although the Foreign Minister repeatedly requested another interview. It became known much later to the Japanese Foreign Office that Chiang had been ordered by his government not to see Shidehara for the time being.

By hindsight the appraisal of the situation in Manchuria by the Nanking government was far more realistic than that of Japan's Foreign Office. They had but two choices: either fight or appeal to the League. They chose the latter.

In direct contrast, the Foreign Office of Japan failed to understand the designs of the Kwantung Army. In the latter part of September the Foreign Office sent Morishima Gorō, Chief of the First Section of the Asia Bureau, to Mukden. Upon arrival, he is said to have remarked earnestly to Consul General Hayashi, "It is the consensus of the Japanese cabinet not to expand the conflict. Will you see to it that this policy is observed." Hayashi retorted, "That's impossible" and indicated the manner in which the Kwantung Army was enlarging its operations each day. When Morishima returned to Tokyo, he reported that even the Consul General's own safety was in jeopardy, since some of the extremist members of the Kwantung Army who were annoyed by Hayashi's interference harbored designs on his life.[7]

Equally in the dark regarding the true state of affairs in Manchuria were Japan's diplomats stationed abroad. A case in point was Ambassador Yoshizawa Kenkichi, who played a leading role at Geneva during the early months of the Manchurian crisis. En route to Tokyo he stopped at Berlin and was flabbergasted to learn for the first time from Ambassador Obata Torikichi the story of the conspiracy by Itagaki and Ishihara of the Kwantung Army.[8] There was little that Japan's foreign representatives could do except to palliate the fait accompli in Manchuria. In

7. *Harada Diary, 2,* 77. Author's translation.
8. Morishima, *Conspiracy,* pp. 70–71.

their thankless task of transmitting to foreign governments the empty pronouncements and proposals of their home government, they earned for themselves an unwished-for reputation for duplicity.

Although the Nanking government was more astute in penetrating the true intentions of the Kwantung Army than was Wakatsuki's government, it too fell short in assessing the extent to which the army was prepared to defy the League. At the cabinet meeting on October 1 Shidehara said it was desirable that Japan should make her intentions known before the League Council met on October 14. The Foreign Minister said, "There would be no problem if Japan evacuated her troops by then. Though it would be permissible to maintain some troops for the purpose of self-protection, it would be ill-advised to leave troops in numbers over and above the requirements at such points as Kirin and Tunhua."

War Minister Minami countered by saying, "If we withdraw our troops now, we will no longer be able to maintain control over Mukden and Kirin and will place ourselves in a vulnerable postion. Why in the world do we not withdraw from the League?"[9] Wakatsuki was helpless in the face of this attitude.

The Bombardment of Chinchow

On the afternoon of September 23 the resolution of the League Council,[1] together with Yoshizawa's report, reached the Foreign Office in Tokyo. On the 25th a reply was drafted and made public. The following morning Wakatsuki had an audience with the Emperor and explained the delicate situation: "The reply to the

9. The exchange of views between Shidehara and Minami is from the *Harada Diary, 2,* 84. Author's translation.

1. In the present work the actions taken by the League will be mentioned only insofar as they had a direct bearing on the decisions made in Tokyo. For the details of the proceedings at Geneva during the Manchurian crisis see Sara R. Smith, *The Manchurian Crisis, 1931–32: A Tragedy in International Relations* (New York, 1948). With respect to Japan's reaction to the proceedings in Geneva see Takeuchi, *War and Diplomacy in the Japanese Empire,* pp. 354–66.

League was deliberately withheld because there were misgivings that the army might not withdraw its troops despite the decision of the cabinet and the promise made by the Minister of War. We were fearful that the army might later commit acts which would contradict our pronouncement and thereby place our nation's honor in serious jeopardy."[2]

Wakatsuki's suspicion was not unfounded for on October 8, within two weeks of Japan's profession of peaceful intentions to the League, the Kwantung Army bombed Chinchow. The fact was that army headquarters in Tokyo and the headquarters of the Korean Army were still in the midst of ironing out differences over the unauthorized crossing of the Yalu River by the Thirty-Ninth Mixed Brigade.

When General Kanaya read the coded message from Mukden at noon on October 8, the bombing of Chinchow was over. The language of the telegram was enigmatic: "Chinchow is the headquarters of Chang Hsueh-liang. It is the center of disturbances in Manchuria. The Kwantung Army contemplates taking some sort of action against it. Please be so advised." The same evening army headquarters in Tokyo was startled by a follow-up telegram from Mukden boldly stating: "Chinchow was bombed. We beg your thoughtful disposal of the matter."[3]

Meanwhile the Big Three of the army—Generals Minami, Kanaya, and Mutō—met to formulate terms of settlement for the Manchurian crisis which would be acceptable to the army. They were: (1) outstanding Sino-Japanese issues, including the railway and land-lease problems, had to be settled immediately; (2) settlement was to be reached with the local authorities, not with the Nanking government; (3) until a new government was formed in Manchuria, Japan should maintain the status quo; the League was not to be permitted to intervene in the affairs of Manchuria.[4]

2. *Harada Diary, 2,* 75. Author's free translation.
3. Matsumura, *Miyakezaka,* p. 44. Author's translation.
4. *Tōkyō Asahi,* October 9, 1931, cited in Takeuchi, pp. 357–58.

These army demands obviously ran directly counter to the policy the Wakatsuki government was desperately trying to carry out. However, the cabinet's authority was already waning so rapidly that it could not bring itself to ask the Minister of War to soften the army's extreme demands. And at its meeting on October 9 no member of the cabinet even dared censure Honjō for the bombing of Chinchow. Having wrested the initiative from Tokyo, the Kwantung Army had begun to expand its military ventures at will, leaving Tokyo no choice but to accept. Each army action that defied the government had the effect of sapping the cabinet's strength. The body politic of Japan was already afflicted with creeping paralysis; although it still made decisions, it could no longer enforce them.

In utter desperation the Premier made a round of calls on senior statesmen and opposition leaders on October 12 and 13. They included Admiral Count Yamamoto Gonbei, Count Kiyoura Keigo, Takahashi Korekiyo, Baron Yamamoto Tatsuo, Inukai Tsuyoshi, Prince Konoe Fumimaro, and Tokugawa Iesato. Kido Kōichi,[5] critical of Wakatsuki's irresoluteness, wrote in his diary: "The cabinet at the time, despite the fact that the responsibility lay with it, did not attempt to work out a policy of its own. Instead, it indiscriminately sought aid from outside, which was most reprehensible."[6]

Wakatsuki was disturbed by the fact that the passage quoted above was read into the record at the Tokyo Trials, and he refuted Kido's charge as unfounded. He explained that despite the fact that he viewed with alarm the Kwantung Army's flaunting disregard of governmental authority, he deemed as ill advised any move to appeal directly to the people even if the Diet were in session at the time, because such an act might cause the cabinet to topple. Instead, he reasoned that it was in the best interest

5. Kido's official position at the time was Chief Private Secretary to the Keeper of Privy Seal.

6. *Wakatsuki Memoirs,* p. 379. Author's translation. For explanations of the dilemma which Wakatsuki faced see Scalapino, *Democracy and the Party Movement in Prewar Japan,* p. 240.

of the country that these disinguished men who were versed in the affairs of the nation be informed about the crisis.

It would seem that more credence ought to be given to Wakatsuki's own explanation of his purpose in visiting these men of eminence than those of his critics. Nevertheless, it was all too patent that he was at his wit's end trying to bring the rampaging Kwantung Army under the control of the cabinet.

On the evening of October 12 Wakatsuki summoned Harada and complained:

> We are in real trouble. In the interest of Japan, I have done all I can to improve her relations with other nations. I have repeatedly called the attention of the Minister of War at cabinet meetings to the fact that our armed forces stationed abroad must exercise utmost prudence not to engage in any action that would betray the professions which the government has already made to its people and to the world. I have constantly endeavored to base the conduct of our foreign relations on good faith.
>
> I would summon the Minister of War to explain to him at great length the necessity of maintaining orderly conduct of our troops abroad. He would then agree, "Indeed, it is as you say. I shall send out an instruction right away." Then what would happen? The troops stationed abroad would commit acts which would run completely counter to the agreement that the Minister of War and I had just made. This is followed by immediate repercussions at Geneva. I am as good as betrayed. Too, they are blemishing Japan's reputation. I am at a loss as to what to do. I cannot go on like this. Yet, I cannot very well resign at this point. Indeed, matters have come to a serious pass.[7]

7. *Harada Diary, 2,* 91–92. Author's translation.

On the 14th, Harada departed for Kyoto to convey Wakatsuki's depressing thoughts to Prince Saionji.

The October Plot[1]

The Wakatsuki cabinet was tottering from the effects of the Manchurian crisis when another conspiracy, the October Plot, was uncovered. It died at birth, like its predecessor the March Plot; the news was so shocking, however, that it hastened the collapse of the Wakatsuki government.

On August 4 Lieutenant Colonel Hashimoto told Major Tanaka Kiyoshi, "A thorough reform is being planned to take place about the middle of September. It will capitalize on an incident which is to occur in Manchuria. Understanding has been reached already with the key men of the General Staff with respect to the nature of domestic reconstruction. Will you, therefore, draw up a plan for the military to spearhead a movement to wrest power from the present government?"[2]

Briefly, the plot[3] called for Lieutenant Colonel Hashimoto and Major Chō to rally the extremists of the Cherry Society and with the cooperation of the Ōkawa and the Kita-Nishida[4] factions to stage a coup on October 24. To be mobilized were some twelve companies of army troops, thirteen naval bombers, and three or four army planes. Their plan of attack was threefold: (1) to bomb the Premier's residence while the cabinet was holding

1. See Storry, *The Double Patriots,* pp. 86–93. As in the case of the March Plot, my account of the October Plot was written without any knowledge of Mr. Storry's publication.

2. Mori, *Senpū Nijūnen,* p. 80. Author's translation. The staff under General Kanaya consisted of Lieutenant General Ninomiya, Assistant Chief of the General Staff, and Major Generals Umezu, Chief of the General Affairs Department, Tatekawa, Chief of the First Department, and Hashimoto Toranosuke, Chief of the Second Department. Matsumura, *Miyakezaka,* p. 51.

3. For details, see Mori, *Senpū Nijūnen,* pp. 76–82.

4. Nishida Zei, a former army officer, and Kita Ikki, author of *Nihon Kaizō Hōan Taikō* (An Outline of Measures for the Reconstruction of Japan) were advocates of an extreme form of national socialism.

a meeting and to wipe out the Wakatsuki government; (2) to occupy the Metropolitan Police Office, the War Ministry, and the General Staff Office; and (3) to eliminate such undesirable army officers as Major General Katsuki Kiyoshi, Director of the War College, and Major Nakano Naozō of the Military Academy. These men had strongly opposed the Cherry Society. Included among the undesirables were also the top officials of the Imperial Household, key figures in political parties, and executives of the zaibatsu.

Except for the premiership, important cabinet posts in the proposed new government were to go to active participants in the coup: Hashimoto, Home Minister; Tatekawa, Foreign Minister; Ōkawa Finance Minister; Chō, Superintendent General of the Metropolitan Police Board; and Rear Admiral Kobayashi, Commander of Kasumigaura Airbase, Navy Minister. The posts of Premier and War Minister were to be proffered to Lieutenant General Araki Sadao. It is a moot point whether General Araki's reaction had been obtained in advance.

The October and March Plots differed from each other in several respects. By the time of the October Plot the locus of decision had shifted from the officers of general grade to those of field grade. In part this was due to Hashimoto's decision to cut his group off from high-ranking officers and concentrate on company-grade officers. There is evidence that civilians were excluded despite the interest shown in Hashimoto's plot by the Kita-Nishida wing and the Inoue Nisshō faction. These two groups, which had a strong following among the young extremist army and navy officers, met on August 26 at the Outer Garden of Meiji Shrine to discuss what position they ought to assume with respect to this new plot.

Ōkawa's clique also may have been excluded, although there seems to be evidence to the contrary. Thus on August 31 Inoue is said to have instructed one Fujii Sei to approach Ōkawa with a proposal that their clique be allowed to participate in the October Plot. Another source, "Major Tanaka's Notes," states that

Ōkawa and his group were the only civilians utilized in the October Plot.[5]

General Tanaka Ryūkichi, testifying at the Tokyo Trials, said, "Hashimoto, Chō, and Ōkawa planned the October Plot in 1931 for the purpose of overthrowing the Government then in power and setting up in its place a new Government which would support the Manchurian Incident. Tatekawa said he would support such a Government."[6] Moreover, it is difficult to believe that Ōkawa could have been promised a post in the new cabinet unless he had played a significant role in plotting the fall of the government.

All this, however, is hearsay or secondary evidence. Hashimoto himself denied that Ōkawa participated in the October Plot. At the Tokyo Trials, Hashimoto was asked point-blank, "Did Dr. Ōkawa assist you in the October Plot?" He replied, "No, Dr. Ōkawa did not. In the March Plot, Ōkawa and I were co-conspirators. However, I began to entertain misgivings about the advisability of allowing civilians to participate in a plot of this nature lest they become a source of leakage. It was therefore decided that no civilian would be let in on the October Plot."[7]

What caused the collapse of the October Plot? Above all, the conspirators brought failure upon themselves by their personal misbehavior. Hashimoto and Chō were said to have thrown a round of extravagant geisha parties, to which were invited a number of company-grade officers who were persuaded to cast their lot with the cause. The more serious-minded young officers joined an extreme ultranationalist group called the Kokutai Genri-ha (National Foundation Principle faction) which, under the leadership of Captain Sugaha Saburō, had close ties with the Kōdō-ha.

Serious disagreements arose within the Cherry Society over the question of the means to bring about national reconstruction.[8]

5. IMTFE, *Proceedings,* p. 19,676.
6. Ibid., p. 2013.
7. Ibid., p. 28,815.
8. See above pp. 96–97.

The extremists insisted that the old political order must first be completely demolished, after which the new order would emerge from the ruins like a phoenix. Hashimoto and his followers belonged to this school of thinking. Opposing them was the more moderate faction, which argued that destruction need not go quite so far and that it should in fact be kept to a minimum. These men thought of reform in terms of concrete proposals and of a new ideology which would be appealing enough to attract a mass following.

Closely identifying themselves with these young officers of ultranationalist bent were Muranaka Kōji and Isobe Asaichi.[9] So disturbed did they become with the flamboyant attitude of Hashimoto and his group that the two collaborated in writing a pamphlet entitled *Views Regarding Housecleaning in the Army*.[10] In it they gave their reasons for their opposition, stating that "because we had begun to entertain misgivings about the soundness of the ideology of the ringleaders even before we reached the point of drawing up plans for the October Plot, we decided to make a clean break with them. It was from this time on that the officers interested in national reconstruction were split into roughly two camps . . . resulting in oppression of and malicious slander being directed against the younger officer group."

Another defector was Major Tanaka Kiyoshi, who until the October Plot had worked closely with Hashimoto. In his "Notes" he writes: "Hashimoto's plot violated the founding principle of the Japanese army. It would have inflicted untold damage on the army, which was the only body able to effect national reconstruction. Thereupon I decided to block the coup by any means."

9. Later both men resigned from the army and were executed as civilian leaders in the February 26, 1936, uprising of young officers.

10. The Japanese title is *Shukugun ni Kansuru Ikensho*. It is interesting to note that the leaders who brought down the Tokugawa rule were acting under an impulse closely parallel to that of the leaders of the October Plot. See Yoshio Sakata and John W. Hall, "The Motivation of Political Leadership in the Meiji Restoration," *Journal of Asian Studies, 16* (1959), 50.

Also prominent among these who had a change of heart was Lieutenant Colonel Nemoto Hiroshi. The circumstances of his defection are not clear.

Apart from the information filtering into the Ministry of War through the mouths of those who, like Colonel Nemoto, had defected, plans for the coup also became known as the unrestrained talk of Hashimoto and his men drifted beyond the confines of their favorite places of rendezvous. Their plans and every move were known to the gendarmery and the civil police. However, the gendarmery did not dare take positive action because it was alleged that Prince Chichibu and Prince Kaya were implicated in the plot.[11]

The army leaders, however, became alarmed when on October 15 Colonel Hashimoto confronted General Sugiyama, Vice Minister of War, and demanded that he, too, lend his moral support to the coup. Meanwhile, queries from worried government officials singled out as targets for the coup continued to pour into the Ministry of War.

Minami, Minister of War, and Kanaya, Chief of the General Staff, were anxious to pacify the rebellious officers with a minimum of commotion lest this latest evidence of internal strife discredit the army in the eyes of the Japanese people. On an earnest request by these two generals, General Araki visited the scene of a party on the night of October 16[12] to placate the officers. Major

11. The two quotations from preceding paragraphs are from Shiraki, *Nihon Seitōshi,* pp. 89 and 90. Author's translations. Tanaka Sōgorō, *Nihon Fashizumu no Genryū* (The Wellspring of Japanese Fascism) (Tokyo, 1949), p. 324. This is the only book that makes an allegation of this nature, and its veracity is open to doubt for Tanaka does not give the source of his information. It should be pointed out that the October Plot is sometimes dubbed "The Imperial Flag Revolution" (Kinki Kakumei). However, this is not because members of the imperial family were allegedly implicated in the plot but because those who participated in the October Plot had planned to hoist a banner with the phrase "Kinki Kakumei" near the Land Survey Department in the General Staff Office which was to be their headquarters. Mori, *Senpū Nijūnen,* p. 80.

12. Testimony by General Araki, IMTFE, *Proceedings,* p. 28,126. Also *Harada Diary, 2,* 106–07.

Chō, according to one source, is said to have responded angrily by flinging down the gauntlet. There is another version which states that Araki had to promise the unruly officers to prosecute the Manchurian crisis to a successful conclusion and to overthrow the Wakatsuki cabinet.

On the same evening Minami summoned a number of his subordinates to his residence for an all-night conference. It was not until 3 o'clock the following morning that a decision was reached. At 4, Hashimoto, Nemoto, Chō, and nine others were arrested, bringing the October Plot abruptly to an end.[13]

There is evidence indicating that toward the end Hashimoto himself grew faint-hearted; Major Tanaka believes that Hashimoto deliberately confronted the Vice Minister of War with his demand so that the Ministry would officially quash the plot. This would have enabled Hashimoto to save face. Another source cites the fact that one day Hashimoto came to Lieutenant General Araki begging him to take the lead in voicing opposition to the scheme.

When the conspirators were arrested in Tokyo, one of them—perhaps Colonel Hashimoto—blurted out, "You might make arrests in Tokyo, but in Manchuria the Kwantung Army will attain autonomy just the same." The army leaders received another jolt from a rumor that Colonel Itagaki of the Kwantung Army had provided 200,000 yen to finance the October Plot.[14]

In a flurry of nervous excitement, a severe warning was wired to the Kwantung Army under the joint signature of the three subchiefs of the supreme command in Tokyo—Sugiyama, Vice Minister of War, Ninomiya, Assistant Chief of Staff, and Araki, Assistant Chief Inspector of Military Education. The wire read: "Any act of conspiracy, such as one aimed at attainment of independence of the Kwantung Army or the like, will not be toler-

13. Testimony of Marquis Kido, IMTFE, *Proceedings,* p. 30,739.

14. Matsumura, *Miyakezaka,* p. 51. It is possible that the 200,000 yen was not from Itagaki but a sum which Marquis Tokugawa Yoshichika gave Ōkawa. Author's translation.

ated." In addition, Sugiyama wired a coded message to detachments of the Kwantung Army warning them that "even if the headquarters of the Kwantung Army rise in open revolt, detachments are not to lend their support." These wires were followed by a visit of General Shirakawa to Mukden. The Kwantung Army, in anger, retorted in a wire: "What manner of misjudgment would you call this?" Army headquarters had taken another slap in the face.[15]

As in the case of the March Plot, we are again confronted with a question: Was there collusion between the instigators of the Mukden Incident and the conspirators of the October Plot? It is tempting to link the March Plot, the Mukden Incident, and the October Plot together as part of a unified conspiracy masterminded by a single intelligence operating behind the scenes, but this was not the case. Many popular writers, including those in Japan and particularly those with leftist leanings, have found it convenient to lump all these outrages together as the doings of the "military clique," a vague collective term for a group of men bent on saber rattling and continental expansion. As has been demonstrated, the so-called military clique, composed primarily of army men, in the early thirties was far from an efficient, unified body.

Moreover, since all three occurred within a period of seven months and were all in violent reaction against Shidehara's foreign policy and the corruption and inefficiency of the parliamentary form of government, the temptation is all the stronger to presume that collusion of one sort or another must have existed between, perhaps, Colonel Itagaki of the Kwantung Army and Lieutenant Colonel Hashimoto in Tokyo. Nevertheless, the evidence developed at the Tokyo Trials seems to point in another direction. According to the testimony of Lieutenant General Wachi Takaji, who was on intimate terms with Hashimoto and was once his subordinate, Hashimoto had never met Itagaki, Ishihara, and Doihara up to the time of the Manchurian crisis.

15. Ibid., pp. 51–52. Author's translation.

Wachi stated that Hashimoto had no occasion to communicate with these men by telephone, telegraph, or any other means.

At the Tokyo Trials, Wachi recounted his experiences during the October Plot when he was arrested and sent to Utsunomiya, a city sixty miles north of Tokyo. There he met two other army officers who had been similarly detained for having taken part in the Plot as private secretaries of Hashimoto. During their fifteen days of confinement they had ample time to compare notes. One of these men said that he had personally handled all of Hashimoto's telephone calls, telegrams, and correspondence, but he had found nothing in these communications to indicate that Hashimoto was acting in collusion with staff members of the Kwantung Army.[16]

On the other hand, it is inconceivable that a tacit understanding of some sort did not exist between Koiso and Tatekawa of the General Staff and Itagaki of the Kwantung Army. One recalls only too well how Tatekawa deliberately forestalled seeing General Honjō until the Liutiaohu Incident had occurred on the night of September 18.[17]

The case of Major Chō may be somewhat different from that of Hashimoto. Our information on Chō is incomplete for the reason that he committed ceremonial suicide after the Battle of Okinawa. Nevertheless, he may have been an important link between the Kwantung Army and the conspirators of the October Plot in Tokyo. According to the testimony of Major General Tanaka Ryūkichi at the Tokyo Trials, Chō told Tanaka that he was the virtual leader in planning the October Plot[18] and that its object was to found a new government in Japan which would facilitate internal reconstruction and the settlement of Manchurian issues by the total mobilization of Japan's national resources.

Chō, because of his violent personality, was under surveillance of army authorities in Tokyo, and in September 1931 was

16. IMTFE, *Proceedings*, pp. 1956–79.

17. See above, pp. 158–59.

18. IMTFE, *Proceedings*, pp. 2015–16.

abruptly transferred to Peking as a military attaché. Highly incensed at the move, which he regarded as tantamount to banishment, Chō balked at the order and would not go until sternly reprimanded by his superior. Within a week after his arrival in Peking, however, he left the capital city and was again back in Tokyo, a few days prior to the date on which the coup was to be engineered. One must presume therefore that his unauthorized presence in Tokyo was made possible by the connivance of influential superiors stationed on the continent; the alternative is that he was simply absent without leave. If the story of 200,000 yen supplied by Colonel Itagaki has any credibility, Major Chō might have had something to do with transferring the funds to Tokyo to supervise their usage.

General Tanaka's testimony[19] bears out another fact which tends to corroborate the notion that Chō must have had some connection with the Kwantung Army. Chō told Tanaka once that Lieutenant Colonel Ishihara was unalterably opposed to the October Plot. Just after the collapse of the plot, Ishihara was en route to North China when he stopped at Mukden. There he is said to have reprimanded Chō for taking an active part in it.

Several pertinent implications might be drawn from General Tanaka's testimony. It is obvious that Ishihara had nothing to do with the October Plot. If any officer of the Kwantung Army had anything to do with it, that officer most likely was Itagaki. This points up the existence of a vast gulf in political outlook between Itagaki and Ishihara, although the two worked as teammates in the Mukden Incident.

Lacking the most essential ingredient of any successful revolution, a unified ideology, it is no wonder that the army coups d'état ended in failure. Not only was the leaders' thinking appallingly slipshod in the planning stage, but as a group they were wholly lacking in the organization and discipline which is found only in a tightly knit group fired by a doctrine that permits no deviation. The conspirators were often torn asunder by mutual

19. Ibid., p. 2016.

suspicion and jealousy and by the deliberate attempts of opposing factions to obstruct each other. This was true both of army and of civilian groups, as was shown in the discussion of the Ugaki and anti-Ugaki factions and the Ōkawa and Kita-Nishida factions. Although the conspiracy fell apart, the mere disclosure of what might have happened was a terrible blow to the Wakatsuki government. Members of the cabinet were shocked when they learned that they were marked as targets for bombing attack from the air.

The army disposed of the October Plot in utmost stealth by administrative measures. Lieutenant Colonel Hashimoto, the ringleader, received a sentence of twenty days in confinement, while Major Chō, Captain Tanaka Wataru, and others each received ten days. They were escorted by military police to resorts in the vicinity of Tokyo and were entertained royally for the duration of their detention.

The gravity of the plot necessitated a shake-up in personnel at the top. As a result of a meeting of the Big Three of the army, the Minister of War and the Chief of the General Staff agreed to resign. Kanaya stuck to his word, but Minami made an unsuccessful attempt to stay on as the Minister of War, only to be replaced by Araki, a member of the rival faction, when the Wakatsuki cabinet collapsed shortly thereafter.

Minami, as in the case of Ugaki in the March Plot, strove to cover up the abortive plot. He dared not prefer charges against the conspirators, since he was fearful that his immediate subordinates and the extremist field-grade officers might openly defy him. It has already been mentioned that on the night of October 16 Minami had to plead with Araki personally to postpone his departure for Kumamoto in order that he might go to Hashimoto and his group to placate them. Had Minami chosen to prosecute the plotters publicly, he would have made himself the target of the undying resentment of the entire Japanese army for discrediting it in the eyes of the nation.

The effect of the October Plot on the Foreign Office was startling, to say the least. "Secretary Stimson noticed that Baron Shidehara had been compelled to adopt in his communications a position supporting his government, which strained the credulity of Americans, especially since his excuses for Japan's action did not tally with the facts that had already been disclosed."[20] Among other things, the Foreign Minister abandoned his previous stand that Japanese troops would be evacuated from Manchuria when and if negotiations were concluded, and showed signs of veering toward the point of view of the army—nonrecognition of Chang Hsueh-liang's regime and the fostering of a local political force to supplant Chang's government. Indeed, Stimson was not the only person to be startled, for even Japan's own delegates at Geneva were astonished by Shidehara's abrupt démarche.[21] It has been suggested that this sudden shift in Shidehara's policy was occasioned by the October Plot. The Foreign Minister feared that if the government continued its policy of restraining the Kwantung Army's action in Manchuria, the army's urge to expand would become internalized and result in a major explosion at home—an explosion that would bring down the entire Japanese government and would be followed by a reign of terror.

Baron Harada, too, observed that the Foreign Office was yielding ground to the army. On October 19 he wrote: "After seeing the Premier . . . I went over to the Foreign Office. There I was told that the younger officers of the Foreign Office were effecting a rapprochement with the army, and relations were working out smoothly." Earlier in his diary we come across an incident that may have marked the beginning of the meeting of minds between the Foreign Office and the army. Under date of September 27 Harada wrote:

> Three or four days ago, Shiratori Toshio,[22] Lieutenant Colonel Suzuki Teiichi, and I dined together. It appeared that the two saw eye to eye on many mat-

20. Yanaga, *Japan since Perry*, p. 554.
21. Kurihara, *Tennō*, p. 63.
22. Chief of the Information Bureau of the Foreign Office. Together

ters. Thus, after I had left the place, the two stayed on and talked until late that night.

On October 1, I came back to Tokyo and saw Shiratori at the Foreign Office. He said, "As I talked with Suzuki, I realized that he too was going about his task [national reconstruction] with strong determination. Though I do go along with many things which he had to say, if the military were to be given free rein there is no telling how far and where they will push it [the reconstruction]. Therefore, we [referring to like-minded members of the Foreign Office and other non-military men] too would like to get in on this [the movement] so we can get in on the ground floor. How about you coming along too?" So I said, "Of course, let's get together and see what this is all about," and we parted company that day.

According to Shiratori, there is a prevailing sentiment among them [the military clique of which Lieutenant Colonel Suzuki was a member] that some kind of drastic action ought to be taken during the Diet session in December.[23]

Further evidence of a high-level shift in policy by the Foreign Office is revealed by Prince Konoe Fumimaro's own words: "Immediately after the Mukden Incident, Shiratori began to move completely in the same direction as Mori Kaku. That Shiratori took to championing the cause of withdrawing from the League was due in large measure to Mori's influence."[24]

The army's inability to do its own housecleaning had an unhealthy effect on itself and on the nation. Instead of bringing to trial the army officers who had conspired to overthrow the gov-

---

with the Chiefs of the Asia, Europe, and America Bureaus, he was a ranking career officer, second only to the Vice Minister of Foreign Affairs.

23. *Harada Diary, 2,* 83. Author's translation.

24. Yamaura, *Mori Kaku,* p. 789. Author's translation.

ernment, the leaders of the army defended the young officers on the ground that they were sincere and well meaning, but in the same breath they condemned the corrupt practices of party government. This attitude by officers in high places only fostered the notion that as long as revolutionary activities were committed in the name of national reconstruction punitive action would not be taken. The upshot was that while discipline in the army deteriorated woefully, the fever to engage in direct action was heightened among the young officers.

Further Military Operations on the Continent

After the bombing of Chinchow, Japanese military operations were suddenly shifted to the northwestern part of the Manchurian plain. The initial encounter with Chinese troops began with skirmishes around the Nonni River bridges in mid-October 1931 and ended with the occupation of Tsitsihar. Only a general outline of the military operations is given here, since there is very little to be gained by going into the details, which are elaborated in the *Lytton Report*.[1] Our primary concern is to seek an explanation for the unabated extension of military operations by the Kwantung Army despite frantic efforts of the Wakatsuki government to confine it. For the answer we must turn to behind-the-scene activities within the Kwantung Army and in Tokyo.

In early October, General Chang Hai-peng advanced with his troops along the Taonan-Angangchi Railway to seize Tsitsihar, the seat of the provincial government of Heilungkiang. The Japanese, it is said, incited the General into opening the offensive.[2] Ma Chan-shan, the defending general, ordered the destruction of the bridges over the Nonni River.

The South Manchuria Railway Company had reason to be concerned, since it had advanced the necessary capital for the construction of the Taonan-Anganchi Railway in the form of a

1. *Lytton Report,* pp. 72–75. Asahi, *Taiheiyō, 2,* 49–84.
2. *Lytton Report,* p. 72.

loan. Even more pressing was the prospect that shipments of soybeans, the all-important product of the northern plains, might be interrupted at the height of the harvest season. At the Kwantung Army's suggestion, the South Manchuria Railway Company applied to the government in Tokyo for armed protection while the bridges were being repaired.

The Japanese Consul General at Tsitsihar asked General Ma Chan-shan to repair the bridges as soon as possible. The situation became aggravated when a small party, consisting of employees of the Taonan-Angangchi Railway and the South Manchuria Railway, was fired upon while it was inspecting the damage to the bridges. The Kwantung Army now stepped into the picture. It served an ultimatum to both Chinese generals: if Ma Chan-shan did not repair the bridges by November 3, the South Manchuria Railway Company would feel free to do the repairing itself, in which event obstruction by the troops of either general would be regarded as an unfriendly act. The Japanese detachment was under orders to advance to Tahsing Station on the north side of the valley in the event of hostilities.

On November 4 a joint commission consisting of Major Hayashi, a representative from the Japanese Consulate General, and Chinese military and civil officials made two visits to the bridges in a last-minute effort to forestall an outbreak of hostilities. The Kwantung Army would not accede to the request made by the Chinese representative for the postponement of Japanese action, and that same morning engineers under the command of Captain Hanai began the repairs. By noon one infantry company was headed in the direction of Tahsing Station. Fierce fighting then broke out. The following day, Chinese troops repeatedly repulsed determined Japanese attacks from a strong line of trenches. On the second day of the encounter the troops fought the Japanese to a standstill, and turned their flanks in a counterattack, taking a heavy toll of the enemy. It was only after the Japanese received reinforcements of two battalions that they were able to capture Tahsing Station. This was as far as army headquarters in Tokyo permitted the Kwantung Army to advance in support of the bridge-repairing operation.

Meanwhile, although there was talk of postponing or canceling the army's annual grand maneuvers on account of the Manchurian crisis, the maneuvers were held as usual, for it seemed unlikely that there would be a further enlargement of military operations. The Emperor left Tokyo for Kumamoto, site of the maneuvers, on November 8 and did not return until November 21. He was accompanied by a sizable cortege consisting of cabinet officials and high-ranking military officers headed by General Kanaya, Chief of the General Staff. Since many of the key officials were in Kumamoto, government activities in Tokyo languished for about two weeks. A more opportune moment could hardly have presented itself for the Kwantung Army to make its next bold move. It was not without reason that the Wakatsuki government bided its time uneasily during the interim.

Foremost among the government's concerns was the disappearance from Tientsin of Henry Pu-yi, heir to the old Manchu dynasty. There were rumors that Colonel Doihara had gone to Tientsin in an attempt to entice him from hiding and that he might appear in Mukden at any moment. The government was equally apprehensive over the likelihood that the Kwantung Army might advance beyond the Nonni River to Tsitsihar. Finally, the government suspected that the riots of November 8 in Tientsin had been instigated by Japanese ruffians, despite the assurance of Chang Hsueh-ming[3] to the contrary. Since the next meeting of the League Council was scheduled for November 16, the government had all the more reason to be cautious, for any untoward incident could jeopardize Japan's precarious status in Geneva.

It was thought in some quarters that the outcome of these issues could well determine the fate of the Wakatsuki cabinet. There were some in the Foreign Office who felt that if these

3. Younger brother of Chang Hsueh-liang and Chief of the Bureau of Public Safety, Tientsin municipal government.

issues took a turn for the worse, the cabinet should be put out of office to show the world that Japan was resolutely against any act committed in violation of international treaties. Only by taking drastic action was it thought that the nation could hope to retain a semblance of her former reputation.[4]

The concerns of army headquarters were quite different from those of the government. Uppermost in its mind was the setting up of a new regime in South Manchuria as rapidly as possible, leaving the thankless task of diplomatic adjustments to the Foreign Office. It has been indicated already that Major General Tatekawa was an outspoken proponent of this view, in opposition to Lieutenant Colonel Ishihara, who was strongly tempted to occupy Harbin in North Manchuria to head off a possible Soviet thrust from Siberia.[5]

Closely associated with the question of instituting an independent political regime in South Manchuria was the question whether to inaugurate Henry Pu-yi as head of a new government. Apparently the decision was cast in his favor for, as many had expected, he appeared in Mukden on November 13, 1931, as the result of the machinations of Colonel Doihara.[6] Doihara testified at the Tokyo Trials that although General Honjō, commanding officer of the Kwantung Army, was responsible for issuing orders to proceed to Tientsin, the details of his meeting with Henry Pu-yi were arranged by Colonel Itagaki. The latter cautioned Doihara when he was about to depart for Tientsin that Henry Pu-yi was not to be coerced into returning to Manchuria and that the matter ought to be left to his own discretion. If Pu-yi were willing, that would be all the better.[7] This rather minor incident again corroborates the view that, in matters of political strategy affecting the Kwantung Army, Colonel Itagaki was the real power and General Honjō was merely a figurehead.

4. *Harada Diary, 2,* 126–27.
5. See above, pp. 178–79.
6. See Hanaya, *Himerareta Shōwashi,* p. 50, for details.
7. IMTFE, *Proceedings,* pp. 15,727–28.

The Kwantung Army would not brook any interference from the Foreign Office on the question of Pu-yi. Kawashima, the Consul General at Tientsin, in describing the defiant attitude of the army in a top secret telegram[8] to Foreign Minister Shidehara on November 3, stated that Doihara had reminded the staff of the Japanese Consulate General at Tientsin that it had been solely through the actions of the Kwantung Army that Manchuria had been brought under Japanese control. If the time should come that enthronement of Pu-yi was necessary, the army would not tolerate interference from the government.

Doihara made it clear that if the Tokyo government persisted in obstructing the actions of the Kwantung Army, the army would secede from the government, and once it had attained autonomy, there was no telling what action it might choose to take. He then made the veiled threat that, in such an event, political troubles would descend upon Japan from unexpected quarters—such as from political assassins, who for the time being were under confinement.[9]

Although War Minister Minami did not say so outright, answers he made to Premier Wakatsuki on several occasions hardly left room for doubt that not only did he favor the establishment of a new regime in South Manchuria but he took its inevitability for granted. During the first week of October 1931 Wakatsuki summoned the Minister of War and explained:

> We should not have any part in setting up a new regime in Manchuria. If we do, we shall be going back on our own profession that we have no territorial ambitions. Not only would we be violating the Nine-Power Treaty, we would be making enemies of the whole world. We

8. Ibid.
9. IMTFE, *International Prosecution Section Document* (Tokyo, 1948), no. 290. IPS documents which are designated as IMT in *Uyehara Checklist* consisted of depositions, publications, memoirs, reports, etc. used for exhibits in the Tokyo Trials.

> stand a chance of being isolated by means of economic sanctions. Whatever the nature of the political entity which may attain independence in Manchuria, our negotiations must be carried out with the central Government [of China].[10]

To this the Minister of War retorted, "Then the status of Manchuria would revert right back to where it stood prior to the Mukden Incident."

About two weeks later Premier Wakatsuki was again sorely tried by an intemperate statement made by War Minister Minami: "There is no need to be restrained in our attitude toward the League and the like. What's wrong with quitting it? . . . If we are set on engaging the rest of the world in a war—that is, if we have the fortitude to do so—what is there to be feared?"[11]

Army headquarters favored General Tatekawa's views, however, with the result that few advocated military operations in northern Manchuria. The military protection which headquarters had sanctioned while the bridges over the Nonni River were being repaired was unavoidable, since the South Manchuria Railway Company claimed that the unimpeded flow of the soybean crop at the height of the harvest season was essential to the survival of this segment of the railway. But headquarters had grave misgivings that the Kwantung Army might advance too far north and stir the Russian army into action, in which event Japan would have had to cope with a real menace.

Meanwhile as repairs to the Nonni River bridges got under way, it was found that Lieutenant Colonel Ishihara had, for rather obvious reasons, been placed in charge of guarding the repair crews. While he was on his detail, he thought:

10. This statement was made by the Japanese government on September 24, 1931, after the Mukden Incident. *Harada Diary, 2,* 89, 482–83. Author's translation.

11. Ibid., p. 105. Author's translation.

> While we are taking time repairing the bridges, it is more than likely that Ma Chan-shan's forces will concentrate toward Tsitsihar and Angangchi. Meanwhile, we shall quietly assemble the Kwantung Army's main strength around Taonan and crush Ma's forces with a single blow. Russia has no intention of intervening at this stage. Therefore, if we cannot advance on Harbin directly,[12] we might as well clinch the control of northern Manchuria from the northwest region.[13]

Just as Ishihara had anticipated, the Heilungkiang troops—twenty to thirty thousand strong—converged on Tsitsihar and Angangchi. On November 7 the Kwantung Army opened an attack on the provincial forces stationed at Sanchienfang, twenty miles north of Tahsing. Between November 6 and 12 the Kwantung Army made four separate demands, each increasingly stringent, in which General Ma Chan-shan was asked to resign from the governorship of Heilungkiang Province in favor of General Chang Hai-peng and to withdraw his troops from Tsitsihar and Angangchi. In each instance General Ma replied that Tsitsihar had nothing to do with the Taonan-Angangchi Railway.

Wakatsuki, again deeply distressed, spoke to Harada of the government's plight:

> Please tell this only to Prince Saionji. At the cabinet meeting the Minister of War tried to push through a proposal to increase the number of troops in Man-

12. General Tatekawa was not the only one who objected to extending military operations into the northern plains of Manchuria. Premier Wakatsuki, concerned that the Kwangtung Army might extend its operations to Harbin, had Assistant Chief of General Staff Ninomiya wire the Kwantung Army on two separate occasions. See *Harada Diary, 2,* 73, 86. Another factor that delayed the Kwantung Army's direct assault on Harbin was the difference in gauge of the South Manchuria and Chinese Eastern Railways, necessitating alterations on the rolling stock. Morishima, *Conspiracy,* p. 64.

13. Matsumura, *Miyakezaka,* p. 53. Author's translation.

> churia, but he failed. At the time I told him firmly to halt the Kwantung Army this side of the Chinese Eastern Railway. So far I have made every effort to maintain our country's face by offering to the League explanations regarding the Kwantung Army's actions which, though at times rather flimsy, still had some semblance of truth. But if the army should ever advance beyond the Chinese Eastern Railway and attack Tsitsihar, I can no longer assume responsibility for its actions.[14]

On November 14 the Kwantung Army renewed its attacks, with the support of four airplanes. On the 16th General Honjō demanded that General Ma withdraw his troops to a point north of Tsitsihar and the Chinese Eastern Railway; Ma refused. On the 18th General Tamon launched an attack and occupied Tsitsihar the following day. With this the Kwantung Army attained the objective of its military operations in the northwest sector of Manchuria. General Ma retreated to Hailun, to which the temporary seat of the provincial government was also removed.

It is a truism to say that quite often activities that take place behind the scenes are more revealing of the true state of affairs than those that occur publicly. An episode of this kind, which suggests that there existed sharp differences in opinion among high-ranking officers of the General Staff, occurred at the temporary headquarters at Kumamoto during the closing days of the grand maneuvers. It appears that bitter words were exchanged by General Umezu Yoshijirō[15] and General Tatekawa, because Umezu had taken the liberty of altering the text of a telegram drafted initially under Tatekawa's supervision. Although General Matsumura, the narrator of the incident, does not recall the

14. Excerpts from statement made on November 16, 1931. *Harada Diary, 2,* 132–33. Author's translation.

15. As Chief of the General Affairs Department, General Umezu was immediately below the Assistant Chief of General Staff in rank and therefore General Tatekawa's superior.

exact content of the telegram, he is certain that it was addressed to the Kwantung Army. And if the episode occurred, as he states, very near the end of the maneuvers, it must have been on November 16, 17, or 18, when the Kwantung Army was girding itself for the assault on Tsitsihar.

When Umezu and Tatekawa took their arguments to General Kanaya, the Chief of the General Staff ruled in favor of Umezu. Knowing as we do something of the character of both Kanaya and Tatekawa, there is hardly a doubt that the text of the telegram drawn up by Tatekawa represented a point of view more extreme than that held by Umezu. Tatekawa left Kumamoto in a huff. Umezu, however, stayed on with the imperial cortege in order that the Emperor might be advised of any sudden new developments in North Manchuria.

At about the same time General Ninomiya, Assistant Chief of the General Staff, left for Manchuria to improve the rapidly deteriorating liaison between army headquarters in Tokyo and the Kwantung Army. During the absence of Ninomiya it fell upon Tatekawa to substitute for him, since General Umezu, next in the line of command, was still in Kumamoto. Tatekawa saw an opportunity to take revenge on Umezu. Instead of assuming Ninomiya's duties from his own office, Tatekawa took it upon himself to move into Ninomiya's office. One can well imagine the embarrassment of Umezu when he returned to Tokyo. Tatekawa had interposed himself betwen Umezu and General Kanaya and intercepted all the administrative papers from Kanaya to Umezu.

Officials of the Foreign Office in Manchuria also did not always see eye to eye with each other in regard to Japan's continental strategy. Shimizu Momokazu, Japanese Consul at Tsitsihar, was anxious to head off the Kwantung Army's assault on Tsitsihar. On or about November 16 he went to Mukden and met Itagaki, the Chief of Staff, and pleaded with him not to attack Tsitsihar. He stressed the fact that the safety of the Japanese residents there would not be jeopardized so long as the Kwantung Army did not bomb the city. Shimizu's plea fell on deaf ears, since Itagaki was bent on marching on Tsitsihar in any case. The Kwantung Army, soon after Shimizu's visit to Mukden, resorted to the now familiar ruse of ordering a hired ruffian to spark off a shooting incident in Tsitsihar, and the attack on the city was on.

Ōhashi Chūji, the Consul General at Harbin, was quite a different person. From the beginning of the Manchurian crisis he favored the actions of the Kwantung Army and strongly advocated sending an expeditionary force to North Manchuria.[16] It is therefore not at all surprising that he was at odds with the Foreign Office in Tokyo. Ōhashi, anticipating the occupation of Tsitsihar, sent a troupe of female entertainers from Harbin, who were turned back by Shimizu, fearful that they would corrupt public morale. Ōhashi then sent them to Tsitsihar, only to have them turned back again. The shuttling of the troupe back and forth reminded at least one observer of a scene from a comic opera.[17]

Once the Tsitsihar operation was under way, army headquarters at Tokyo ordered the Kwantung Army to withdraw to the railroad zone of the South Manchuria Railway as soon as Tsitsihar was taken. From Mukden came the reply: "The Ssu-Tao line[18] is damaged. It is hardly fit for use. If we detour and return by the Chinese Eastern Railway via Harbin, not only shall we be using a Russian line but we shall take about two weeks." Headquarters at Tokyo conceded that some part of the line might have been damaged, since only recently the railway areas had been the scene of battle. Nevertheless, headquarters reiterated its order in a second telegram: "Since the government has already committed itself at home and abroad to evacuate the troops to the railroad zone, withdraw from Tsitsihar as soon as possible."[19]

On November 26 a riot broke out in Tientsin for the second

16. Between September 22 and 24 Ōhashi sent, all told, three telegrams to Mukden requesting that troops be dispatched, in view of the extremely acute situation around Harbin. IMTFE, *Proceedings,* pp. 18, 912–14.

17. Morishima, *Conspiracy,* p. 66.

18. Railway running from Ssupingkai to Taonan.

19. Matsumura, *Miyakezaka,* pp. 56–57. Author's translation.

time.[20] It was engineered by the Army Special Service Agency of Colonel Doihara.[21] The staff officers of the Kwantung Army saw in the threatening situation at Tientsin a long-coveted opportunity to attack Chinchow under the pretext of sending reinforcements to the small Japanese garrison at Tientsin. Much to Tokyo's astonishment, the evacuation of Tsitsihar, which was supposed to require two weeks, was accomplished in a matter of a few days. By the time army headquarters received a telegram stating, "Disturbance in Tientsin, Kwantung Army is immediately advancing to Chinchow," one armored train, one troop train, and two airplanes had crossed the Liao River.[22] Incensed by the precipitate action of the Kwantung Army, army headquarters sent out a terse reminder that the "Kwantung Army must not advance beyond the Liao River." But from Mukden came an equivocal reply, "Cannons are booming at the front. Telephone line is down. No contact with the front yet." However, even after contact was established with the front, the Kwantung Army continued to advance in the direction of Chinchow.[23]

20. The first outbreak occurred on November 8, 1931. For details of both see the *Lytton Report,* pp. 75–77. Asahi, *Taiheiyō, 2,* 93–95.

21. When Harada went to Okitsu on November 24, Saionji said, "I am inclined to think that the Kwantung Army will not attack Chinchow. However, caution must be exercised, since this is a grave issue. Will you therefore approach Ugaki [then Governor General of Korea] in private and ask him to exert his every effort, so that an attack on Chinchow will be absolutely averted? Tell him that Saionji is extremely concerned." The same day Harada returned to Tokyo and saw Ugaki at his daughter's wedding reception at the Imperial Hotel. Ugaki said, "I have just had a talk with the Chief of the General Staff and the Minister of War. Neither thought Chinchow would be attacked, but I shall make further efforts to stress this point." *Harada Diary, 2,* 141–42. Author's translation.

22. Matsumura, *Miyakezaka,* p. 57. Author's translation. This unauthorized mobilization of the Kwantung Army must be distinguished from an order that army headquarters at Tokyo sent to Port Arthur to dispatch one battalion to Tientsin. The action was taken in accordance with the decision reached at a special cabinet meeting on November 27. *Harada Diary, 2,* 143. It is presumed that this expeditionary force proceeded by ship from Port Arthur to Tientsin. It could have been a countermove to head off the Kwantung Army's unauthorized movement by railway.

23. It was alleged that the code officer failed to insert the negative par-

After news of the army's movement toward Chinchow began trickling into Tokyo, Shidehara had to wait a whole day before he saw the Minister of War who had gone away for the weekend. When Shidehara told Minami about the rumor, the latter asked the Foreign Minister to wait while he checked the news with Kanaya, but Kanaya had received no communication about a march on Chinchow. He said that he would investigate immediately, since quite often bureau and departmental chiefs disposed of incoming telegrams on their own responsibility.

That night Minami, clad in full-dress uniform and apparently unconcerned about Chinchow, left for the Imperial Palace to attend a ceremony. His parting words to Shidehara were that the Chief of the General Staff would get in touch with him later. Shidehara, on the other hand, declined the invitation from the palace and waited all evening in his office at the Foreign Office for the report from Kanaya. Finally, at about 11 P.M., he received a telephone call. Kanaya had looked everywhere but had not located the telegram from the Kwantung Army. He promised that he would continue the search and report again.

The following morning an adjutant came to Shidehara from the office of the General Staff and reported, "At this very moment, the Chief of the General Staff is being received by the Emperor. He has received an imperial instruction ordering the troops sent to Chinchow to be withdrawn to Mukden."[24] At last Shidehara felt momentary relief from anxiety.

The *Lytton Report* refers to the crisis as follows: "The Kwantung Army repeatedly bombed Chinchow, but news of the improved situation at Tientsin soon deprived the expedition of its original object and, on November 29, to the great surprise of the Chinese, the Japanese forces were withdrawn to Hsinmin."[25]

---

ticle *zu* in the telegram which ordered the Kwantung Army "not" to cross the Liao River. Matsumura, *Miyakezaka*, p. 58.

24. *Shidehara Memoirs*, pp. 79–80. Author's translation.

25. *Lytton Report*, p. 77.

Henry L. Stimson, in his *Far Eastern Crisis,* expressed his admiration for Shidehara's stout heart—how single-handedly he had compelled the withdrawal of the Kwantung Army from Chinchow.[26] However, Shidehara, in his *Fifty Years of Diplomacy,* disclaims any credit for the alleged feat and ascribes it to General Kanaya, who without even consulting him had compelled the withdrawal of the Kwantung Army.[27]

Only later did it become known that the young officers of the Kwantung Army on the scene had become so incensed by the restraining order that they had gone on a rampage marked by vandalism and property destruction. But, since General Kanaya[28] remained adamant, they had given in and retreated to Mukden.

26. Stimson wrote: "But whatever the reason, Shidehara made on this occasion a very vigorous effort and for once was temporarily successful." *The Far Eastern Crisis* (New York, Harper, 1936), p. 78.

27. *Shidehara Memoirs,* p. 80.

28. An episode indicative of General Kanaya's character is cited by Shidehara in his *Memoirs.* It occurred some time in the early part of 1932. The General by then had resigned from the post of Chief of the General Staff, because of the October Plot. Shidehara was also no longer associated with the Foreign Office, the Inukai cabinet of the opposition party having taken over in the preceding December. One day Kanaya sent a note to Shidehara, who was then residing in Kamakura in semi-retirement, inviting him to dinner in Tokyo. Shidehara, reluctant to go to Tokyo, at first declined, but since Kanaya persisted by sending his aide, Shidehara gave in and went to the Japanese restaurant which Kanaya had designated. There, much to Shidehara's surprise, he found Kanaya with only two or three of his aides. When Shidehara took his place in the room, the General bade the waitresses to withdraw to an adjoining room. Thereupon Kanaya approached Shidehara. As the General solemnly bowed on his hands and knees, he said, "No person is more painfully aware of the untold troubles I have caused you while you were the Minister of Foreign Affairs. I am responsible and feel deeply mortified that matters have been allowed to come to such a pass on account of my incompetency. That is why I have asked for your presence in order that I may at least tender my sincere regrets. I therefore beg you to understand my motive for having invited you here today." Shidehara related that he was deeply impressed by Kanaya's forthrightness, so much so that after World War II he reported the incident to a member of the prosecution section of the International Tribunal for War Crimes. *Shidehara Memoirs,* pp. 183–84. Author's translation.

7.
COLLAPSE OF THE WAKATSUKI CABINET

The Kwantung Army stalked the Chinese army like a beast after its prey. The League Council meanwhile passed a resolution stipulating that Japanese troops withdraw within the railway zone by November 16. This made the helpless Premier Wakatsuki all the more nervous. Equally at a loss was Tani Masayuki, Chief of the Asia Bureau of the Foreign Office, who deplored the fact that the reckless actions of the Kwantung Army had brought Japan to the brink of ruin. As a diplomat he felt he could no longer bear the brunt of the censures directed against Japan from many quarters of the world.

At this juncture the nation's conduct of foreign relations was further compromised by forces bent on subverting the government from within. Foreign Minister Shidehara had to back down and make a series of concessions to the army lest extremist elements attempt another coup d'état on the order of the March and October Plots. Despite Japan's rapidly deteriorating reputation, Shidehara no longer dared insist that the Kwantung Army comply with the League resolution and retreat within the railway zone. Needless to say, the Foreign Minister's decision left the position of Japan's delegation at Geneva virtually untenable.

After the October Plot was foiled, it was decided at a meeting of the Big Three that the Chief of the General Staff and the Minister of War should jointly assume the responsibility for the abortive plot and resign. Wakatsuki, confronted with the task of appointing a successor to Minami, wondered whether it would be at all possible to obtain closer cooperation from a new war minister than he had received from Minami. The Premier was exasperated with Minami's laxity in carrying out the cabinet's decision during the crisis. In his memoirs Wakatsuki states:

> I came to the conclusion that the reason the Kwantung Army slighted the government's order was that the cabinet consisted only of the members of the Minseitō. Therefore, it represented the opinion of only a segment of the public and did not necessarily reflect the views of the majority. Hence, if a coalition cabinet were to be formed, the Kwantung Army might obey the government's orders, since such a cabinet would then represent the wishes of the whole nation. Thereupon, I decided to find out if it were feasible to form a coalition government under the existing party system.[1]

Still, Wakatsuki was not completely convinced of either the desirability or feasibility of a coalition government, and he turned to elderly Adachi Kenzō,[2] his Minister of Home Affairs,

1. *Wakatsuki Memoirs,* pp. 383–84. Author's translation. Wakatsuki, to be sure, was aware of the grumbling voiced from quarters outside his own party. To cite a few, Lieutenant General Matsui Iwane told Harada that a quick change of cabinet was imperative, since the military harbored intense enmity toward Wakatsuki and Shidehara. The tension would be greatly lessened were Adachi Kenzō to become premier and Inukai Tsuyoshi vice premier, thereby forming a coalition cabinet of the Minseitō and the Seiyūkai. Mori Kaku, the Seiyūkai extremist, told Harada that unless there was a change in the government "the present unrest will not be quelled." On another occasion, looking forward to the 60th Session of the Diet to convene on December 26, Mori said: "Even if it means bloodshed, we will not permit the majority party [the Minseitō] to act willfully." Shiraki, *Nihon Seitōshi,* p. 92. Author's translation.

2. Adachi, a man of sixty-eight, was a veteran politician who had good reason to feel that the Premier should defer to him in matters of such importance. He was Wakatsuki's senior in age, and when Hamaguchi had resigned, he had stepped aside, because of his rapidly advancing years, and personally solicited Wakatsuki to assume the presidency of the Minseitō, though he had coveted the position himself.

for advice. When Wakatsuki asked Adachi, if there were any way to stabilize the political situation, Adachi replied that at this juncture, there was no formula but to rise above party differences and form a coalition cabinet. Since Wakatsuki was at his wit's end, he must have lent an attentive and conceivably even a sympathetic ear to Adachi's proposal.

On October 31 Wakatsuki admitted to Harada that for several days after his conversation with Adachi he was in favor of the idea, but he had to give it up. Shidehara and Inoue, the two most influential members of the cabinet, were firmly against any form of coalition. Their principal objection was that if the Minseitō were to join hands with the Seiyūkai, the current foreign and financial policies would have to be overhauled, to the detriment of the nation's best interests. The two ministers earnestly besought Wakatsuki to give up the idea.

Wakatsuki now showed signs of wavering. His vacillation, however, only incited Adachi to advocate even more vociferously the cause of a coalition cabinet. Therefore, to put an end to any further exploratory talk, Wakatsuki summoned Adachi and asked him to drop the idea, because influential members of the cabinet had voiced strong objection to the proposal. Adachi persisted that his idea was an inspired one, but, since Wakatsuki would not yield, Adachi acquiesced for the time being, and soon afterward joined the imperial cortege and left for Kumamoto to attend the army's grand maneuvers.

Meanwhile, the members of the Wakatsuki cabinet,[3] alarmed by the turn of events, consulted each other while Adachi was away. They agreed to fight to the bitter end any attempt to form a coalition cabinet and also to dissuade Wakatsuki from entertaining such a notion.

Adachi, having arrived in Kumamoto, called on General Araki

3. This group included Inoue Junnosuke, Finance; Tanaka Ryūzō, Education; Machida Chūzō, Agriculture and Forestry; Sakurauchi Yukio, Commerce and Industry; Koizumi Matajirō, Post Office; and Hara Shūjirō, Railroads.

several times. Araki had by then become the Commander of the Fifth Division. Although no one knows the subjects of these private conversations, it is highly probable that the two touched upon a change in the government.

It has been alleged that on the night of October 16, when General Araki went to placate and to dissuade Hashimoto, Chō, and his group from staging the October Plot, he was forced to promise them that he would help overthrow the Wakatsuki government.[4] It is thus likely that there was a close meeting of minds between Adachi and Araki. Adachi must have felt emboldened after having received the backing of a general who was the idol of young officers and whose star was rapidly rising. Actually, Adachi had been intrigued by the idea of a nonparty pro-military government even before he had gone to see Araki in Kumamoto. On the night of November 4 Adachi summoned Harada to his residence and confided, "I am intent on pushing this through on the basis of coalition. I believe the way to go about it is to get the military's understanding, then make the Minseitō and the Seiyūkai join hands."[5]

In a buoyant mood, Adachi had started back to Tokyo when he was cornered by press reporters at Shimonoseki. When the question of coalition government was put to him, he no longer could resist the temptation. Despite Wakatsuki's repeated requests not to speak on the question of a coalition government, Adachi stated that the political situation called for just that. Since the pronouncement came directly from the mouth of the Minister of Home Affairs, it created a great sensation. Moreover, it gave rise to many adverse rumors, undermining the nation's confidence in the Wakatsuki government. Wakatsuki waited until Adachi arrived in Tokyo and remonstrated with him for his ill-advised utterances. Adachi again countered with his pet theory that it was the initial inspiration which was always the most natural and the best.

4. See above, p. 199.
5. *Harada Diary, 2,* 116. Author's translation.

On the Seiyūkai side, Tokonami Takejirō, Kuhara Fusanosuke, and even Hatoyama Ichirō, were said to be in favor of coalition government. Only Mori Kaku and members of the Suzuki clique were staunchly opposed to it. Nevertheless, to undermine the position of the Minseitō, the Seiyūkai on November 11 passed a resolution at their party caucus favoring a ban on the export of gold. The resolution had an immediate effect on the coalition movement.[6] President Inukai was now certain that the two parties would be unable to agree on a working arrangement, since his party had spelled out a financial policy at complete variance with that of the opposition. Inukai is quoted as observing: "British political parties vie with each other over the choice of policy. Therefore, if several parties can reach accord over a matter of policy, parties can join hands. However, in Japan, the prime object of parties is to dominate the government, so it is not within the nature of political parties to coalesce."[7] Furthermore, Inukai was of the opinion that the political situation was not particularly suitable for a coalition cabinet.

On the Minseitō side, after the Seiyūkai resolved to ban gold exports, party interests dictated that Wakatsuki assume an uncompromising attitude toward any proposal to form a coalition government. Any abrupt change of cabinet would have affected adversely the financial interests operating in line with the free and flexible exchange policy of Inoue, the Minister of Finance. Furthermore, Wakatsuki feared that the rumor of an imminent change in government might spread panic in the financial world and induce a flight of capital.

Kuhara Fusanosuke, Secretary General of the Seiyūkai, was quick to see that the breach between Wakatsuki and Adachi was pregnant with possibilities for furthering his own political fortunes. By astute manipulation of the coalition theme he could not only hasten the collapse of the Wakatsuki cabinet but steal a march on his political rivals by ushering in a reconstructed gov-

6. See below, pp. 227–29.
7. Shiraki, *Nihon Seitōshi,* p. 95. Author's translation.

ernment oriented toward the new political movement spearheaded by army men. It appeared that he might be able to kill two birds with one stone.

However, Wakatsuki himself was largely responsible for abetting the coalition movement. It was he who had first lent a sympathetic ear to Adachi's proposal. But even more far-reaching in effect was the prevalent notion that Wakatsuki was too weak a premier to face the crisis on two fronts—at home and in Manchuria. Allusion has already been made to the fact that at the time of the Mukden Incident, Kido Kōichi had criticized Wakatsuki's timidity.[8] Later, on New Year's Day of 1932, Harada reports having heard Saionji say, "When I learned that Wakatsuki was going around calling on the Elder Statesmen, I had a strong premonition that he had made a fatal move."[9]

Because of the official positions Kuhara and Adachi held in their respective parties, neither man dared approach the other openly.[10] However, Kuhara found ready collaborators in Tomita Kojirō[11] and Nakano Seigō,[12] both of whom were members of Adachi's clique. On December 10 Tomita suddenly confronted Wakatsuki with a Tomita-Kuhara agreement. In brief the pact provided that, irrespective of the party affiliation of the individual

8. See above, pp. 192–94.

9. *Harada Diary, 2,* 169. Author's translation.

10. Kuhara had told Prince Saionji, "I have not met with Adachi, but have met with Mr. Tomita in regard to coalition government" (*Harada Diary, 2,* 151). Despite Kuhara's profession to Saionji, it is inconceivable that the two men did not have a tacit understanding. Their names were inseparably linked in the minds of the public as men who plotted the downfall of the Wakatsuki cabinet. That Kuhara had committed himself to the cause of a coalition cabinet is borne out by the following incident. After Inukai became the premier, he asked Kuhara to become the chief secretary of the party. Kuhara was greatly troubled and the story was that he consented only after he had cleared himself with Adachi. Tsugumo Kunitoshi, "Kuromaku, Kuhara Fusanosuke" (Kuhara, The Wire Puller), *Fūun Jinbutsu Tokuhon,* p. 187.

11. A member of the Lower House of the Diet, a counselor of the Minseitō.

12. A member of the Lower House of the Diet and the manager of the Minseitō.

who would be asked to form the next cabinet by imperial mandate, the heads of both parties would meet and distribute the portfolios for cabinet officials and parliamentary vice ministers equally among the men of both parties. Needless to say, the pact had been reached in private between Kuhara and Tomita only and did not bear the official stamp of approval of either party.

The coalition government envisaged by Adachi, Kuhara, or Tomita did not represent a last stand of the party men to bury the hatchet and unite in order to stave off the encroachment of army men on party government. Quite the contrary, these men saw in the rising tide of military influence in government an opportunity by which they might further their own political fortunes. Publicly they may have paid lip service to the preservation of a party form of government, but privately they curried the favor of influential military men.[13] Adachi was doing exactly the same thing Mori had done in January of the same year: he was employing the army as a lever to dislodge the opposition.

It has been noted that among the members of the Seiyūkai, only Mori and those of Suzuki's clique were opposed to any kind of coalition government. Mori's long association with the army from the days of Premier Tanaka made him an avowed foe of Shidehara's China policy, and he saw no reason why party government should be allowed to continue in decrepit form. It may be recalled that during the March Plot the three generals—Ninomiya, Koiso, and Tatekawa—summoned Lieutenant Colonel Suzuki Teiichi to the official residence of the Minister of War one night and summarily ordered him: "Go immediately to

13. Reference has been made earlier to Adachi's visits to General Araki during the former's stay in Kumamoto at the time of the grand maneuvers. To cite another instance, at a cabinet meeting in the latter part of September when Shidehara put a difficult question to Minami regarding the unauthorized movement of the Kwantung Army, Adachi defended Minami. After this minor incident, Adachi is said to have curried the good will of the army. See *Harada Diary, 2,* 85. With respect to Nakano Seigō, Harada wrote, "Take, for instance, Nakano Seigō. There is even a rumor that he has been calling on General Araki every day." Ibid., p. 127. Author's translation.

Mori of the Seiyūkai and explain to him that you come on order of the Minister of War, and instruct Mori to take measures to keep the Diet in a state of confusion."[14] Again during the period immediately preceding the October Plot, it was Mori who apparently had advance information on the doings of the young officers.[15] He is said to have gone about predicting the big coup d'état which was to come any day.

On the same day that Tomita confronted Wakatsuki with the Kuhara-Tomita agreement, the Premier summoned all cabinet ministers who were members of the Minseitō party to his residence for a conference. Only Adachi failed to appear. Those who were present decided to continue the cabinet as it was then constituted. Meanwhile, Wakatsuki sent three men to Adachi urging him to join the meeting, but he refused in each instance. The last to go was Tanaka Ryūzō, Minister of Education. He urged Adachi to submit a letter of resignation, but Adachi would not do so, stating that he would resign only on condition that all the other members of the cabinet did likewise. Wakatsuki's time was

14. Ibid., pp. 22–23. Author's translation.

15. Mori's true colors became increasingly apparent with the passage of time. In the spring of 1932, as the army became disgruntled with Inukai's government, it sought to replace Inukai with a cabinet headed by Hiranuma. Mori promptly parted company with his former friends of the Seiyūki, such as Hatoyama (see the following for details), and set out to engineer the collapse of the Inukai cabinet from within with the backing of the Araki-Mazaki clique—the Kōdō-ha. Inukai quickly saw Mori's design and allied himself with Kuhara. But Inukai's long political career came to an abrupt end when he fell at the hands of the young officers in the May 15 Incident of 1932. Hatoyama said: "It was during the days of the Inukai cabinet that I got into a heated argument with Mori in the Chief Secretary's Office [of the Seiyūkai]. Mori disapproved the path I was treading, saying that times had changed. He said that if I persisted in adhering to my type of thinking, my life would be in peril." Mori said, "I will assure your position and reputation for you; so let me handle this matter my way. Do not interfere with me. I have no political ambition except to see that the problem of China is settled. In matters of domestic politics, I shall respect your opinion to the bitter end." Hatoyama retorted, "I'll take care of my own life so do not worry. However, your idea is mistaken." And they parted company in tears. Yamaura, *Mori Kaku,* p. 506. Author's translation.

up. The following day, December 11, all the members of the cabinet, including Adachi, submitted their resignations. Thereupon, Adachi, Tomita, Nakano, and six other members of Adachi's clique seceded from the Minseitō.

Although no one has succeeded in determining whether the two events are interrelated, it is often alleged that the heavy purchase of dollar funds by large business interests in Japan throttled the coalition movement and thereby hastened the fall of the Wakatsuki cabinet.

When London chose to go off the gold standard on September 22, 1931, it is a fact that the major banks in Japan had to build up their dollar funds in New York. Taking the British action as a sign of the future, Japanese financiers suspected that it was but a question of time until Japan, too, would have to suspend her shipments of gold. In such an event the value of the yen on the exchange market would inevitably decline, and those who waited until then to convert their dollar funds into yen would receive more yen for the dollar than those who converted before the ban on gold shipments. Initially, the purchase of dollar funds began as a measure of expediency, but it later turned into a speculative venture, especially after the Seiyūkai at its party caucus passed a resolution favoring a ban on gold shipments.[16] From then on, the flight of capital from Japan shifted into high gear.

Inoue, Minister of Finance, countered the Seiyūkai's public statement with an announcement that the Minseitō government would under no circumstance resort to a ban on gold shipments.

16. On September 12, 1917, Japan followed America in placing a ban on the export of gold. In the summer of 1929 the Minseitō party returned to office. Inoue Junnosuke, the Finance Minister, was a firm believer in balanced budgets and free gold movements—in short, in "orthodox" financial policy. Inoue managed to convince his colleagues and the business world that exchange fluctuations were in the long run more detrimental to Japan's future development than any inconveniences that would attend a return to the gold standard. The gold embargo was lifted on November 21, 1929. Perhaps the most authoritative account of the "purchase of dollars" is Ikeda Seihin's own story in Yatsugi, *Shōwa Jinbutsu Hiroku,* pp. 100–18.

Nevertheless, during the months of October and November 1931 gold shipments out of Japan reached 285 million yen, heavily depleting the supply of gold specie held by the Bank of Japan. Ikeda Seihin, managing director of the Bank of Mitsui, estimated that the total capital flight in this period ranged between 500 and 600 million yen. This was a sizable part of the funds held by the Bank of Japan, for immediately prior to the resumption of gold shipments in 1929 it had amounted to over one billion yen.

Thus, many were able to argue that the large business interests of Japan, by heavy buying of dollars, had irrevocably committed themselves to a policy of waiting for the expected depreciation in the exchange rate of the yen that would follow a gold embargo. They had thus assumed a position from which they could not withdraw. Either the Seiyūkai had to replace the Minseitō or big business interests stood to sustain a heavy loss. Therefore, the suspicion grew that there may have been collusion between the Adachi-Kuhara coalition cabinet movement and the big business interests which had invested heavily in dollar funds.

As maintained previously, evidence has not been uncovered to substantiate the suspicion that the large financial interests abetted Adachi, Kuhara, or Tomita in upsetting the Wakatsuki cabinet. Moreover, Ikeda Seihin, the mainstay of Mitsui interests, has stated that in the capital transfer from yen to dollar, Japanese banks actually sustained huge net losses, running into the millions: Mitsubishi Bank, 80 million yen; Bank of Mitsui, 10 million yen; and Sumitomo Bank, about 5 million yen.

Ikeda further has stated that when he became Minister of Finance in 1938 under the first Konoe government, he ordered a thorough study of the incident, and it was substantiated that the purchase of dollar funds did not result in profits.

Nevertheless, the public could not overlook the fact that, after the ban on gold shipments, the exchange rate of the yen in relation to the dollar declined by 20 per cent. With it there was an appreciable rise in the price of consumer goods. The night the ban went into force, two department stores in Tokyo had their clerks work all night to retag their merchandise with higher prices. The rise in wages lagged behind, with the result that wage earners were caught in a squeeze.

When Baba Tsunego, a well-known journalist, wrote a scathing editorial about the alleged exorbitant profits—60 million yen—reaped by the zaibatsu in a time of acute depression, it fanned the resentment of the public all the more. The term "purchase of dollars" thus came to be associated with a change of government, and became a byword for the corruption of the political parties and big business interests. And such a trend in public opinion gave the national reconstruction movement centered around the military a convenient pretext for resorting to direct action to liquidate these two alleged sources of evil in Japan: big business interests and party government.

8.
PRELUDE TO TRAGEDY

Despite the mounting crisis at home and abroad, it did not appear in the spring of 1931 that Japan as a nation was on the verge of large-scale revolution. Quite the contrary, the bureaucracy went about its routines at a seemingly unhurried pace, and it may well have been its complacency that spurred the military and the extremists to proceed with their plans with so much zeal.

Certain public figures, moreover, despite a belief that the correct policy lay in maintaining the status quo at home and preserving peace abroad, found it expedient for political reasons to pay lip service to expansionist sentiments. For some this may have been the reaction of an innate conservatism to the unrestrained liberal tendencies of the twenties. Tanaka belonged to this category; Premier and simultaneously Minister of Foreign Affairs, he was never the architect of the China policy that bore his name.

While Tanaka as an old soldier decried Japan's waning influence in China and blamed the conciliatory policy of the opposition party for it, his confidant was furtively engaged behind the scenes in negotiations with the Chinese authorities. This was not to the liking of the expansionists, who were clamoring for more forceful means to break the momentum of the fiery rights recovery movement and thus restore Japan to her former position of influence in Manchuria and China.

Behind Premier Tanaka stood the true molder of his China policy—Mori Kaku, Parliamentary Vice Minister of Foreign

Affairs, who in the early months of Tanaka's government convened the Eastern Regions Conference in Tokyo to outline to the diplomats and military officials summoned from China and Manchuria his own version of the "positive policy." The occasion was momentous, for Mori at this conference finally sanctioned the kind of direct action which the extremists of the Kwantung Army had for some time been advocating. In short, by his action Mori gave direct impetus to a development that ended with the Mukden Incident.

Mori had no scruples about arousing the antagonism of the Chinese. Despite the misgivings voiced by both Tanaka and the army and despite strenuous opposition from the officials of the Foreign Office stationed in China, in 1927 and 1928 Mori willfully sent military expeditions to Shantung. The second expedition brought on a direct clash between Chinese and Japanese troops, which required more than two years of painstaking negotiations to settle.

Mori planned to occupy Manchuria in May 1928, and only Tanaka's veto at the final moment prevented a precipitating incident from occurring at that time. Although Tanaka momentarily restrained the Kwantung Army from going on the warpath, the irate officers gave vent to their anger by assassinating Chang Tso-lin. Thus again a Sino-Japanese clash became only a question of time, since under Chang Hsueh-liang, his successor, relations between the two countries became even more strained.

At home Mori advocated withdrawal from the League, so that Japan could pursue unimpeded her expansionist goals in Manchuria. In order to strengthen Japan's war potential, he declared that free enterprise should be restrained, that essential industries such as insurance, banking, navigation, fishing, and silk should be nationalized. He decried trading practices which permitted basic staples such as rice to become objects of speculation on the open market.

Mori's prescription for creating a highly centralized form of government was for politicians and the military to join hands in forming a single mass party. In practice, however, he drew much more heavily on the army than on civilians to back his expansionist program and to exert pressure upon the rival party in government. By utilizing the army as his political tool Mori, more than any other individual in Japan's recent history, provided the military with convenient access to Japan's political structure. This, indeed, is a grave accusation, for in the end it was the reckless behavior of the army in China which brought onto Japan her disastrous defeat in World War II.

Less obvious but highly important was the all-pervasive influence exerted by Mori's political philosophy upon many up-and-coming officials in the government. Most notable among this group was Prince Konoe Fumimaro, who thrice became premier between 1937 and 1941, a decisive period in Japan's modern history. He described his debt to Mori in 1940:

> Because of the stimulus I received from Mori, my face was turned toward a new political order. It was through him that I was afforded the opportunity of meeting men in military and other walks of life who were adherents of the philosophy underlying the new political order. Again it was through Mori that I began to entertain deep concern for Manchuria. Indeed, Mori was the predecessor who drew me into the circle of the new political order.[1]

Although Tanaka's name has over the years become a byword for Japan's sinister designs on the continent, he was neither a chauvinist nor an expansionist.[2] He was in large measure a victim of his subordinates—men like Mori Kaku and his firebrands of the Kwantung Army who stopped at nothing to fulfill their

1. Yamaura, *Mori Kaku,* pp. iii–iv. Author's free translation.
2. See *Ugaki Memoirs,* pp. 315–17, for General Ugaki's account of Tanaka's own formula for the solution of the international problems posed by Manchuria.

expansionist ambitions, and, in the process, together with the Seiyūkai's policy toward China, brought upon Tanaka the unearned opprobrium of the world.

Mori was a proponent of expansionism, the direct actionists attempted to implement his type of program through a series of conspiracies, plots, and assassinations. Notable among this group were Colonel Kōmoto Daisaku, Ōkawa Shūmei, Lieutenant Colonel Hashimoto Kingorō, and Major Hanaya Tadashi. The boastful utterances and chauvinistic actions of these men can hardly be considered as coming from stable individuals, and in fact they would have made appropriate subjects for psychiatric study.[3] They behaved contemptuously toward those who sought compromise solutions, including even their immediate superiors. Many were woefully lacking in any sense of responsibility even toward the immediate members of their families, not to speak of the society of which they were a part.

It should not occasion surprise, therefore, to find that individuals whose dealings with their own society were irresponsible behaved with criminal irresponsibility in the international sphere. The fact was that these extremists regarded the efforts of the Foreign Office to abide by the terms of international agreements as sheer cowardice and lack of patriotism. In seeking an explanation for their excessive behavior, we become aware that we are studying what might be termed the anatomy of over-reaction.

In the most general terms, when the status or the existence of a nation or a group with a strong identity is threatened from within or without, it is not uncommon for an individual or a group of individuals to decide to risk their personal welfare in

3. In this connection attention is called to four very penetrating essays by Professor Maruyama Masao: "Chō-kokka Shugi no Ronri to Shinri" (The Rationale and Psychology Underlying Ultranationalism), "Nihon Fashizumu no Shisō to Undō" (Ideology and Movements Pertaining to Japanese Fascism), "Gunkoku Shihaisha no Seishin Keitai" (The Gestalt of the Elites of Militarism), and "Nihon ni Okeru Nashonarizumu" (Nationalism in Japan). These articles, together with supplementary footnotes, are included in his *Gendai Seiji no Shisō to Kōdō* (Thoughts and Actions Underlying Contemporary Politics), *1* (Tokyo, 1958).

what they feel to be the best interests of the nation or group. That the individual thereby catapults himself into the limelight tends to reinforce his sense of mission—as a hero, Messiah, martyr, patriot, or whatever. This tendency, if one may hazard a guess, seems especially strong in an authoritarian society such as Japan, where the ego's needs are often submerged in the interests of the group without leaving the individual any socially acceptable means of redress. Thus rebellion against authority, when it comes, tends to be more violent and irrational than in a less suppressive society, and it characteristically starts under the banner of patriotism or national interest. Only by positing such assumptions can the behavior of the direct actionists in Japan be properly understood. In the early thirties certain self-styled patriots felt that a need existed to surmount the domestic and international crisis. And in view of the—to them—hopelessly inadequate political means available for a solution, they felt driven to resort to erratic, irresponsible, and desperate actions which seriously jeopardized the long-term national interests of Japan. The assassinations of Chang Tso-lin and Premier Hamaguchi, the abortive March and October Plots, and the Mukden Incident belong to this category.

The welling crises in Manchuria and at home patently demanded decisiveness in thinking and action by the government, but decisiveness was sadly lacking. While Saburi and Shigemitsu as representatives of the Japanese government made every effort to keep channels of communication open with the Chinese, Shidehara and Wakatsuki dared not take steps which even suggested a conciliatory attitude, lest such a move provoke the army extremists to go on a rampage and create untoward incidents.

At this point the crux of the problem reveals itself as the old question of the place of the military in the Japanese government. We may note in passing that for a variety of reasons Itō and his legal advisers found it necessary to clothe the Meiji Constitution in the garb of constitutional monarchy and yet provide for the independence of the supreme command. In the late twenties and early thirties, societal strains and inequities of every description that had been contained for many years under the governmental program of forced modernization came to a head in the form of a crucial question: Should not this fiction inherent in Japan's political structure be resolved once and for all?

Wakatsuki cannot be absolved from the charge that he failed to provide strong political leadership when Japan needed it most. Vigorous action was a necessity if only to revive the confidence of the people in the parliamentary form of government, but Wakatsuki, a former bureaucrat, may well have lacked confidence in the future of parliamentary government. A revealing incident in this regard is cited by Harada Kumao.

Shortly before the Mukden Incident, Harada asked Premier Wakatsuki's opinion on the Emperor's role in forming a cabinet. Should the Emperor remind a party president forming a new cabinet to exercise care in the selection of ministers so that only men of upright character and reputation would be appointed, thereby restoring the confidence of the people in political parties?

Wakatsuki's reply is interesting because it reveals his mental reservations on parliamentary government: "If it should ever become the practice for the Emperor to direct his queries exclusively toward the presidents of parties, this would carry a strong overtone that the Emperor himself sanctions party rule as being the proper mode of His Imperial Highness' government in the future."[4]

If Wakatsuki was powerless to restrain the unruly Kwantung Army, was this not the moment for the Premier or Prince Saionji to advise the Emperor to invoke his prerogative to bring the army into line? Prince Saionji was firmly set against it. Did he perform an effective role as the last surviving Elder Statesman?

Prince Saionji in his youth had spent ten years in France absorbing the liberal political traditions of the West and was undoubtedly the most enlightened of the Elder Statesmen who in their lifetime had often acted as a balance wheel between the

4. *Harada Diary, 2,* 59–60. Author's free translation.

parliamentary forces and the military. Two factors, however, left him relatively powerless in the herculean task of restraining the military both at home and abroad in the critical thirties: his personality and his age. As a scion of the effete court nobility of Kyoto, he tended to be overly gentle and lacking in the militant spirit and iron resolve necessary for his role as arbiter; and his advanced years—he was already in his eighties and in failing health—further robbed him of the energy required for his exacting role.[5]

The Emperor, who sternly disapproved of the arbitrary actions of the Kwantung Army and indeed on a number of occasions expressed his desire for the restoration of friendly relations with China, often volunteered to assume the arbiter's role, perhaps to compensate for the weak role Saionji was performing. The Emperor suggested in late October of 1931 that he summon Premier Wakatsuki and War Minister Minami to discuss the current Manchurian situation.

This meeting never took place, however, because Saionji firmly advised against it. Not only did he seriously doubt that such meetings could accomplish anything of consequence, he also suspected that should a decision be reached only to be disobeyed by the army, the position of the throne would be compromised. Saionji therefore insisted to the bitter end that the Emperor should never be made to assume personal responsibility for any act of state.

One wonders if Saionji ever fully appreciated the crippling effect which the passing of the institution of the Elder Statesmen from the political scene in Japan had on practical aspects of government.[6] As the solitary surviving Elder Statesman, Saionji

5. For an excellent portrayal of Prince Saionji, see "Saigo no Genrō, Saionji Kinmochi" (Saionji, The Last Elder Statesman), in Oka Yoshitake, *Kindai Nihon no Seijika* (Statesmen of Recent Japan) (Tokyo, 1960), esp. pp. 203–04, 227–28, 235.

6. After the death of two Elder Statesmen from Satsuma, Kuroda Kiyotaka in 1900 and Saigō Tsugumichi in 1902, the balance of power in that body shifted to the Chōshū faction with Itō Hirobumi, Yamagata

no longer enjoyed the powerful influence previously wielded by this extraconstitutional body in directing the domestic and foreign policies of Japan. While he retained in his person the important function of nominating premiers, he no longer performed the function which the exigencies of the time made even more essential—reconciling the differences between the cabinet and the high command. During the Meiji era joint sessions of the Elder Statesmen and the principal cabinet officials, or of these two bodies with the high command, had been held to iron out differences and to facilitate the unimpeded operation of these governmental agencies.

Once the powerful institution of Elder Statesmen wasted away, who would step in to resolve the dualism inherent in the constitutional structure of Japanese government? That there existed a genuine need for such a body was brought to a sharp focus under the stresses of the Manchurian crisis when Premier Wakatsuki, out of desperation, made a round of calls on senior statesmen and opposition leaders to effect some sort of solution.

Saionji, however, was deeply distressed by Wakatsuki's precipitate action and told Harada, his aide, that any action which tended to revive obsolete bodies such as the conference of Elder Statesmen was anachronistic and ran contrary to the growth of constitutional government. It is true that Japan possessed a written constitution, but because of its origin and structure it was not the sort from which the eventual evolution of a responsible government in the Western sense could be expected.

A pragmatic approach to one of the gravest political crises that beset Japan would have demanded that countervailing forces of every description be marshaled to check, if only momentarily, the mounting strength of the military. Saionji prescribed no such all-out effort. Instead he resorted to a stop-gap measure

---

Aritomo, and Inoue Kaoru pitted against Matsukata Masayoshi and Ōyama Iwao of Satsuma. The subsequent addition of Katsura Tarō and Saionji Kinmochi did not affect the predominance of the Chōshū faction, since the former was also from Chōshū.

by calling on individuals, such as General Ugaki and Admiral Saitō, to man the crumbling defenses as best they could.

From time to time the assertion has been made that the Mukden Incident marked the beginning of the unfolding of Japan's master plan to dominate the whole of the Far East. This simplistic and linear view of history, already discredited, requires modification, since it ignores the thesis developed here that the crises with which Japan was confronted at home and in Manchuria from the late twenties were intrinsically such as to invite radical solutions; and that self-styled patriots, excited by the belief that the solution lay in conquest and domination, internally and externally, sought by direct extremist action to realize their vision of a perfect world.

It is known for a fact that Japan's creeping expansion in the Far East from Manchuria in 1931 and down through North China in 1937 and southward into French Indo-China and the Dutch East Indies in 1941 hardly represented a well-coordinated drive masterfully directed from Tokyo. The true significance of the Mukden Incident was that its instant success not only enabled the army to regain stature and influence but also permitted it to make inroads into the weakened fabric of Japan's political structure, gradually supplanting the old order with a political system more in consonance with its own views and goals.

However, the army in so doing accentuated the deep-seated factional struggle which had been going on within the ranks since the early twenties. The bitter feud raging between the factions tended to strengthen the political influence of the ultranationalists, whose backing certain army factions tried to enlist, and conversely weakened the status of the liberal elements which had hitherto exercised a moderating, though limited, influence inside the government as well as in Japanese society in general.[7] Therein lay the roots of Japan's prewar tragedy.

7. "The crisis may be exploited by rival groups within the elite in the process of internal power striving. The thrusts implicit in the crisis situation for the elite as a whole provide a point of leverage for the dominant

It is significant that, despite the extremely shaky position of cabinet government following the abortive March and October Plots, no leader rose from the ranks of the commoners as in Italy and Germany to become the symbol of a regenerated Japan. Although the young officers of the Kōdō-ha may have toyed with the idea of replacing the Emperor with his younger brother, Prince Chichibu, it was unthinkable for any loyal Japanese subject to defy the imperial tradition, rooted in over a thousand years of history, and rule Japan as a dictator. Even a military dictator after the fashion of the Tokugawa Shogunate would have been improbable in the Shōwa era; for unlike the warrior class or samurai of the Tokugawa period, who owed their fealty to local feudal lords, the rank and file of the Japanese army and navy were recruited from the common people and owed their allegiance to the Emperor. This explains why right-wing revolutionaries showed very little interest in mass uprisings as a means of grasping power and resorted instead to assassinations and coups d'état.

Westerners are prone to look upon any act of defiance by the military which undermines the authority of the duly constituted government as something grievous and monstrous, since we have come to assume that the rigid subjection of armies and navies to the civil authorities is the perfectly normal state for a civilized society. The truth of the matter is that military hegemony in some form or other has been the rule rather than the exception in human history. Events in many parts of the world today attest to the fact that, even in better-ordered societies, a serious dislocation of the established order quite often results in reversion to rule by a military dictator or junta.

In Japan, owing to the exceptionally acute nature of the crises with which she was confronted at home and abroad in the early

---

faction to improve its power position over against the opposition factions." Lasswell and Kaplan, *Power and Society* (New Haven, Yale University Press, 1950), p. 245. In the case of Japan, from about the middle thirties the dominant faction was the Tōsei-ha.

thirties and to a firmly entrenched tradition of military dictatorship, this phenomenon—the mounting influence of the military in the affairs of government—developed more rapidly and with less resistance after the Manchurian crisis than most Western nations were prepared to believe.

CHRONOLOGY

1927

	IN JAPAN		ABROAD
		Mar. 24	Nanking Incident
Apr. 18	Bank of Taiwan fails	Apr. 18	Chiang Kai-shek forms gov't in Nanking Chang Tso-lin threatened in North China
20	Tanaka forms a cabinet Tanaka launches railroad negotiations with Chang Tso-lin		
		May 30	Japanese troops land at Tsingtao
June 27–July 7	Second Eastern Regions Conf. convenes in Tokyo		
		July 20	Yamamoto Jōtarō assumes Presidency of South Manchuria Railway Co.
Aug. 13	Mukden Conference (Mori Kaku)		
Aug. 14	Dairen Conference (Mori Kaku)	Aug.	Chiang Kai-shek relinquishes command of Nationalist Army
Aug. 15	Port Arthur Conference (Mori Kaku)		
		Sept. 8	Japanese troops evacuated from Shantung
		16	Coalition of Nanking and Wuhan governments

1927 (Continued)

	IN JAPAN		ABROAD
Sept. 29–Nov. 8	Chiang Kai-shek in Japan		
		Nov.	Yamamoto Jōtarō visits Chang Tso-lin in Peking
		Dec.	Chiang Kai-shek allies with Feng Yu-hsiang

1928

Feb.	First popular election		
		Apr. 19	Kumamoto Division dispatched to Shantung
		May 3	Tsinan Incident
May 20–25	Eastern Regions Conf. Emergency Session, Tanaka stops invasion of Manchuria		
		June 4	Death of Chang Tso-lin Kōmoto's demand to mobilize Kwantung Army meets rebuff
		July 7	Nationalists announce abolition of extraterritoriality, abrogation of unequal treaties
		Aug. 27	Signing of Kellogg-Briand Pact
Oct.	Army grand maneuvers in Iwate Prefecture	Oct. 1	U.S.S.R. begins first Five-Year Plan
		Dec. 29	Chang Hsueh-liang raises Nationalist flag in Manchuria

1929

		Jan. 10	Assassination of Yang Yu-ting
June 28	Tanaka's report rejected by Emperor		

1929 (Continued)

	IN JAPAN		ABROAD
July 2	Tanaka cabinet resigns, Hamaguchi forms cabinet	July 21	Severance of Soviet-Chinese diplomatic relations over Chinese Eastern Railway
Sept. 29	Tanaka Giichi dies		
		Oct. 23	Crash of N.Y. stock market
Nov. 29	Saburi Sadao dies		

1930

	IN JAPAN		ABROAD
Jan. 11	Ban on gold export lifted	Jan. 21	London Naval Conference opens
Feb. 19	Kanaya appointed Chief of General Staff		
Apr. 2	Chief of Naval General Staff appeals directly to Emperor	Apr. 22	London Naval Treaty signed
June 14	Gen. Ugaki signifies intention to resign as Minister of War		
Sept.	Small Cherry Society organized; critical drop in price of rice and silk		
Oct. 1	Privy Council ratifies London Navy Treaty		
Nov. 4	Premier Hamaguchi attacked by assassin		

1931

	IN JAPAN		ABROAD
Mar.	March Plot		
Apr. 14	Second Wakatsuki cabinet formed		
June 13	Uchida appointed Pres. of South Manchuria Railway	June	Nakamura Incident
17	Ugaki replaces Saitō as Gov. Gen. of Korea		

1931 (Continued)

IN JAPAN		ABROAD	
		July	Wanpaoshan Incident
		Sept. 18	Mukden Incident
		21	Korean Army crosses Yalu River and Manchuria
Oct.	October Plot	Oct. 8	Bombing of Chinchow
		Nov. 19	Kwantung Army enters Tsitsihar
		26	Tientsin Incident
Dec. 11	Wakatsuki cabinet resigns		
13	Inukai forms cabinet, ban on gold shipment		

1932

IN JAPAN		ABROAD	
		Jan. 3	Kwantung Army enters Chinchow
		28	Shanghai Incident
		Feb. 5	Kwantung Army enters Harbin
Feb. 9	Inoue Junnosuke assassinated		
		29	Arrival of Lytton Commission
Mar. 5	Dan Takuma assassinated	Mar. 1	Manchukuo established
		15	America announces nonrecognition of Manchukuo
May 15	May 15 Incident, Inukai assassinated		
26	Saitō cabinet formed		
Sept. 15	Japan recognizes Manchukuo		
		Oct. 2	Lytton Report released
Dec. 12	Mori Kaku dies		

GLOSSARY

Aikoku Kinrōtō—Patriotic Workers' Society.

Chōshū—Geographical designation for most of what is now Yamaguchi Prefecture. A number of Genrō and high-ranking military men from this area formed a clique which wielded powerful influence in government and military circles.

Daimyō—Feudal lord(s).

Elder Statesmen (Genrō)—An extraconstitutional body of highly venerable statesmen and military men which met to discuss matters of extreme importance and advise the Emperor.

Fengtien Army—The army under Marshal Chang Tso-lin and, later, Chang Hsueh-liang.

Ketsumeidan—Blood Brotherhood League.

Kōdō-ha—The Imperial Way Faction. Consisted primarily of army officers of company grade who rallied around Generals Araki Sadao and Mazaki Jinzaburō. Members of this clique were determined to eliminate zaibatsu and political parties. Civilian counterparts of this group included men such as Kita Ikki and Nishida Zei.

Kwantung Army—Japanese Army stationed in Kwantung Territory and Manchuria with headquarters in Port Arthur.

Manchurian Crisis (or Incident)—The extended military operations of the Kwantung Army which began with the Mukden Incident and continued with the occupation of strategic cities of Manchuria by November 19 of the same year (1931); and to the efforts made at Geneva to reconcile the differences between China and Japan resulting in Japan's notification to withdraw from the League of Nations on March 27, 1933.

Minseitō—One of Japan's large political parties formed by the union of Kenseikai and Seiyūhontō in June 1927 with Hamaguchi Osayuki as president. It maintained close ties with the Mitsubishi interests.

Mukden Incident—The alleged explosion of a bomb on the tracks of the South Manchuria Railway a few miles north of Mukden on the night of September 18, 1931, following which the Kwantung Army went into action and occupied Mukden and neighboring cities before the night was over.

Musantō—Proletarian party.

Rōdō Nōmintō—Labor Farmer party.

Sakurakai—The Cherry Society.

Samurai—Warrior(s) or warrior class.

Satsuma—Geographical designation for what is now a portion of Kagoshima Prefecture. Like Chōshū, this area produced a number of able statesmen and military men who, as a clique, wielded powerful influence in Japanese government and military circles.

Shakai Minshutō—Social Democratic party.

Seiyūkai—Political party founded in 1900 by Itō Hirobumi, Saionji Kinmochi, and Hara Kei. Worked closely with Mitsui interests and older military men. In general, supported the "positive" policy toward China.

Teikoku Nōkai—Imperial Agricultural Society.

Tōsei-ha—The Control Faction. Major General Nagata Tetsuzan and General Tōjō Hideki were leading members of this group. It sought political ascendancy by means of gradualism and legitimate procedures. After eliminating the Kōdō-ha in 1936, it was in an unassailable position.

Wuhan government—A Nationalist government with Soviet form which existed in Hankow, China, from 1926 to 1927.

Young officers—A collective term denoting several factions of army and naval officers, principally of company grade but including a few army officers up to the rank of lieutenant colonel. Their primary goal was internal reconstruction of

Japan along the lines of national socialism. Although they were involved in continental expansion, this was incidental to the successful accomplishment of domestic reform. As a means of initiating their program, the "young officers" relied solely on individual assassination and coups d'état rather than on general strikes or mass uprisings, tactics more frequently employed by revolutionaries in the West.

Zaibatsu—Japanese financial-industrial combines.

BIBLIOGRAPHY

PUBLIC DOCUMENTS

In English

International Military Tribunal for the Far East, *Exhibits,* Tokyo, 1948.

International Military Tribunal for the Far East, *International Prosecution Section Document,* Tokyo, 1948.

*International Military Tribunal for the Far East, *Judgment, 4, 6,* Tokyo, 1948.

*International Military Tribunal for the Far East, *Proceedings,* Tokyo, 1948.

*League of Nations, *Appeal by the Chinese Government—Report of the Commission of Enquiry,* Geneva, 1932.

U.S. Foreign Relations, 1931, 3, Washington, D.C.

U.S. Foreign Relations, Japan (1931–41), 1, Washington, D.C.

In Japanese

Japan, Ministry of Home Affairs, Public Peace Section, comp., *Nihon Kakushin Undō Hiroku* (The Secret Records of Japanese Reform Movements), Tokyo, 1938.

Japan, Chief of Staff, *Manshū Jihen-shi* (The History of the Manchurian Incident), compilation no. 3, Tokyo, 1932.

*Asterisks denote sources especially relevant to this study.

BOOKS

In English

Allen, G. C., *Japan: The Hungry Guest,* New York, Dutton, 1938.
*Allen, G. C., *A Short Economic History of Modern Japan, 1867–1937,* London, Allen and Unwin, 1946.
Bemis, Samuel F., *A Diplomatic History of the United States,* New York, Holt, 1951.
Borton, Hugh, *Japan's Modern Century,* New York, Ronald Press, 1950.
Briggs, Herbert W., *The Law of Nations,* New York, Appleton-Century-Crofts, 1952.
Brown, Delmer M., *Nationalism in Japan,* Berkeley, University of California Press, 1955.
Burton, John W., *Peace Theory: Preconditions of Disarmament,* New York, Knopf, 1962.
Chien, Tuan-sheng, *The Government and Politics of China,* Cambridge, Harvard University Press, 1950.
Colegrove, Kenneth W., *Militarism in Japan,* Boston, World Peace Foundation, 1936.
Craig, Albert M., *Chōshū in the Meiji Restoration,* Cambridge, Harvard University Press, 1961.
Grew, Joseph C., *Ten Years in Japan,* New York, Simon and Schuster, 1944.
Jones, F. C., *Japan's New Order in East Asia: Its Rise and Fall, 1937–45,* New York, Institute of Pacific Relations, 1954.
Lasswell, Harold D., and Kaplan, Abraham, *Power and Society,* New Haven, Yale University Press, 1950.
Linebarger, Paul Myron Anthony, *Government in Republican China,* New York, McGraw-Hill, 1938.
MacNair, H. F., *China in Revolution,* Chicago, University of Chicago Press, 1931.
MacNair, H. F., and Lach, Donald G., *Modern Far Eastern International Relations,* New York, Van Nostrand, 1951.
Maki, John M. *Japanese Militarism, Its Causes and Cure,* New York, Knopf, 1945.

Maxon, Y. C., *Control of Japanese Foreign Policy: A Study of Civil–Military Rivalry, 1930–1945,* Berkeley University of California Press, 1957.

Morley, J. W., *Japanese Thrust into Siberia, 1918,* New York, Columbia University Press, 1957.

Morris, Evan I., *Nationalism and the Right Wing in Japan,* New York, Oxford University Press, 1960.

Nakano, Tomio, *The Ordinance Power of the Japanese Emperor,* Baltimore, Johns Hopkins Press, 1923.

*Norman, E. Herbert, *Japan's Emergence as a Modern State,* New York, Institute of Pacific Relations, 1940.

Norman, E. Herbert, *Soldier and Peasant in Japan: The Origins of Conscription,* New York, Institute of Pacific Relations, 1943.

Reischauer, Edwin O., *Japan, Past and Present,* New York, Knopf, 1954.

Reischauer, Karl Robert, *Japan Government—Politics,* New York, Nelson, 1939.

Rowe, David Nelson, *China Among the Powers,* New York, Harcourt, Brace, 1945.

*Scalapino, Robert A., *Democracy and the Party Movement in Prewar Japan,* Berkeley, University of California Press, 1953.

Schumpeter, E. B., Allen, G. C., Gordon, M. S., and Penrose, E. F., *The Industrialization of Japan and Manchukuo, 1930–40,* Toronto, Macmillan, 1940.

Smith, Sara R., *The Manchurian Crisis, 1931–32: A Tragedy in International Relations,* New York, Oxford University Press, 1948.

Stimson, Henry L., *The Far Eastern Crisis,* New York, Harper, 1936.

Storry, R., *The Double Patriots,* Boston, Houghton Mifflin, 1957.

*Takeuchi, Tatsuji, *War and Diplomacy in the Japanese Empire,* New York, Doubleday Doran, 1935.

Tang, Peter S. H., *Russian and Soviet Policy in Manchuria and Outer Mongolia, 1911–1931,* Durham, Duke University Press, 1959.

Toynbee, Arnold J., *Survey of International Affairs, 1931,* London, Oxford University Press, 1933.

Tsunoda, R., de Bary, W. T., and Keene, D., *Sources of the Japanese Tradition,* New York, Columbia University Press, 1958.

Uyehara, Cecil H., comp., *Checklist of Archives in the Japanese Ministry of Foreign Affairs, Tokyo, Japan, 1868–1945,* Washington, D. C., Library of Congress, 1954.

Vespa, A., *Secret Agent of Japan: A Handbook to Japanese Imperialism,* London, Little, 1938.

Vinacke, Harold M., *A History of the Far East in Modern Times,* New York, Appleton-Century-Crofts, 1950.

Weale, Putnam (Bertram Lenox Simpson), *Why China Sees Red,* New York, Dodd, Mead, 1925.

Woodward, E. L., and Butler, Rohan, eds., *Documents on British Foreign Policy, 1919–39,* 2d Ser., *2,* London, H. M. Stationary Office, 1930.

Wright, Quincy, *A Study of War, 1,* Chicago, University of Chicago Press, 1942.

*Yanaga, Chitoshi, *Japan since Perry,* New York, McGraw-Hill, 1949.

Yanaga, Chitoshi, *Japanese People and Politics,* New York, Wiley, 1956.

Young, A. Morgan, *Imperial Japan 1926–1938,* New York, Allen, 1938.

Young, C. Walter, *Japan's Special Position in Manchuria,* Baltimore, Johns Hopkins Press, 1931.

Young, C. Walter, *Japanese Jurisdiction in the South Manchuria Railway Areas,* Baltimore, Johns Hopkins Press, 1931.

Young, John, comp., *Checklist of Microfilm Reproductions of Selected Archives of the Japanese Army, Navy, and other Government Agencies, 1868–1945,* Washington, D. C., Georgetown University Press, 1959.

In Japanese

Akamatsu Katsumaro, *Nihon Shakai Undō-shi* (History of Social Movements in Japan), Tokyo, 1952.

*Aoki Tokuzō, *Taiheiyō Sensō Zenshi* (History of Events Leading to the Pacific War), *1,* Tokyo, 1953.

*Asahi Shinbun-sha *Taiheiyō Sensō e no Michi* (The Road to the Pacific War), *1, 2,* Tokyo, 1962.

Baba Tsunego, *Gendai Jinbutsu Hyōron* (Character Sketches of Contemporary Figures), Tokyo, 1930.

*Harada Kumao, *Saionji-kō to Seikyoku* (Prince Saionji and Political Developments), *1, 2,* Tokyo, 1950.

Hatoyama Ichirō, *Aru Daigishi no Seikatsu to Iken* (Life and Thoughts of an M.P.), Tokyo, 1952.

*Hirano Reiji, Manshū no Inbōsha (A Conspirator in Manchuria), Tokyo, 1959.

Horiuchi Kanjō, *Chūgoku no Arashi no Naka de* (In the Storms in China), Tokyo, 1950.

Hosokawa Ryūgen, *Tanaka Giichi,* Tokyo, 1958.

Hosoya Chihiro, *Shiberia, Shuppei no Shiteki Kenkyū* (Historical Study of Military Expedition to Siberia), Tokyo, 1955.

Ishii Itarō, *Gaikōkan no Isshō* (A Life Story of a Diplomat), Tokyo, 1950.

*Itō Masanori, *Gunbatsu Kōbōshi* (The History of the Rise and Fall of the Military), *2,* Tokyo, 1958.

Iwabuchi Tatsuo, *Gunbatsu no Keifu* (The Lineage of Military Cliques), Tokyo, 1948.

Iwabuchi Tatsuo, *Seikai Gojūnen-shi* (Fifty Years of Japanese Politics), Tokyo, 1948.

Kinoshita Hanji, *Nihon Fashizumu-shi* (History of Japanese Fascism), *1,* Tokyo, 1949.

Kinoshita Hanji, *Nihon no Uyoku* (The Right Wing of Japan), Tokyo, 1953.

*Kurihara Ken, *Tennō* (The Emperor), Tokyo, 1955.

*Maruyama Masao, *Gendai Seiji no Shisō to Kōdō* (Thoughts and Actions Underlying Contemporary Politics), *1,* Tokyo, 1958.

*Matsumura Hidesugu, *Miyakezaka,* Tokyo, 1952.

Minami Jirō Denki Kankōkai, *Minami Jirō,* Tokyo, 1957.

*Mori Shōzō, *Senpū Nijūnen* (Twenty Turbulent Years), Tokyo 1955.

*Morishima Morito, *Inbō, Ansatsu, Guntō* (Conspiracy, Assassination, and the Sword), Tokyo, 1950.

Nakamura Kikuo, *Shōwa Seiji-shi* (Shōwa Political History), Tokyo, 1958.

Nakano Tomio, *Tōsuiken no Dokuritsu* (The Independence of Supreme Command), Tokyo, 1934.

Nashimoto Yūhei, *Chūgoku no naka no Nihonjin* (Japanese in China), *1,* Tokyo, 1958.

Nezu Masashi, *Dai Nihon Teikoku no Hōkai* (Collapse of Imperial Japan), *1,* Tokyo, 1961.

*Okada Keisuke, *Okada Keisuke Kaikoroku* (Okada Memoirs), Tokyo, 1950.

Ozaki Yoshiharu, *Rikugun o Ugokashita Hitobito* (Figures Who Wielded Influence in the Army), Odawara, 1960.

Ozawa Eiichi, Takai Hiroshi, Oda Yasumasa, *Shiryō Nihon-shi* (A Source History of Japan), Tokyo, 1958.

Satō Kenryō, *Tōjō Hideki to Taiheiyō Sensō* (Hideki Tōjō and the Pacific War), Tokyo, 1960.

Shidehara Heiwa Zaidan, *Shidehara Kijūrō,* Tokyo, 1955.

*Shidehara Kijūrō, *Gaikō Gojūnen* (Fifty Years of Diplomacy), Tokyo, 1951.

*Shigemitsu Mamoru, *Gaikō Kaisōroku* (A Diplomatic Memoir), Tokyo, 1953.

*Shigemitsu Mamoru, *Shōwa no Dōran* (Political Disturbances of Shōwa Period), *1, 2,* Tokyo, 1952.

*Shiraki Masayuki, *Nihon Seitōshi (Shōwa-hen)* (History of Japanese Political Parties [Shōwa Period]), Tokyo, 1949.

*Takakura Tetsuichi, ed., *Tanaka Giichi Denki* (The Biography of Tanaka Giichi), *2,* Tokyo, 1960.

Tanaka Ryūkichi, *Haiin o Tsuku* (Probing the Cause of Defeat), Tokyo, 1946.

Tanaka Ryūkichi, *Nihon Gunbatsu Antō-shi* (An Account of the Secret Strifes between the Japanese Military Cliques), Tokyo, 1947.

Tanaka Sōgorō, *Nihon Fashizumu no Genryū* (The Wellspring of Japanese Fascism), Tokyo, 1949.

Tōyama Shigeki, Imai Seiichi, and Fujiwara Akira, *Shōwa-shi* (History of the Shōwa Era), Tokyo, 1955.

Ueda Katsuo, *Nikka Kōshō-shi* (History of Sino-Japanese Relations), Tokyo, 1948.

*Ugaki Kazushige, *Shōrai Seidan* (Refreshing Discourse at Shōrai Villa: A Memoir), Tokyo, 1951.

*Ugaki Kazushige, *Ugaki Nikki* (Ugaki Diary), Tokyo, 1954.

Wakatsuki Reijirō, *Kofūan Kaikoroku* (Memoirs of Kofūan [Wakatsuki's pseudonym]), Tokyo, 1950.

Yamada Yūzō, *Nihon Kokumin Shotoku Suikei Shiryō* (Statistical Estimates of Japan's National Income), Tokyo, 1951.

Yamaguchi Shigeji, *Ishihara Kanji—Higeki no Shōgun* (Ishihara Kanji, The Tragic General), Tokyo, 1952.

*Yamamoto Katsunosuke, *Nihon o Horoboshita Mono* (Those who Brought about the Downfall of Japan), Tokyo, 1949.

*Yamaura Kanichi, *Mori Kaku,* Tokyo, 1940.

*Yatsugi Kazuo, *Shōwa Jinbutsu Hiroku* (Inside Stories of Personalities of the Shōwa Era), Tokyo, 1954.

ARTICLES AND PERIODICALS

In English

*Brown, Delmer M., "Recent Japanese Political and Historical Materials," *American Political Science Review, 43* (1949), 1010–17.

Burns, C. Delisle, "Militarism," *Encyclopedia of Social Sciences, 10* (1930), 446–50.

Colegrove, Kenneth W., "The Japanese Cabinet," *American Political Science Review, 30* (1936), 903–23.

Conroy, Hilary, "Government vs. 'Patriot': The Background of Japan's Asiatic Expansion," *Pacific Historical Review, 20* (1951), 31–42.

Conroy, Hilary, "Japanese Nationalism and Expansionism," *American Historical Review, 60* (1955), 818–29.

Crowley, James B., "Japanese Army Factionalism in the 1930's," *Journal of Asian Studies, 21,* (1962), 309–26.

Dorfman, Ben, "The 'Manchurian Incident' of 1931," *Harpers, 169* (1934), 449–52.

Dull, Paul S., "The Assassination of Chang Tso-lin," *Far Eastern Quarterly, 11* (1952), 453–63.

*Ferrell, R. H., "The Manchurian Incident," *Journal of Modern History, 27* (1955), 66–72.

*Iriye, Akira, "Chang Hsueh-liang and the Japanese," *Journal of Asian Studies, 20* (1960), 33–43.

Lasswell, H. D., "Garrison State," *American Journal of Sociology, 46* (1941), 455–68.

Lauterbach, Albert T., "Militarism in the Western World," *Journal of History of Ideas, 5* (1944), 446–78.

Lerner, Max, "Assassination," *Encyclopedia of Social Sciences, 2* (1930), 271–75.

Moore, Barrington, Jr., "Notes on the Process of Acquiring Power," *World Politics, 8* (1955), 1–18.

Nakayama Ichirō, "Accumulation of Capital in the Japanese Economy," *The Annals of the Hitotsubashi Academy, 3* (1953), 139–63.

New York Times, 1930–1932.

Palyi, Melchior, "Economic Foundations of the German Totalitarian State," *American Journal of Sociology, 46* (1941), 469–86.

Sakata, Yoshio and Hall, John W., "The Motivation of Political Leadership in the Meiji Restoration," *Journal of Asian Studies, 16* (1956), 31–50.

Sprout, Harold, "Trends in the Traditional Relations Between Military and Civilian," *Proceedings of American Philosophical Society,* October 25, 1948, pp. 264–70.

Wright, Quincy, "The Military and Foreign Policy," in *Civil-Military Relationships in American Life,* ed. Jerome Kerwin, Chicago, 1948.

In Japanese

Gushima Kanesaburō, "Nitchū Kankei to Kokusai Jōsei: Nichiro Sensō kara Taiheiyō Sensō made" (Sino-Japanese Relation in World Affairs: From Russo-Japanese War to the Pacific War), *Nihon Gaikō-shi Kenkyū* (Studies of Diplomatic History of Japan), Tokyo, March 1961, pp. 1–16.

*Hanaya Tadashi, "Manshū Jihen wa Kōshite Keikaku sareta" (This is how the Manchurian Incident was Planned), *Himerareta Shōwashi* (Hidden History of the Shōwa Era), Supplement to *Chisei,* December 1956, pp. 40–50.

Hatoyama Ichirō, "Mori Kaku Tsuioku" (In Memory of Mori Kaku), *Chūō Kōron, 48* (1933), 249–58.

*Ikeda Sumihisa, "Tōsei-ha to Kōdō-ha" (Tōsei Faction and Kōdō Faction), *Bungei Shunju, 34* (1956), 92–108.

Imamura Hitoshi, "Manshū Hi o Fuku Koro" (When Fire was Raging in Manchuria), *Himerareta Shōwashi,* Supplement to *Chisei,* December 1956, pp. 60–71.

*Inada Masaji, "Taiheiyō Sensō Boppatsu to Tennō, Genrō oyobi Jūshin no Chii" (The Outbreak of the Pacific War and the Emperor, Position of Elder Statesmen and Senior Statesmen), *Taiheiyō Sensō Genin Ron* (Causes of the Pacific War), ed. Ueda Katsuo, Tokyo, 1953, pp. 26–96.

Kiyose Ichirō, "Go-ichi-go Jiken no Bengo ni Tachite" (In Defense of the May 15 Incident), *Kaizō, 15* (1933), 283–91.

Kiyozawa Retsu, "Go-ichi-go Jiken no Shakaiteki Konkyo" (Social Origin of the May 15, 1932, Incident), *Kaizō, 15* (1933), 262–71.

Kōmoto Daisaku, "Watakushi ga Chō Sakurin o Koroshita" (I Killed Chang Tso-lin), *Bungei Shunju, 32* (1954), 194–201.

Machino Takema, "Chō Sakurin Bakushi no Zengo" (Events Preceding and Following Chang Tso-lin's Death from Bombing), *Chūō Kōron, 727* (1949), 72–80.

Maruyama Masao, "Nihon ni Okeru Nashonarizumu sono Shisōteki Haikei" (Nationalism in Japan and its Ideological Background), *Chūō Kōron, 66* (1951), 295–304.

Mazaki Jinzaburō, "Ankoku Saiban: Ni-ni-roku Jiken" (The Black Trials of February 26, 1936, Incident), *Bungei Shunju,* Special Issue, April 1957, pp. 124–32.

Morton, William F., "Sainan Jihen, 1928–29" (Tsinan Incident, 1928–29), *Nihon Gaikō-shi Kenkyū,* Tokyo, March 1961, pp. 103–18.

Muramatsu Yūji, "Taiheiyō Sensō Boppatsu to Nihon Keizai" (The Outbreak of the Pacific War and the Japanese Economy), *Taiheiyō Sensō Genin Ron,* 1953, pp. 513–71.

Nomura Kōichi, "Manshū Jihen Chokuzen no Higashi Sanshō Mondai" (Problem of Three Eastern Provinces Immediately before the Manchurian Incident), *Nihon Gaikō-shi Kenkyū,* Tokyo, March 1961, pp. 103–18.

Oka Yoshitake, "Saigo no Genrō, Saionji Kinmochi" (Saionji, the Last Elder Statesman), *Kindai Nihon no Seijika* (Statesmen of Recent Japan), Tokyo, 1960, pp. 199–252.

*Shinmyō Takeo, "Shōwa Seiji Hisshi—Chō Sakurin Bakusatsu" (Secret Political History of the Shōwa Era—The Bombing of Chang Tso-lin), *Chūō Kōron, 69* (1954), 190–201.

Suzuki Teiichi, "Hokubatsu to Shō: Tanaka Mitsuyaku" (The Northern Expedition and Chiang Kai-shek: Tanaka's Secret Agreement), *Himerareta Shōwashi,* Supplement to *Chisei,* December 1956, pp. 20–25

*Takamiya Taihei, "Waribashi kara Umareta Manshū-Jihen" (The Manchurian Incident which Started from a Fall of a Chopstick [i.e. flipping of a coin]), *Shōwa Memo,* Supplement to *Bungei Shunju,* July 1954, pp. 22–31.

Tōkyō Asahi, 1927–1932.

Toyoshima Fusatarō, "Chōsengun Ekkyō Shingeki su" (Japan's Korean Army Crosses the Border and Advances), *Himerareta Shōwashi,* Supplement to *Chisei,* December 1956, pp. 52–58.

Tsugumo Kunitoshi, "Kuromaku—Kuhara Fusanosuke" (Kuhara, The Wire Puller), *Fūun Jinbutsu Tokuhon* (Review of the Men of the Hour), Supplement to *Bungei Shunju,* June 1955, pp. 184–89.

Usui Katsumi, "Chō Sakurin Bakushi no Shinsō" (The Truth Regarding the Assassination by Bombing of Chang Tso-lin), *Himerareta Shōwashi,* Supplement to *Chisei,* December 1956, pp. 26–38.

*Yamaura Kanichi, "Bōshō Mori Kaku" (Mori Kaku, The Arch-Schemer), *Fūun Jinbutsu Tokuhon,* Supplement to *Bungei Shunju,* June 1955, pp. 60–65.

MICROFILMS

Documents pertaining to London Naval Conference preserved by the Japanese Embassy in London, DLC* 5039, Reels UD 32, 33, 34.

Japanese Editorials and Articles concerning the Supreme Command, April-June, 1930, DLC, Reel S612.

Japanese Foreign Ministry, Correspondence, Instructions, Communiques, etc., June 1929 to May 1931, DLC, Reel S112.

Japanese Foreign Ministry, DLC 5040, Reels 42, 43. (Consular Reports, principally from China Proper, some from Manchuria, 1932–33.)

Japanese Naval Attaché Reports: Captain Nakamura Incident, Manchurian Incident, DLC, Reels R26, R27.

Japanese Navy, Documents relevant to London Naval Conference, DLC, UD55–2.

Kido (Kōichi) Diary, July 11, 1931–December 9, 1945, DLC, Reel WT5.

Kwantung Army, Army General Staff: Intelligence Reports on Manchurian Incident, DLC, Reel 132.

Public Speeches relevant to London Naval Conference and Treaty made by Hamaguchi, Wakatsuki, Takarabe, etc., August 1929–October 1930, DLC, Reel S113.

*DLC denotes microfilm at Library of Congress.

OTHER SOURCES

In English

Kobayashi, Key Kiyokazu, "The Kwantung Army and the Manchurian Incident," submitted to the East Asian Institute, Columbia University, 1956.

Tiedman, Arthur E., "The Hamaguchi Cabinet, First Phase, July 1929–February 1930: A Study in Japanese Parliamentary Government," doctoral dissertation, Columbia University, 1960.

Wald, Royal J., "The Young Officers Movement in Japan, ca. 1925–37: Ideology and Action," doctoral dissertation, University of California at Berkeley, 1949.

In English and Japanese

Ōkawa Shūmei, Written Statement Regarding the Manchurian Incident of September 18, 1931. Japanese text and English translation. International Prosecution Section SCAP, no. 815. Designated as IMT 103 in Uyehara, *Checklist of Archives.*

INDEX

YALE STUDIES IN POLITICAL SCIENCE

1. Robert E. Lane, *The Regulation of Businessmen*
2. Charles Blitzer, *An Immortal Commonwealth: The Political Thought of James Harrington*
3. Aaron Wildavsky, *Dixon-Yates: A Study in Power Politics*
4. Robert A. Dahl, *Who Governs? Democracy and Power in an American City*
5. Herbert Jacob, *German Administration Since Bismarck: Central Authority versus Local Autonomy*
6. Robert C. Fried, *The Italian Prefects: A Study in Administrative Politics*
7. Nelson W. Polsby, *Community Power and Political Theory*
8. Joseph Hamburger, *James Mill and the Art of Revolution*
9. Takehiko Yoshihashi, *Conspiracy at Mukden: The Rise of the Japanese Military*

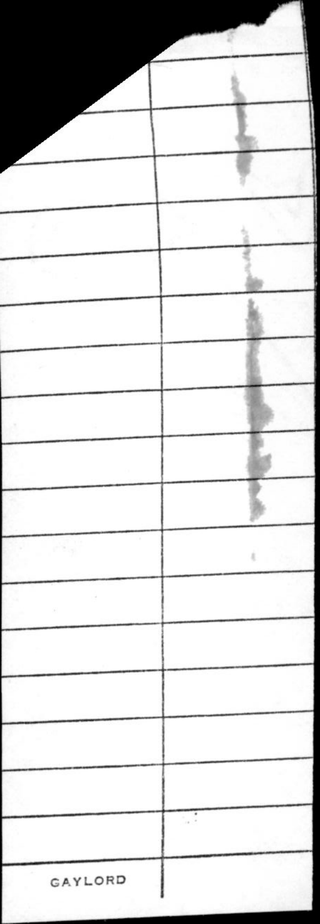